Technology, Work and Globalization

Series Editors

Leslie P. Willcocks, Department of Management, London School of Economics and Political Science, London, UK
Mary C. Lacity, Sam M. Walton College of Business, University of Arkansas, Fayetteville, AR, USA

The Technology, Work and Globalization series was developed to provide policy makers, workers, managers, academics and students with a deeper understanding of the complex interlinks and influences between technological developments, including information and communication technologies, work organizations and patterns of globalization. The mission of the series is to disseminate rich knowledge based on deep research about relevant issues surrounding the globalization of work that is spawned by technology.

Nikita Singhal · Shikha Goyal · Tanmay Singhal

Potential, Risks, and Ethical Implications of Decentralized Insurance

palgrave
macmillan

Nikita Singhal
IIMT University
Meerut, Uttar Pradesh, India

Shikha Goyal
Amity University
Noida, Uttar Pradesh, India

Tanmay Singhal
STM & Associates
Chartered Accountant
New Delhi, Delhi, India

ISSN 2730-6623 ISSN 2730-6631 (electronic)
Technology, Work and Globalization
ISBN 978-981-97-5893-7 ISBN 978-981-97-5894-4 (eBook)
https://doi.org/10.1007/978-981-97-5894-4

This Palgrave Macmillan imprint is published by the registered company Springer Nature Singapore Pte Ltd.
The registered company address is: 152 Beach Road, #21-01/04 Gateway East, Singapore 189721, Singapore

"Dedicated to my loving parents"

Thank you for your unwavering support, boundless encouragement, and endless sacrifices. You have been my guiding light, nurturing my dreams with your love and wisdom. This book is a tribute to your belief in me and a testament to the values you have instilled in my heart. Your love and guidance have shaped me into the person I am today, and I am eternally grateful. Thank you for always believing in me and for being my constant source of strength and inspiration.

With all my love and gratitude

Preface

In the dynamic landscape of insurance, a seismic shift is underway, driven by the transformative power of innovative technologies. As we stand at the precipice of this digital revolution, we must explore decentralized insurance comprehensively—a realm brimming with promise, peril, and profound ethical implications.

This book represents a concerted effort to navigate the uncharted waters of decentralized insurance, probing its potential, uncovering its risks, and interrogating its ethical dimensions with scholarly rigour and intellectual curiosity. By delving into the depths of this emergent field, we aim to equip readers with the knowledge, insights, and critical perspectives necessary to navigate the complexities of decentralized insurance with clarity and confidence. At its core, this book is driven by a singular purpose: to advance the discourse surrounding decentralized insurance and catalyze informed dialogue among stakeholders across academia, industry, and regulatory bodies. By fostering a deeper understanding of decentralized insurance and its multifaceted implications, we aspire to empower individuals and organizations to harness its transformative potential responsibly and ethically. This book seeks to transcend disciplinary boundaries, drawing upon insights from diverse fields such as finance, technology, law, ethics, and sociology. By synthesizing knowledge from disparate domains, we aim to give readers a holistic perspective on decentralized insurance, facilitating interdisciplinary dialogue and collaboration in pursuing innovative solutions to complex challenges.

Embarking on an intellectual journey through the pages of this book, readers will delve into the multifaceted realm of decentralized insurance, exploring its technological intricacies, innovative business models, regulatory challenges, and ethical considerations. Each chapter is meticulously crafted to provide readers with valuable insights, critical analyses, and actionable recommendations, enriching their understanding of this rapidly evolving field. Through clear explanations and real-world examples, readers will unravel the complex concepts of blockchain, smart contracts, and decentralized autonomous organizations (DAOs), gaining a nuanced understanding of how these technologies reshape insurance practices, from policy issuance to claims processing.

Moreover, the book navigates the diverse landscape of decentralized insurance business models, shedding light on peer-to-peer, parametric, and mutual insurance approaches. By examining each model's strengths, weaknesses, and potential pitfalls, readers are equipped with the knowledge needed to discern viable strategies for fostering innovation and sustainability within the industry. Concurrently, the book scrutinizes the regulatory frameworks governing decentralized insurance, offering insights into the legal and compliance challenges that insurers, regulators, and policymakers face. Through case studies and comparative analyses, readers gain a comprehensive understanding of the global regulatory landscape and its implications for decentralized insurance solutions. Additionally, the book confronts the ethical dilemmas inherent in decentralized insurance, grappling with questions of privacy, transparency, and social equity. By engaging with ethical theory and real-world scenarios, readers are challenged to critically evaluate the ethical implications and consider strategies for promoting ethical conduct within the industry.

Ultimately, this book is more than a mere scholarly endeavour; it is a call to action to embrace the transformative potential of decentralized insurance while remaining steadfast in our commitment to ethical principles, social responsibility, and human flourishing.

Meerut, India
Noida, India
New Delhi, India

Nikita Singhal
Shikha Goyal
Tanmay Singhal

Acknowledgements

Decentralized insurance has captured the attention of enterprise leaders owing to its intricate and multifaceted nature, which presents unique challenges during implementation. As researchers, we embarked on a journey to address pivotal questions that lay the groundwork for our investigation. These questions include: What are the fundamental technologies that serve as the backbone of decentralized insurance, such as blockchain, smart contracts, and decentralized autonomous organizations (DAOs)? How do these technologies reshape traditional insurance practices, from policy issuance to claims processing? What innovative business models propel decentralized insurance forward, and how do they effectively cater to diverse customer needs while fostering financial inclusion? We sought to understand the regulatory landscape surrounding decentralized insurance, exploring the challenges and opportunities it presents and examining how regional variations in regulatory frameworks impact the sector's evolution. We delved into the ethical considerations inherent in decentralized insurance, particularly regarding privacy, transparency, and social equity. We aimed to provide insights into how stakeholders can navigate these ethical dilemmas and promote ethical conduct within the industry. Finally, we explored emerging trends and prospects for decentralized insurance, considering the influence of technological advancements, regulatory developments, and societal shifts.

These questions served as the cornerstone of our research endeavour. We extend our heartfelt gratitude to the anonymous reviewers whose meticulous assessment of our book proposal provided invaluable suggestions and constructive feedback. Special recognition is owed to Prof. Dr Syed Husain Ashraf and Prof. Dr SibhgatUllah Farooqui from Aligarh Muslim University for their invaluable guidance throughout our research journey.

We are indebted to the Indian Council of Social Science Research (ICSSR) for their generous support, particularly for awarding Dr Nikita Singhal the ICSSR Major research project. Dr. Singhal spearheaded the project, and this book is a direct outcome of the research sponsored by ICSSR. It is important to emphasize that while this book is a product of the ICSSR-funded project, the views expressed herein are solely those of the author. Our sincere appreciation extends to all individuals administering the grant and providing invaluable guidance and assistance during the project's execution.

Our exploration of decentralized insurance has been both intellectually stimulating and rewarding. We hope that scholars, practitioners, and enthusiasts alike will find value in the insights presented within this book and that it will inspire further exploration and research in the dynamic realm of decentralized insurance.

Contents

About the Authors

Dr. Nikita Singhal is an Associate Professor at IIMT University. Her areas of specialization are Insurance, Banking, Taxation, and Sustainability. She has published around 35 research papers in ABDC listed, Web of Science, and SCOPUS index journals, including Journals of Taylor and Francis, Springer, Sage, Willey, and national and international repute conferences. She also has various books and chapters in the Edited book. She has spoken and organized various faculty development programs and conferences. She is also a managing editor of the IJAST Journal of IIMT University. She completed her PhD from the Department of Commerce, Aligarh Muslim University, and was awarded JRF (Commerce) in 2013 and JRF (Management) in 2012. Dr Nikita Singhal is also an awardee of a Major Research project titled "Insurance claim settlement during Covid-19: A new challenge for Indian insurance sector" sponsored by the Indian Council of Social Science Research.

Dr. Shikha Goyal is an Assistant Professor at Amity University. Her area of specialization is Banking, Taxation, Insurance, and Sustainability. She has published around 25 research papers in ABDC listed, Web of Science, and SCOPUS index journals, including Journals of Taylor and Francis, Springer, Sage, Willey, and national and international repute conferences. She completed her PhD from ACCF, Amity University.

Tanmay Singhal is a fellow member Institute of Chartered Accountants of India and he is working as a partner with a chartered accountancy firm M/s STM & Associates established in 1986. He is extensively exposed to audit and assurance, internal financial control, insurance risk assessment, secretarial compliances, tax planning, assessment, and other taxation matters. He has 2 research papers in the Journal of Taylor and Francis, which is SCOPUS indexed and listed in ABDC.

Abbreviations

AI	Artificial Intelligence
AIG	American International Group, Inc.
AML	Anti-Money Laundering
APIs	Application Programming Interfaces
APRA	Australian Prudential Regulation Authority
AR	Augmented Reality
ASIC	Australian Securities and Investments Commission
AWS	Amazon Web Services
CAGR	Compound Annual Growth Rate
CBI	Community-Based Insurance
CFTC	Commodity Futures Trading Commission
DAOs	Decentralized Autonomous Organizations
DApps	Decentralized Applications
DeFi	Decentralized Finance
DLT	Distributed Ledger Technology
DoS	Denial-of-Service
EC	European Commission
EIOPA	European Insurance and Occupational Pensions Authority
ESG	Environmental, Social, and Governance
EU	European Union
FCA	Financial Conduct Authority
FCRA	Fair Credit Reporting Act
FEAT	Fairness, Ethics, Accountability, and Transparency
FSA	Financial Services Agency
FTIG	Financial Technology and Innovation Group
GC&C	Generali Global Corporate & Commercial

GCP	Google Cloud Platform
GDPR	General Data Protection Regulation
GFIN	Global Financial Innovation Network
HIPAA	Health Insurance Portability and Accountability Act
IA	Insurance Authority
ICS	Insurance Cloud Services
IDC	International Data Corporation
IoT	Internet of Things
IRDAI	Insurance Regulatory and Development Authority of India
KYC	Know-Your-Customer
MAS	Monetary Authority of Singapore
MiCA	Markets in Crypto-Assets
ML	Machine Learning
NAIC	National Association of Insurance Commissioners
NLP	Natural Language Processing
OIC	Office of Insurance Commission
P2P	Peer-to-Peer
PoS	Proof of Stake
PoW	Proof of Work
PRA	Prudential Regulation Authority
RBAC	Role-Based Access Control
RBC	Risk-Based Capital
RegTech	Regulatory Technology
RPA	Robotic Process Automation
SEBI	Securities and Exchange Board of India
SEC	Securities and Exchange Commission
SupTech	Supervisory Technology
SUSEP	Superintendence of Private Insurance
TVL	Total Value Locked
UBI	Usage-Based Insurance
VR	Virtual Reality
ZKPs	Zero-Knowledge Proofs

List of Figures

List of Tables

List of Boxes

CHAPTER 1

Decentralized Insurance: Reshaping the Future of Coverage

1.1 Insurance: Business, Ethics, and Technology

Insurance represents a fundamental concept of pooling the risk. When individuals find the chances of potentially devastating financial losses, they turn to insurance to mitigate that risk. Insurance companies facilitate risk mitigation by creating risk pools, where individuals collectively contribute premiums to shoulder the burden. The soul of insurance lies in the fact that each individual's premium is significantly lower than the potential cost of the catastrophic event they seek to protect against. Insurance providers operate on the belief that the total amount collected from policyholders will exceed the payouts for claims.

Even though profitability is an important aspect of any business, the insurance industry is uniquely responsible for protecting individuals, businesses, and communities from unforeseen risks. This ethical obligation is deeply rooted in the historical development of insurance. Insurance, in its essence, is a system of risk management designed to distribute the financial burden of losses among a group of policyholders. Its origins can be traced back to ancient civilizations, where communities supported individuals who experienced misfortunes like fire, theft, or natural disasters. These early forms of mutual aid and assistance established the foundation of insurance based on principles of solidarity, fairness, and social responsibility (Fang et al., 2023).

N. Singhal et al., *Potential, Risks, and Ethical Implications of Decentralized Insurance*, Technology, Work and Globalization,
https://doi.org/10.1007/978-981-97-5894-4_1

As insurance evolved, it became formalized into a structured industry. Insurance companies emerged to provide coverage in exchange for premiums to ensure financial stability for individuals and businesses. However, the ethical dimension of insurance remained significant as the industry's purpose continued to protect policyholders.

One of the fundamental ethical principles in insurance is the concept of indemnification. When policyholders suffer a loss covered by their insurance policy, the insurer must reimburse them to the extent agreed upon in the contract. This principle reflects the ethical duty of insurers to honour their promises and provide financial support to those in need.

Furthermore, insurance plays a crucial role in promoting social and economic stability. By spreading risks across a large pool of policyholders, insurers help individuals and businesses recover from unexpected events without suffering severe financial hardship. This aspect is particularly relevant when considering catastrophic events such as natural disasters, where insurance coverage can aid in recovering and rebuilding affected communities.

Historically, numerous insurance practices and regulations have emerged to protect policyholders and ensure ethical conduct within the industry. For example, the concept of utmost good faith, or uberrimae fidei, has long been a fundamental principle in insurance contracts. It requires both parties, the insurer and the insured, to disclose all material information honestly and in good faith. This principle aims to create a fair and balanced contractual relationship, emphasizing the ethical duty of honesty and transparency. The ethical dimension of insurance is also evident in its role as a facilitator of trust and reliability. Insurers must maintain financial stability to fulfil their obligations when policyholders need them the most. This ethical responsibility fosters trust between insurers and policyholders, enabling a sustainable and reliable insurance market.

Furthermore, insurance regulatory bodies and government agencies have been established to oversee the insurance industry, ensuring compliance with ethical standards and protecting the interests of policyholders. These entities enforce regulations on solvency, reserve requirements, consumer protection, and fair claims handling practices, among others, to maintain the ethical integrity of the insurance business.

Insurers can fulfil their ethical obligations towards policyholders and society by upholding principles such as indemnification, stability, trust, and regulatory oversight. This commitment to ethics safeguards the interests of individuals and businesses and contributes to communities' overall stability and welfare.

Ethical considerations become more crucial in today's scenario where insurers leverage technology. Data privacy and security must be prioritized, with transparent data collection, robust security measures, and responsible use of customer information in compliance with data protection regulations. Fairness and bias must be addressed, as algorithms and AI systems can inadvertently perpetuate biases. Insurers must ensure fairness and prevent discrimination in their use of technology (Kantur & Bamuleseyo, 2018). Transparency and explainability of algorithms are essential to building trust with policyholders. Ethical frameworks and guidelines should be established to guide the responsible use of technology in the insurance industry (The Geneva Association, 2018).

The revolutionization of the insurance industry through decentralized principles and the use of technology presents huge opportunities for improved business practices, enhanced customer experiences, and greater product innovation. However, technological advancements must accompany ethical considerations to protect customer privacy, ensure fairness, and promote transparency. By navigating the ethical dimensions of technology, the insurance industry can harness its full potential while upholding the principles of integrity, accountability, and social responsibility.

1.2 The Symphony of Decentralized Insurance

Traditional insurance operates on a centralized model, transferring risk from insured individuals to insurers. This system establishes a bilateral contract between the insured party and the insurer. However, as the same contract is typically sold to numerous insured individuals, the insurer is a central service provider for all policyholders. In contrast, decentralized insurance functions within a community of participants, where risks are shared and transferred collectively (Abdikerimova & Feng, 2022). In a decentralized insurance scheme, participants engage in a multilateral agreement rather than relying on a central authority to dictate the terms and conditions of financial arrangements. Instead of a single entity setting the rules, decentralized insurance is characterized by mutual support and cooperation among its participants.

Decentralized insurance represents a groundbreaking shift in the traditional insurance paradigm, where control, decision-making, and operations are distributed across a network of participants rather than centralized in a single authority. This transformative approach aims to foster a more transparent, efficient, and inclusive insurance ecosystem. In a decentralized insurance framework, distributed technology, decentralized governance, blockchain technology, smart contracts, and other decentralized mechanisms are pivotal in reshaping how insurance is conceptualized, executed, and experienced (Deloitte, 2017).

The impetus for decentralization in the insurance sector stems from the evident drawbacks embedded in the centralized insurance paradigm. The existing model grapples with myriad challenges—limited options, lack of customization, exorbitant costs, delayed claims settlement, and security vulnerabilities. Adding to these challenges is the overarching authority wielded by insurance providers, compelling policyholders to provide extensive evidence and justifications subjected to rigorous scrutiny. In contrast, decentralized insurance introduces a collaborative model where users collectively contribute funds to create specialized risk pools and are subject to their own rules on governance and decision-making, which liberates individuals from intermediaries and endows them with unprecedented autonomy (Bohnert et al., 2019). The decentralization insurance, viewed through various lenses, reveals a dynamic and inclusive environment where traditional notions of risk pooling and claims management undergo revolutionary metamorphoses, ushering in an era where individuals actively shape the trajectory of their insurance experiences.

Decentralization within the insurance sector encompasses both technological and non-technological dimensions. The non-technological aspect involves decentralizing decision-making, governance, and risk assessment without exclusive reliance on technology. This form of decentralized insurance, or alternative insurance, refers to models that operate independently of conventional centralized insurance systems and do not heavily depend on technological platforms or innovations. Instead, these models typically rely on principles such as cooperation, risk-sharing, and community involvement to offer insurance coverage.

For instance, Takaful exemplifies a cooperative insurance model rooted in Islamic principles of mutual assistance and shared responsibility. In Takaful, participants contribute to a communal fund, which is utilized to cover losses incurred by any group member. Operating on the principle of "tabarru," or voluntary contribution, Takaful adheres to

Shariah-compliant practices. Mutual aid societies represent another form of alternative insurance, characterized by member-driven organizations extending their members' insurance benefits. Members contribute dues or premiums to the society, which then allocates funds to provide financial assistance, healthcare coverage, or other benefits to members facing hardships. These societies often cater to specific communities or professional groups and emphasize solidarity and collective support. Catastrophe risk pooling involves aggregating resources from multiple entities to collectively address the financial ramifications of catastrophic events, such as natural disasters or large-scale emergencies. By spreading the risk across a broader pool of participants, catastrophe risk pooling aims to mitigate the individual financial burdens faced by insurers or policyholders in the wake of such events. Community self-help schemes entail informal insurance arrangements established within local communities or social circles. Community members contribute resources or offer assistance to one another during times of need, such as emergencies or unforeseen circumstances. These schemes rely on mutual trust, social bonds, and reciprocal support to furnish financial protection and aid to community members. These non-technological decentralized insurance or alternative insurance models offer diverse risk management and financial protection approaches, emphasizing community solidarity, mutual aid, and shared responsibility principles. While they may lack the technological sophistication of modern insurance platforms, these models underscore the enduring value of collective action and social cohesion in addressing insurance needs within communities and societies.

Technologically, decentralized insurance represents a paradigm shift in the insurance industry, leveraging various innovative technologies to transform traditional insurance processes. These technologies include blockchain, Distributed Ledger Technology (DLT), Decentralized Applications (DApps), Internet of Things (IoT), Decentralized Autonomous Organizations (DAOs), Artificial Intelligence (AI), and Machine Learning (ML). These technologies uniquely decentralize insurance operations and enhance efficiency, transparency, and security within the ecosystem. The advent of blockchain technology brings a compelling turn by marking a new chapter in decentralized insurance. A distributed and tamper-resistant ledger becomes the guardian of truth, recording and verifying transactions with unyielding precision (Popovic et al., 2020). Smart contracts, architects of automation, seamlessly execute intricate insurance processes. Blockchain, with its immutable record accessible to all participants, becomes the cornerstone of trust, solidifying transparency and security. Tokenization introduces fractional ownership and increased liquidity to insurance assets, expanding possibilities within decentralized insurance (The Geneva Association, 2023).

The Internet of Things (IoT) is crucial in decentralized insurance by enabling real-time data collection from connected devices. IoT devices, such as smart sensors and wearables, gather valuable information about insured assets, enabling insurers to assess risks more accurately and offer personalized insurance products. By leveraging IoT data, decentralized insurance platforms can enhance risk management and improve underwriting processes. Decentralized applications, or DApps, run on decentralized networks like blockchain platforms. In the context of decentralized insurance, DApps facilitate various insurance-related activities, including policy issuance, claims processing, and risk assessment. These applications operate autonomously without centralized control, giving users greater control over their insurance activities. AI and ML technologies are vital in decentralized insurance by enabling automated data analysis, risk prediction, and customer service. AI algorithms can analyse vast amounts of insurance data to identify patterns, detect fraudulent activities, and optimize insurance processes. ML models can also personalize insurance offerings based on individual customer preferences and behaviour, enhancing customer satisfaction and retention. Consensus algorithms, such as Proof of Work (PoW) and Proof of Stake (PoS), ensure the integrity and security of decentralized insurance transactions. These algorithms enable network participants to reach a consensus on the validity of transactions without relying on centralized authorities. Decentralized databases, built on blockchain or DLT, provide a secure and transparent infrastructure for storing insurance-related data, reducing the risk of data manipulation or tampering.

Hence, decentralized insurance does not merely represent a technology change; it is a cultural shift, an evolution in insurance philosophy. It is a departure from the top-down approach, where decisions are imposed, to a bottom-up approach, where participants actively contribute and shape the insurance landscape. The emphasis is on redefining the essence of insurance by giving individuals more agency and democratizing the entire process. Decision-making is distributed to participants without a central authority, creating a more democratic and participatory environment. This decentralized governance model ensures that all participants have a role in shaping the decentralized insurance ecosystem's rules, policies, and future developments (Feng, 2023).

Decentralized insurance is particularly impactful in addressing the limitations of the traditional insurance model. One of the significant drawbacks of centralized insurance is the limited array of options and lack of personalized solutions. Policies are often one-size-fits-all, leaving many users with coverage that may not align with their specific needs. Through its collaborative and customizable approach, decentralized insurance allows for a more tailored and flexible insurance experience. Moreover, the exorbitant operational costs associated with centralized insurance are mitigated in a decentralized model. Decentralized insurance significantly reduces overhead costs by eliminating the need for extensive intermediaries and streamlining processes. This efficiency translates to more cost-effective insurance solutions, making coverage more accessible to a broader audience. The issue of delayed claims settlement, a common pain point in centralized insurance, is also effectively addressed through decentralization. This reduces the time taken for settlements and enhances the overall efficiency and trustworthiness of the insurance system. Security vulnerabilities, another challenge in the centralized insurance model, find a robust solution in decentralized insurance, especially when blockchain technology is used. Blockchain technology ensures a tamper-resistant and transparent ledger, minimizing the risk of fraud or manipulation. The immutable nature of blockchain records adds a layer of security, instilling confidence among participants in the integrity of insurance transactions. The introduction of tokenization further enhances the versatility of decentralized insurance. Fractional ownership becomes possible by representing insurance assets as digital tokens on the blockchain. This innovation increases liquidity in insurance assets and opens up new avenues for investment and participation. Tokenization introduces a novel dimension to the decentralized insurance landscape, allowing for more granular ownership and trading of insurance assets.

Hence, decentralized insurance is a technological advancement and a cultural and philosophical shift in the insurance world. It transcends the limitations of traditional models, offering a more collaborative, efficient, and user-centric approach. Whether through advanced technologies or alternative insurance, the essence of decentralized insurance lies in reshaping the power dynamics, fostering inclusivity, and democratizing the insurance experience. It is a symphony of transformation, resonating with innovation, adaptability, and a commitment to reshaping the future of coverage. Figure 1.1 shows the detailed concept of decentralized insurance.

1.3 Principles of Decentralization

Decentralized insurance operates on a distinct set of fundamental principles that fundamentally redefine how insurance functions. These principles serve as the bedrock of decentralized insurance systems, shaping their design, operation, and ethos. By adhering to these principles, decentralized insurance platforms aim to uphold the values of integrity, efficiency, and fairness, thus distinguishing themselves from traditional insurance models. At its core, decentralized insurance embodies trustless transactions, transparency, immutability, peer-to-peer interactions, autonomous governance, security and privacy, interoperability, scalability, inclusivity, and accessibility.

1.3.1 Trustless Transactions

Trustless transactions refer to the ability to conduct transactions or engage in interactions without relying on trust between parties. In traditional insurance models, trust is placed in centralized entities such as insurance companies or intermediaries to facilitate and validate transactions. In decentralized insurance, trustless transactions can be facilitated through robust contractual agreements. Parties involved in an insurance transaction can establish legally binding contracts that clearly outline the terms and conditions of the insurance policy. These contracts ensure that transactions are enforced without the need for implicit trust in each other. Trustless transactions can also be facilitated through the involvement of third-party mediators or arbitrators. For instance, in a peer-to-peer insurance arrangement, parties may appoint a neutral mediator to oversee the transaction process and ensure that both parties fulfil their obligations. The mediator's impartiality and adherence to established rules help mitigate the need for direct trust between the transacting parties. Reputation-based systems can contribute to trustless transactions by providing transparency and accountability within decentralized insurance communities. Participants can build and maintain reputations based on their past behaviours and interactions. For example, in a decentralized insurance platform, users with a proven track record of honesty and

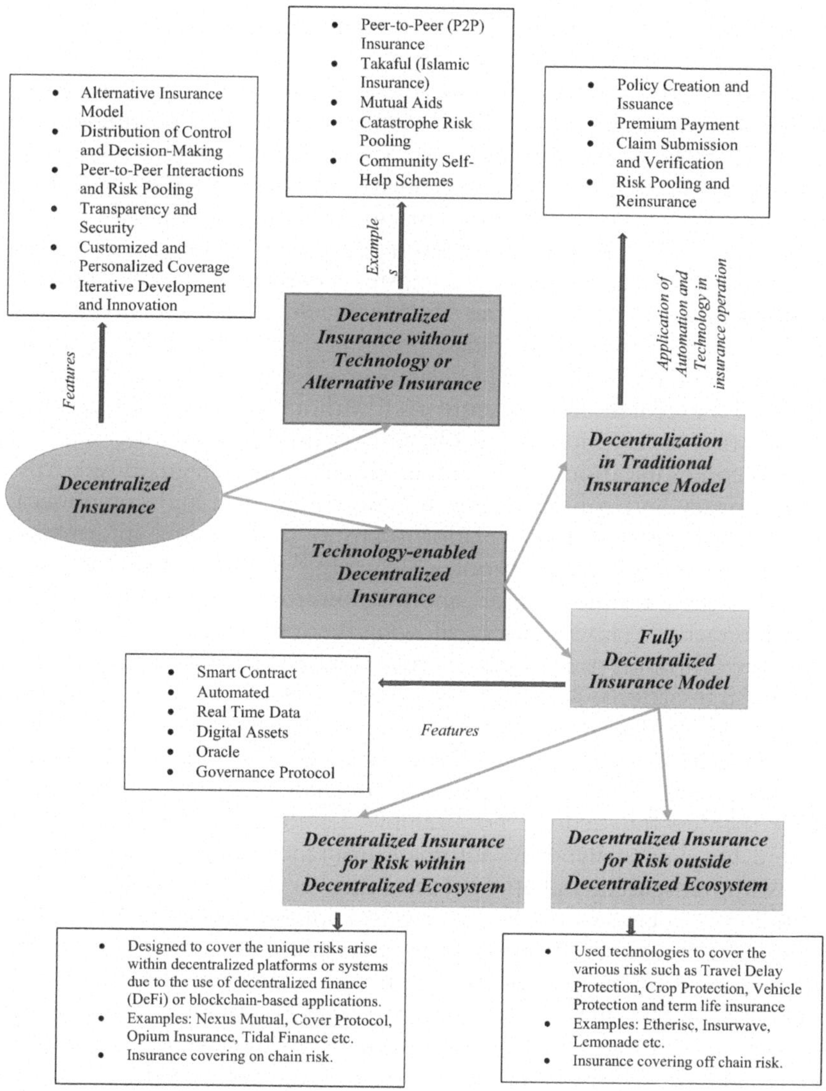

Fig. 1.1 Realm of decentralized insurance (*Source* Prepared by authors)

integrity may be more trusted by other participants, leading to increased confidence in trustless transactions.

Nowadays, the advent of innovative technologies has made trustless transactions quite easier. For example, blockchain technology has provided a transparent, immutable, decentralized ledger that records all transactions. Each transaction is verified and added to the blockchain through a consensus mechanism, making altering or tampering with historical data virtually impossible. As a result, trust is no longer dependent on centralized entities but is instead derived from the inherent security and transparency of the blockchain. Smart contracts, deployed on blockchain networks, automate insurance processes such as policy issuance, premium payments, and claims processing, ensuring that transactions are executed transparently and without the need for trust in third parties. Encryption protocols are essential for securing sensitive data and communications on decentralized platforms, safeguarding participants' privacy and confidentiality. By encrypting data and communications, decentralized insurance platforms ensure that sensitive information remains secure and tamper-proof, enhancing participant trust. Peer-to-peer networking technologies are another powerful technique that enables direct interactions between users, allowing them to transact without intermediaries. Through peer-to-peer networking, participants can engage in trustless transactions, knowing that their interactions are verified and validated by the decentralized network rather than a centralized authority.

Decentralized insurance platforms leverage blockchain technology, smart contracts, encryption protocols, and peer-to-peer networking to enable trustless transactions. For example, Lemonade utilizes blockchain, AI, and big data analytics to automate insurance processes and provide users with transparent and efficient insurance services. By leveraging these technologies, Lemonade ensures trustless interactions between policyholders and insurers, enhancing transparency and efficiency in insurance transactions. Another example is TongJuBao, which employs digital platforms and mobile apps to facilitate peer-to-peer insurance transactions. Through TongJuBao's platform, users can directly engage with each other to share risks and financial burdens without intermediaries. By leveraging digital platforms and peer-to-peer networking technologies, TongJuBao enables trustless transactions and fosters greater transparency and efficiency in insurance. These examples demonstrate how decentralized insurance platforms leverage various technologies to enable trustless transactions, empowering participants to transact confidently and transparently in the decentralized insurance ecosystem.

1.3.2 Transparency and Immutability

Transparency and immutability are fundamental principles in decentralized insurance, contributing to trust, accountability, and reliability within the ecosystem. Transparency ensures that all participants in decentralized insurance have access to the same information regarding policies, transactions, and claims. It fosters trust among stakeholders by providing visibility into the processes and activities within the insurance ecosystem. On the other hand, immutability refers to the inability to alter or tamper with recorded data. This ensures the integrity and permanence of records, preventing unauthorized modifications and preserving the historical accuracy of transactions. Achieving transparency and immutability in decentralized insurance involves various practices and mechanisms prioritizing openness, integrity, and permanence in insurance transactions. One of the primary ways transparency and immutability are achieved in decentralized insurance is through blockchain technology. Blockchain serves as a distributed ledger where all transactions are recorded in a transparent, secure, and immutable manner.

Each transaction, or block, is cryptographically linked to the previous one, forming a chain of blocks that cannot be altered retroactively. This ensures that once data is recorded on the blockchain, it cannot be tampered with or modified, guaranteeing the integrity and permanence of insurance records. Smart contracts, self-executing contracts with terms directly written into code, are significant in ensuring transparency and immutability in decentralized insurance. These contracts automate and enforce the terms of insurance agreements, eliminating the need for intermediaries and reducing the risk of human error or manipulation. Smart contracts execute predefined actions automatically when predetermined conditions are met, providing transparency and certainty in transactions (Goodenough & Salkind, 2021). Decentralized governance mechanisms empower participants in decentralized insurance platforms to participate in decision-making processes that shape insurance policies, premiums, and parameters. Through decentralized governance models, stakeholders can vote on proposals, influence platform policies, and contribute to the design of innovative insurance products. This democratic approach increases transparency, accountability, and responsiveness to user needs, ensuring that the interests of all participants are represented and protected. Independent auditing and verification processes ensure transparency and immutability in decentralized insurance. Auditors and verifiers examine insurance transactions, policies, and claims to verify their accuracy, compliance with regulations, and adherence to predefined criteria. These auditing processes assure stakeholders that insurance transactions are conducted transparently and following established standards, enhancing trust and confidence in the decentralized insurance ecosystem. Decentralized insurance platforms may adopt public reporting and disclosure practices to promote transparency and immutability. Publicly reporting financial statements, claims data, and performance metrics allows stakeholders to assess the platform's operations, financial health, and regulation compliance. By providing access to transparent and comprehensive information, decentralized insurance platforms demonstrate their commitment to accountability and openness, fostering participant trust.

1.3.3 Peer-To-Peer Interactions or Collaborative Risk Sharing

In decentralized insurance, the principle of peer-to-peer interactions, or collaborative risk sharing, underscores the core concept of facilitating direct engagement between individuals in insurance transactions, bypassing traditional intermediaries such as insurance companies or brokers. Within decentralized insurance, participants are empowered to interact directly with one another, negotiating, creating, purchasing, and managing insurance policies without third-party intervention. Collaborative risk-sharing emphasizes the collective approach to managing risks, where individuals pool their resources and share the financial burdens associated with potential losses.

These platforms equip individuals with the tools and infrastructure to engage directly in insurance transactions, fostering a sense of ownership and control over insurance decisions. One of the primary benefits of peer-to-peer insurance models lies in their ability to democratize access to insurance coverage. By eliminating intermediaries, decentralized platforms significantly reduce administrative costs and overheads, resulting in more competitive pricing and greater accessibility to insurance products. Moreover, peer-to-peer interactions facilitate resource pooling and risk sharing among individuals, fostering community and mutual support within the insurance ecosystem.

Platforms like Teambrella, Lemonade, and Friendsurance exemplify peer-to-peer insurance models. Teambrella operates as a peer-to-peer insurance platform that enables collective insurance arrangements among groups of individuals through blockchain-based smart contracts. Lemonade, leveraging artificial intelligence and behavioural economics, streamlines the insurance process by allowing the direct purchase of insurance and pooling premiums to pay out claims. The platform's transparency in disclosing fee structures and donating unclaimed premiums to charitable causes builds trust among users. Friendsurance incentivizes policyholders to form small groups and pool premiums, offering cashback bonuses in the absence of claims, thereby fostering a community-centric approach to risk management.

Peer-to-peer interactions form the cornerstone of decentralized insurance, enabling direct engagement in transactions, collective risk sharing, and community building within the insurance ecosystem. Through innovative platforms and models, peer-to-peer insurance is revolutionizing the insurance landscape, making it more accessible, transparent, and tailored to the needs of individuals and communities. Collaborative risk sharing ensures that the financial burdens associated with potential losses are distributed among participants, promoting shared responsibility and solidarity in managing risks.

1.3.4 Autonomous Governance

Autonomous governance in decentralized insurance refers to the automated and self-executing mechanisms embedded within decentralized platforms, allowing for decentralized decision-making processes without centralized authorities or intermediaries. It involves the establishment of governance frameworks and protocols that enable participants within the ecosystem to collectively govern and manage the platform's operations, policies, and protocols transparently and autonomously.

Before the advent of modern technology, decentralized governance in insurance or any other sector was much more challenging to implement effectively. However, certain decentralized decision-making and governance principles have historically existed, albeit in different forms. In traditional societies, many decisions, including those related to risk management and insurance-like arrangements, were often made at the local community level. Villages or towns would collectively decide how to address risks such as crop failures, property damage, or illness within their community. These community-based approaches allowed participation and consensus-building among local stakeholders. Mutual aid societies have a long history, dating back centuries in various cultures. These societies operated on collective responsibility and support principles, where members contributed funds or resources to a common pool. In times of need, such as illness, disability, or death, members could draw upon these pooled resources for financial assistance. Mutual aid societies exemplified principles of community-driven support and shared risk management. In mediaeval Europe and other regions, guilds and trade associations served as forms of decentralized governance within specific industries or trades. These organizations established rules, standards, and dispute resolution mechanisms for their members, often without direct intervention from centralized authorities. While hierarchical to some extent, guilds and trade associations provided a degree of autonomy and self-regulation within their respective sectors. In many traditional societies, informal agreements and contracts are crucial in governing interactions and managing risks. Individuals or communities would enter into agreements based on mutual trust and understanding, often without the need for formal legal frameworks or intermediaries. These informal arrangements relied on principles of trust, reciprocity, and social norms to govern behaviour and resolve disputes. While these historical examples demonstrate decentralized decision-making and governance to some extent, they were limited in scope, scale, and efficiency compared to contemporary decentralized systems enabled by technology. Nowadays, blockchain technology, smart contracts, and decentralized autonomous organizations provide robust and scalable mechanisms for decentralized governance, allowing for transparent, auditable, and autonomous decision-making processes at a global scale.

Decentralized autonomous organizations (DAOs) are self-governing entities operating through smart contracts and decentralized consensus mechanisms, enabling stakeholders to participate in decision-making processes, vote on proposals, and collectively govern the platform's affairs. Decentralized governance mechanisms, such as DAOs, facilitate decision-making processes in decentralized insurance platforms through various mechanisms:

- Proposal Submission: Participants within the ecosystem can submit proposals for changes, improvements, or new initiatives within the platform. These proposals are typically recorded on the blockchain and open for review and discussion by other stakeholders.
- Voting Mechanisms: Once a proposal is submitted, stakeholders can vote on its approval or rejection. Each participant's voting power is typically determined by their stake or contribution to the platform, ensuring that decisions are made proportionally to each participant's level of involvement.
- Execution of Proposals: Once a proposal is approved through the voting process, smart contracts autonomously execute the agreed upon changes or actions. These smart contracts are programmatically enforced, ensuring that the decisions made by the community are implemented accurately and transparently.

There are several use case studies of autonomous governance in decentralized insurance platforms. Aragon is a decentralized autonomous organization (DAO) platform that enables the creation and management of decentralized organizations. It provides organizations with tools and infrastructure to govern autonomously through transparent and auditable processes. Nexus Mutual is a decentralized insurance platform built on the Ethereum blockchain that provides coverage against smart contract failures and other risks in the DeFi space. It operates as a DAO, where members collectively govern the platform's affairs, including risk assessment, claims adjudication, and premium setting. Members vote on proposals and decisions through the NXM token, representing their ownership and voting rights within the platform. This autonomous governance in decentralized insurance platforms empowers stakeholders to participate in decision-making processes and collectively govern the platform's affairs transparently, audibly, and autonomously.

1.3.5 Security and Privacy

Security and privacy are paramount in decentralized insurance systems, protecting sensitive information and maintaining participants' trust within the ecosystem. In decentralized insurance, security means safeguarding data and assets against unauthorized access, manipulation, or theft. At the same time, privacy is all about protecting individuals' personal information and transactions from being disclosed to unauthorized parties. These principles are critical for building trust and confidence among users and fostering widespread adoption of decentralized insurance platforms. This can be possible through physical security measures, such as locked filing cabinets, restricted access to sensitive documents, and manual verification processes. However, these manual processes and trust-based relationships were somewhat effective but were also prone to human error, fraud, and inefficiencies. Advances in technology, such as digital encryption, secure databases, and automated verification systems, have since revolutionized the way security and privacy are maintained in insurance transactions. Encryption techniques are utilized to secure data transmission and storage within decentralized systems. Cryptographic protocols ensure that sensitive information remains confidential and is only accessible to authorized parties with the appropriate decryption keys. Decentralized insurance platforms leverage distributed ledger technology, such as blockchain, to store transactional data across a network of nodes. This distributed architecture enhances security by eliminating single points of failure and reducing the risk of data tampering or manipulation. Consensus algorithms, such as Proof of Work (PoW) or Proof of Stake (PoS), ensure data integrity on decentralized networks by requiring network participants to agree on the validity of transactions. These mechanisms prevent malicious actors from altering the blockchain's history and ensure only valid transactions are added to the ledger. Role-based access control (RBAC) mechanisms are implemented to manage permissions and access levels within decentralized insurance platforms. By assigning specific roles and privileges to users based on their credentials and responsibilities, RBAC ensures that sensitive data is only accessible to authorized individuals. Privacy-preserving technologies, such as zero-knowledge proofs (ZKPs) and homomorphic encryption, enable transactions to be conducted privately without revealing sensitive information to other parties. ZKPs allow users to prove the validity of a statement without disclosing the underlying data, thereby preserving privacy while still ensuring trust and verifiability.

1.3.6 Interoperability and Scalability

Interoperability and scalability are two fundamental principles that underpin the efficiency and effectiveness of decentralized insurance ecosystems. Interoperability refers to the seamless exchange and utilization of information between different systems, platforms, or networks within the insurance landscape. It ensures that data can flow freely and be accessed and utilized by various ecosystem components without encountering compatibility issues or barriers. On the other hand, scalability pertains to the system's capacity to accommodate increasing workloads and growing demand while maintaining optimal performance and efficiency. This ensures that the infrastructure supporting decentralized insurance can scale up to support a growing number of users, transactions, and data volumes over time without experiencing degradation in performance.

Historically, interoperability in insurance relied on standardized practices, manual processes, and human coordination. Insurance contracts, policies, and claims were documented using standardized forms and protocols to ensure consistency and compatibility across different insurers and markets. However, in the modern era of technologically-enabled decentralized insurance, achieving interoperability requires careful planning and adherence to best practices. A modular architecture design approach is often employed when designing interoperable and scalable decentralized insurance solutions. This approach allows for the development and integration of different components and functionalities within the ecosystem in a modular fashion. By breaking down the system into smaller, interconnected modules, developers can ensure that each component can communicate and interact seamlessly with others, promoting interoperability. Standardization of data formats, protocols, and interfaces is also crucial for achieving interoperability in decentralized insurance. By adopting standardized practices, platforms and networks can ensure that data can be exchanged and interpreted consistently across different systems and platforms, facilitating interoperability. Flexible consensus mechanisms and governance models can facilitate decision-making and coordination among stakeholders, further promoting interoperability and scalability within the ecosystem. Continuous monitoring, testing, and optimization of the infrastructure are essential for proactively identifying and addressing scalability bottlenecks and performance issues. By regularly assessing the system's performance and making necessary adjustments, decentralized insurance platforms can ensure they can scale effectively as they grow. This iterative optimization approach helps maintain optimal performance and efficiency, even as the demands on the system increase over time. Hence, interoperability and scalability are essential principles of decentralized insurance. Through careful planning, standardization, and continuous optimization, decentralized insurance platforms can maximize their interoperability and scalability, enhancing their ability to meet the evolving needs of users and stakeholders in the insurance industry.

1.3.7 *Inclusivity and Accessibility*

Inclusivity ensures that decentralized insurance platforms cater to the needs of a diverse range of individuals, regardless of their socioeconomic status, geographical location, or cultural background. By promoting inclusivity, decentralized insurance platforms can address the needs of marginalized communities and underserved populations with limited access to traditional insurance services. Accessibility, however, ensures that insurance services are easily accessible and user-friendly for individuals across different regions and demographics. By enhancing accessibility, decentralized insurance platforms can break down barriers to entry and empower individuals to protect themselves against risks effectively. There are several strategies for ensuring inclusivity and accessibility. Decentralized insurance platforms should prioritize user-centric design principles to ensure that their interfaces and services are intuitive, easy to navigate, and accessible to individuals with diverse levels of technological literacy. Providing support for multiple languages enables individuals from different linguistic backgrounds to access insurance services in their preferred language, enhancing inclusivity and accessibility. Engaging with local communities and stakeholders can help decentralized insurance platforms understand the unique needs and challenges different demographic groups face, allowing them to tailor their services accordingly. Implementing flexible payment options and affordable insurance products can promote financial inclusion by enabling individuals with limited financial resources to access insurance coverage. By adopting strategies that prioritize the diverse needs of individuals and communities, decentralized insurance platforms can enhance financial resilience, promote social equity, and empower individuals to protect themselves against unforeseen risks effectively.

The principles of decentralized insurance represent core values that drive innovation, trust, and inclusivity in the insurance industry. By adhering to these principles, stakeholders can create a more equitable and accessible insurance ecosystem, fostering transparency, autonomy, and security for all participants.

1.4 Decentralized Insurance Without Technology or Alternative Insurance

It's worth noting that not all decentralized insurance models rely on technologies. Several decentralized insurance approaches operate without technologies, such as peer-to-peer (P2P) insurance, takaful (Islamic insurance), mutual aid, self-help schemes, and catastrophe risk pooling. These decentralized or alternative insurance approaches embody a community-driven ethos based on mutual support and cooperation principles (Swiss Re, 2017a). Instead of relying on a centralized authority dictating the terms and conditions of financial arrangements, these schemes flourish on the bedrock of transparency, trust, and consensus. The intermediary role is obviated, empowering policyholders with unprecedented control over their coverage, premiums, and claims processes. Decentralizing insurance and financial services involves transferring control away from large banks and financial institutions distributing power among a broader public. This approach lowers the costs associated with financial transactions, enables all participants to leverage network effects, and expands their opportunities (Stepanova & Eriņš, 2021).

Decentralized insurance represents a unique and community-driven approach to risk management and assurance. This paradigm refers to traditional principles of mutual support, collaboration, and shared responsibility within a community. The essence lies in fostering human connections, transparency, and collective decision-making to create a decentralized insurance-like system. Communities or groups of individuals establish assurance networks where residents come together, committing to support each other in times of need. This assurance network operates on interpersonal relationships and mutual trust, cultivating a culture of shared responsibility within the community. The approach fosters a sense of community solidarity. Members actively participate in the assurance network, creating a safety net where individuals feel secure knowing their neighbours are committed to supporting them during challenging circumstances. In this model, there is transparent risk assessment through open discussions within the community. Residents collectively identify and assess potential risks faced collectively, whether they be natural disasters, economic challenges, or unforeseen events. This grassroots approach allows for a shared understanding of vulnerabilities. Transparent risk assessment ensures that the insurance-like coverage aligns with the community's genuine risks. It promotes a collective awareness of potential challenges, allowing members to tailor their mutual support network to address specific needs. Decisions related to the decentralized insurance system are made through regular community meetings, emphasizing shared governance.

There is no reliance on complex technological platforms; decisions are shaped through open dialogue and consensus-building among community members. Shared governance enhances transparency and inclusivity. It empowers community members to contribute to establishing and evolving the decentralized insurance model actively, ensuring that policies resonate with the community's collective values. Participants make verbal commitments to assist each other based on reciprocity. Reciprocal commitments create a sense of accountability and reinforce the idea that mutual support is a shared responsibility. This cultural aspect fosters empathy and interconnectedness, where individuals feel secure knowing their community is committed to their well-being. When a community member faces significant challenges, they call upon the collective assurance of the community. Other members step in to provide tangible support, such as sharing resources, offering skills or services, or contributing to a communal fund established for such situations. Collective assistance ensures that no member faces adversity alone.

Various decentralized insurance schemes based on collaborative sharing have emerged worldwide, each with distinctive mechanisms. For instance, online mutual aid platforms in China have gained immense popularity. Here, individuals willingly contribute to a common pool, and when a participant encounters a specific risk, such as medical expenses, the community rallies together, offering financial support following predefined rules and mutual agreements. In the West, peer-to-peer insurance platforms have increased, enabling direct interaction between individuals seeking insurance coverage. By pooling their resources and collectively sharing risks, these platforms prevent the need for traditional intermediaries. In the Middle East, the principles of takaful, deeply rooted in Islamic tenets, shape the cooperative insurance model. Participants contribute to a communal pool guided by the noble concept of mutual assistance. Decentralized insurance mechanisms such as catastrophe risk pooling have been established in regions prone to natural disasters, such as the Caribbean. These pools aggregate risks and extend vital financial assistance to the afflicted areas, distributing the burden across a broader collective. These innovative models have paved the way for decentralized insurance platforms and protocols operating on blockchain networks.

However, incorporating technology significantly enhances decentralized insurance models rooted in traditional principles. Technology brings scalability to accommodate the growth of decentralized networks, fosters transparent and efficient communication through distributed ledgers, automates claims processing with smart contracts, enables tokenization for asset representation, ensures an immutable record for trust, breaks down geographical barriers for global accessibility, allows for programmable rules and governance, and enhances data security and privacy. This seamless integration amplifies the effectiveness, scalability, and accessibility of decentralized insurance, accompanying traditional community-driven values with technological innovation to empower individuals, foster trust, and reshape the future of insurance in a digital age (PWC, 2023).

1.5 Technology-enabled Decentralized Insurance

In a decentralized framework, technology-enabled decentralized insurance refers to a technology-powered model of mutual risk-sharing without a centralized financial intermediary. For instance, Smart contracts represent a transformative tool in the insurance industry, particularly in automating policy issuance. These contracts, encoded with predefined conditions and executed autonomously, streamline operations while enhancing transparency and security (Hirschfield & Duric, 2022). For instance, Etherisc, a decentralized insurance platform, utilizes smart contracts to automate policy issuance for various insurance products, including flight delay and parametric crop insurance. With Etherisc, policyholders can access coverage through decentralized applications (DApps) and smart contracts deployed on blockchain networks. These smart contracts execute predefined conditions, such as a flight delay or adverse weather conditions, triggering automatic payouts to policyholders without needing manual claims processing. The automation enabled by smart contracts expedites the policy issuance process, enhances transparency, and reduces the risk of errors or fraud. Since smart contracts operate on blockchain networks, all transactions and policy-related activities are recorded immutably on the blockchain, providing a transparent audit trail. This transparency builds trust among stakeholders, as they can independently verify the integrity of policy issuance and premium payments. Smart contracts reduce the administrative overhead associated with traditional policy issuance methods, benefiting insurers and policyholders. Insurers can significantly reduce operational costs and improve efficiency by automating premium calculations, policy terms, and payment processing. Conversely, policyholders enjoy a faster and more convenient purchasing experience, with policies issued in minutes rather than days or weeks. Lemonade, a prominent InsurTech company, facilitates rapid policy issuance for renters and homeowners' insurance through its platform. Through its digital platform, customers can apply for coverage, receive quotes, and complete the purchase process entirely online. Behind the scenes, smart contracts handle premium calculations, policy terms, and payment processing, ensuring users' seamless and efficient experience.

Technology-enabled decentralized insurance platforms streamline claims processing by automating claim verification and settlement procedures. These platforms revolutionize the traditional claims processing workflow by automating key steps and introducing transparency and efficiency. Smart contracts, deployed on blockchain networks, play a central role in automating claim verification and settlement procedures. For instance, in the case of flight delay insurance, companies like AXA and Etherisc utilize smart contracts to trigger claims payouts when predefined conditions are met automatically. If a flight delay occurs beyond a specified duration, the smart contract automatically releases funds to the policyholder without requiring manual intervention. The automation facilitated by smart contracts drastically reduces the processing time for claims. Rather than relying on manual review and verification by claims adjusters, smart contracts execute the claims process automatically once the predetermined conditions are met. This accelerates the payout process and minimizes the potential for human error or bias, enhancing the accuracy and fairness of claims settlements.

Furthermore, technology-enabled decentralized insurance platforms leverage blockchain's immutability and transparency to enhance claims processing's security and trustworthiness. Companies like Etherisc and Teambrella utilize blockchain technology to record all claim-related transactions and activities in a tamper-proof manner. This creates an immutable audit trail of the entire claims journey, enabling stakeholders, including policyholders, insurers, and regulators, to independently verify the authenticity and integrity of claims transactions. Another critical advantage of technology-enabled decentralized insurance platforms is mitigating fraudulent claims. Automating the claims process and implementing predefined conditions for claims payouts reduce the possibility of fraudulent activities. For example, Lemonade employs AI algorithms to detect and prevent fraudulent claims, ensuring the integrity of the insurance ecosystem. Technology-enabled decentralized insurance platforms leverage data analytics, AI, and ML algorithms to assess risks accurately. These platforms analyse vast amounts of data from various sources, including IoT devices, social media, and historical insurance data, to evaluate risks and determine appropriate premium rates. By harnessing advanced technologies, insurers can make data-driven decisions and offer personalized insurance products tailored to individual risk profiles. Decentralized insurance platforms facilitate peer-to-peer underwriting, where participants collectively assess and assume risks. Stakeholders collaboratively determine underwriting criteria and policy terms through transparent voting mechanisms and consensus algorithms. This decentralized approach promotes fairness, inclusivity, and community engagement in the underwriting process. Advanced technologies such as AI and ML are crucial in detecting and preventing insurance fraud. These technologies analyse patterns, anomalies, and historical data to identify suspicious claims and fraudulent activities. By leveraging real-time data analysis and predictive modelling, insurers can proactively detect fraud and mitigate potential losses, thereby safeguarding the integrity of the insurance ecosystem. Decentralized insurance platforms enhance customer service through digital channels and self-service options. AI-powered chatbots provide instant support and assistance to policyholders, addressing queries, processing claims, and providing personalized recommendations. Digital platforms offer intuitive interfaces for policy management, premium payments, and claims submissions, enhancing the customer experience.

Peer-to-peer insurance is widely accepted through technology. For instance, peer-to-peer insurance operates using tokens for premium and claims settlements, functioning on a public blockchain like Ethereum, a concept often termed tokenized or token-based insurance. In this system, participants interact directly on the blockchain or any digital platform, theoretically bypassing the need for a middleman. Notably, peer-to-peer decentralized insurance operates independently of traditional insurance companies, catering to a cohort of policyholders with similar insurance requirements, as Nexus Mutual and Teambrella exemplify. This decentralized insurance framework typically involves two primary stages. Initially, participants exchange risks among themselves to attain risk diversification through the blockchain or any digital platform. Subsequently, they transfer risks beyond their collective risk-bearing capacity to third parties, often via reinsurance mechanisms. Despite its potential, decentralized insurance's total value locked (TVL) remains relatively modest, hovering just above USD 500 million as of October 2022, constituting a mere 0.5% of the TVL in the broader decentralized ecosystem. Tokens, also known as crypto tokens, represent a crypto asset tokenized on an existing cryptocurrency's blockchain. For instance, tokens like NXM are built on Ethereum's blockchain and serve various purposes, such as funding peer-to-peer insurance initiatives.

Furthermore, technology can optimize various aspects of the insurance value chain, facilitating internal information sharing, identity verification, and claims validation. Decentralized pension databases at the national level enhance information sharing and data security. Blockchain technology facilitates supply chain finance, credit insurance, crypto-related risk coverage, and innovative services like financing brokerage receivables. The case of Annchain (ZQAlink) illustrates this concept (The Geneva Association, 2023). Originating with Bitcoin, blockchain technology has birthed numerous cryptocurrencies, crypto assets, and stablecoins, enabling secure online payments without traditional financial intermediaries. Cryptocurrencies are integrated into mainstream insurance services, serving as tools for premium and claims payments and investment assets for forward-thinking insurers. Despite experiencing market fluctuations, cryptocurrencies remain integral to the market acceptance of blockchain applications. Blockchain 2.0, exemplified by Ethereum, introduces smart contracts, revolutionizing insurance processes. While insurance contracts are traditionally complex, smart contracts enhance transparency and accessibility for consumers, insurers, and regulators. Smart contracts streamline insurance processes, from quotations and policy administration to claims processing and contract renewal, driving efficiency, and customer satisfaction.

Moreover, blockchain 2.0 significantly improves energy efficiency compared to its predecessor, addressing concerns regarding energy consumption. As the cornerstone of DeFi/blockchain insurance, smart contracts bolster trust between transaction parties, mitigate moral hazard, detect fraud, automate operations, and expedite claims payments. They also enable the codification of regulations, facilitating compliance monitoring and regulatory reporting in an automated fashion.

Hence, technology-based decentralized insurance emerges as a game-changer in an era of technological innovation and a hunger for empowerment. It challenges the status quo, disrupting traditional insurance models and paving the way for a more inclusive and democratized system (Ankitha, 2022; Nath, 2016). By embracing this revolution, individuals reclaim control over their financial well-being, ushering in a future where insurance is no longer a one-size-fits-all concept but a dynamic and personalized safeguard tailored to their unique needs (Deloitte, 2016).

Technology-enabled decentralized insurance encompasses two categories: decentralization within the traditional insurance model and fully decentralized insurance. In the first category, decentralization is introduced gradually into existing insurance frameworks, enhancing certain aspects of traditional insurance operations through technology integration. This approach involves leveraging innovative technologies such as blockchain, smart contracts, and artificial intelligence to optimize specific processes within traditional insurance models. For example, smart contracts automate policy issuance, claims processing, and contract management, streamlining operations and reducing administrative overhead. Similarly, artificial intelligence algorithms are employed to enhance underwriting processes, risk assessment, and fraud detection, improving the efficiency and accuracy of traditional insurance practices. Rather than completely replacing existing insurance processes, blockchain-based solutions can be implemented to automate specific aspects, such as claim processing or managing the insurance-reinsurance or broker-reinsurance relationship. Pioneering initiatives like B3i and Nayms leverage smart contracts and on-chain processes to enhance efficiency, reduce administrative costs, and improve transparency in traditional insurance operations (Meeusen, 2017; Swiss Re, 2017a, b).

On the other hand, fully decentralized insurance represents a more radical departure from traditional insurance models, where the entire insurance process is conducted on decentralized platforms without centralized intermediaries. In this category, technology serves as the foundation for creating peer-to-peer insurance networks, where policyholders interact directly with each other to share risks and pool resources. These decentralized insurance platforms leverage blockchain, decentralized applications (DApps), and tokenization to facilitate trustless transactions, transparent governance, and automated claims processing (Cousaert et al., 2022). By eliminating the need for traditional insurance companies and intermediaries, fully decentralized insurance platforms aim to democratize access to insurance, reduce costs, and foster greater transparency and trust within the insurance ecosystem.

There are two basic models of fully decentralized insurance. These are within and outside the decentralized ecosystem. The first model operates within the DeFi ecosystem, specifically addressing risks unique to this decentralized financial landscape, such as smart contract vulnerabilities and unstable stablecoins. It aims to provide tailored insurance solutions to protect participants against these specific or on-chain risks and ensure the overall stability of DeFi. The second model ventures beyond the DeFi ecosystem and provides decentralized insurance solutions for the broader insurance industry. This model harnesses the power of blockchain technology, smart contracts, and alternative decentralized insurance approaches to cover off-chain risks and streamline traditional value chains. Off-chain risks refer to events outside the blockchain network but can still be insured using the power of blockchain technology. Examples of such risks include parametric flight delay or weather risk coverage. Companies like Teambrella and TongJuBao harness blockchain technology to establish transparent and efficient processes for coverage against these types of risks.

1.5.1 Decentralization in Traditional Insurance Model

Decentralization in the traditional insurance model brings a remarkable transformation by simplifying complex processes. By making the traditional framework interactive, decentralization fosters simplicity, transparency, and efficiency in the insurance industry. Imagine a scenario where policyholders can directly interact with insurers through peer-to-peer networks. This streamlined approach simplifies the insurance experience, allowing policyholders to be more active in managing their policies and claims. Decentralization in the insurance business can occur with or without technology, but technology brings a creative aspect to the traditional insurance model by leveraging advanced technology and digital solutions. Insurance operations can be automated through advanced technologies like blockchain, smart contracts, and artificial intelligence, reducing manual paperwork, and time-consuming processes.

The insurance industry has been relatively slow to embrace the digital revolution due to stringent regulations, extensive existing policies, and the significant capital required to cover insurance risks. However, the industry is not impervious to change. Companies that fail to adapt to digital advancements will face increased pressure from competitors who leverage technology to reduce costs and enhance investment returns. These companies will struggle to keep up as digital innovations continue to disrupt traditional business models. For instance, in the realm of personal auto insurance, the use of vehicle sensors is already driving down premiums as driving safety improves. Observing other industries, it is evident that new digital competitors with substantial customer bases can swiftly enter new markets driven by data and analytics.

This shift presents numerous opportunities for established insurance companies to transform how they deliver products and services, the nature of these offerings, and even their overall business model. Recognizing the need for digital transformation is one thing; effectively managing it is another challenge. There is no foolproof guide to ensure a smooth transition to the digital age. Companies that act quickly and decisively are likely to thrive, while those that hesitate will find it increasingly difficult to achieve profitable returns. The insurance industry remains largely uncharted territory in digital transformation, as no company has completed this journey yet—it may take up to a decade. Nevertheless, some insurance companies have begun to explore using Blockchain for specific applications.

1.5.1.1 Technology Revolutionizing Traditional Insurance Landscape: Instance from Pioneers

AIG, IBM, and Standard Chartered Bank's Blockchain-Powered Policy

American International Group, Inc. (AIG) stands at the forefront as a leading global insurance organization. With a rich history from its founding in 1919, AIG and its member companies have become renowned for providing customers with a wide range of insurance and financial services in over 80 countries and jurisdictions. This creative exploration delves into the collaboration between AIG, IBM, and Standard Chartered Bank plc, resulting in successfully piloting the world's first multinational, "smart contract" based insurance policy using blockchain technology.

The integration of blockchain technology marks a turning point for the insurance industry, igniting excitement among industry experts who anticipate significant cost reductions and a decline in disputes. AIG's policy for Standard Chartered comprises a "master policy" in the United

Kingdom linked to local policies in the United States, Kenya, and Singapore. A master policy is generally issued in the country where a company has its headquarters. At the same time, subsidiaries or affiliated branches often require insurance coverage in countries with different regulations, documentation requirements, and payment terms. The Standard Chartered policy utilizes blockchain technology to enable instant information sharing for a primary policy written in the United Kingdom, which serves as the bank's headquarters, along with three separate local policies in the United States, Singapore, and Kenya (Ralph, 2017).

This pioneering approach eliminates the bottlenecks typically associated with multinational policies by providing a swift and cost-effective solution using smart contracts. International insurance coverage is always challenging due to the complex regulations, paperwork, and payment terms, making managing it cumbersome. However, by converting complex multinational policies into "smart contracts," industry leaders can provide real-time access to policy data and documentation, ensuring visibility into coverage, premium payments, and automated notifications across local and master levels (Faulkner, 2017). Moreover, including third parties such as brokers, auditors, and stakeholders fosters a customized view of policy and payment data, revolutionizing collaboration within the network. The successful pilot of AIG's multinational, blockchain-based insurance policy is a powerful testament to the potential impact of Blockchain in the insurance industry.

The Advent of Blockchain Consortiums

AIG's foray into blockchain experimentation is not a solitary endeavour within the insurance industry. B3i, an industry consortium established in 2016, features prominent names such as Munich Re, Swiss Re, Zurich, Aegon, and Allianz, demonstrating the increasing interest in the potential of Blockchain. Subsequently, in 2017, ten other companies, including Achmea, Ageas, Generali, Hannover Re, Liberty Mutual, SCOR, Sompo, RGA, Tokio Marine, and XL Catlin (now AXA XL), joined the consortium. Willis Towers Watson also participated as a strategic advisory board member (Allianz, 2016; Meeusen, 2017).

In 2018, B3i established a company called B3i Services AG in Zurich, which garnered support from 20 major re/insurer investors by 2020. This collaborative effort implies a comprehensive approach requiring all insurance companies to create smart contracts from the outset. The insurers and reinsurers who invested in B3i aimed to explore the potential of using

Distributed Ledger Technologies (DLT) to reduce costs and uncertainties associated with insurance transactions. An oft-cited example was the aftermath of the September 11 terrorist attacks when the coverage for the World Trade Center was agreed upon, but paperwork was still pending when the towers were hit. This led to protracted legal proceedings. The theory was that lengthy legal disputes could have been avoided if blockchain solutions had been available and the policy had been recorded in a shared, verifiable ledger.

The B3i Initiative secured substantial funding in millions of dollars in the early years and gained support from leading insurance and reinsurance companies worldwide. In fact, as of April 2022, Allianz and Swiss Re utilized the company's technology to execute the first excess of loss (XoL) reinsurance contract on Distributed Ledger Technology (DLT).

Hence, B3i signifies a joint effort to explore the transformative potential of Blockchain in the insurance industry. Moreover, AIG's collaboration with Standard Chartered and the B3i consortium share a distinctive characteristic: the absence of insurance brokers. This new approach challenges the traditional insurance landscape and addresses the increasing tensions between insurers and brokers. Recently, B3i announced a lack of adequate support to sustain its venture, prompting concerns regarding the long-term viability of technological solutions in the insurance industry (Sheehan, 2022). Amid this, Allianz, one of its shareholders, released a statement acknowledging the discontinuation of the B3i consortium comprising 20 insurers. However, the collaboration has yielded successful blockchain applications that Allianz presently utilizes. Allianz maintains its belief in the potential of blockchain technology and is actively exploring avenues to further its development.

Showcasing Innovations: AXA's Flight Delay Insurance

AXA, one of the world's largest insurance companies, and blockchain startup Fizzy have pioneered a decentralized flight delay insurance product, leveraging the power of smart contracts on the Ethereum blockchain (Terekhova, 2017). By automatically recording insurance purchases on an immutable ledger and linking them to global air traffic databases, Fizzy enables instant compensation for a flight delay of over two hours. The smart contract acts as an automated arbitrator, eliminating potential disputes between insurers and customers. This innovative approach simplifies the compensation process and enhances the insurer-customer.

For instance, When customers acquire flight delay insurance through Fizzy's platform, their purchase is permanently recorded on the tamper-proof Ethereum blockchain, ensuring the utmost security and transparency of the insurance agreement. This smart contract is intricately linked to global air traffic databases, enabling swift and automatic compensation initiation when a delay surpassing two hours is detected. This delegation of the compensation decision to an independent network strengthens customer trust in AXA and reinforces the company's commitment to providing reliable insurance services.

AXA's partnership with Fizzy represents a significant milestone in the insurance industry's adoption of blockchain technology. Through the utilization of smart contracts, the complex process of flight delay insurance is simplified. These kinds of investments in insurtechs continue to disrupt the insurance landscape, and legacy players must recognize the urgency to modernize and leverage Blockchain's transformative potential. The future of insurance lies in embracing innovation, meeting consumer expectations, and creating a seamless and efficient experience for all stakeholders involved.

However, in 2020, AXA discontinued its Fizzy flight delay smart contract platform, originally designed to provide flight coverage between the United States and France. The rationale behind this decision is that the product failed to achieve its desired commercial objectives and lacked sufficient demand. However, AXA has introduced several other automated payout solutions, such as the parametric insurance policies offered by the AXA Climate group. This indicates that AXA remains committed to self-executing contracts that eliminate the need for legal involvement in assessing and processing payouts.

1.5.1.2 Driving Innovation in Existing Insurance Landscape: Strategies for Success in the Digital Age

The insurance industry embraces the imperative of innovation as the key to seizing boundless opportunities and triumphing over lurking threats. With innovation as their core capability, insurers embark on a visionary journey, exploring three remarkable avenues to foster fresh ideas and accelerate progress: collaboration, digital-savvy startups, and internal innovation powerhouses. By employing a multifaceted strategy aligned with strategic goals, insurers can harmonize many innovative initiatives, resulting in a powerful and coordinated outcome.

Collaboration with Tech Industry Leaders

Achieving innovation through individual endeavours can present significant challenges for most insurers. However, the emergence of collaboration opportunities has revolutionized the landscape, empowering insurers to explore uncharted territories and swiftly introduce customized policies and sales strategies. Numerous successful collaborations illustrate blockchain technology's power in insurance operations.

Allianz, an exemplar of forward-thinking in the insurance realm, forged a powerful alliance with the Chinese internet giant Baidu. By harnessing the vast data on consumers' online behaviour, Allianz adeptly tailors personalized offers to meet individual needs. For instance, when a customer purchases a plane ticket, the system automatically dispatches an enticing proposition for flight insurance. This collaboration not only unveils new avenues for sales but also provides Allianz with coveted access to the extensive Chinese market.

AIG established collaborations with technology stalwarts like IBM and other esteemed vendors. These collaborations fortify AIG's risk analytics and cybersecurity expertise, reinforcing its position at the forefront of the digital landscape. Acknowledging the pivotal role of technology capabilities, AIG effectively leverages cutting-edge solutions to ensure its competitive edge remains steadfast.

Another noteworthy collaboration emerged between AXA and Microsoft. This collaboration harmoniously combines AXA's profound industry expertise with Microsoft's unparalleled technological prowess. Harnessing the potential of advanced cloud infrastructure and artificial intelligence capabilities, AXA pioneers innovative solutions such as real-time risk assessments, personalized policy recommendations, and streamlined claims processes.

These remarkable collaborations serve as living testaments to insurers' determination to embrace innovation through collaborations.

Investing in Digital-Savvy Startups

Insurance providers have recognized the immense potential of investing in digital-savvy startups. This has led to a shift in their approach to innovation, as they recognize the value of gaining access to cutting-edge technologies, fresh perspectives, and agile working methods. By strategically investing in emerging ventures, insurers position themselves at the forefront of the digital era, poised to redefine industry standards. There are some instances of insurers investing in digital-savvy startups.

AIG, for instance, invested strategically in Human Condition Safety, an innovative provider of wearable devices designed to enhance workplace safety. Similarly, Munich Re's subsidiary, Hartford Steam Boiler, invested in Augury, utilizing advanced sensors and analytics to monitor heating, ventilation, and air conditioning systems that improve maintenance practices and prevent breakdowns.

Furthermore, some insurers have taken a proactive approach by funding technology incubators. Swiss Re, for example, established an insurtech accelerator in Bangalore, India, to support startups in developing innovative products and services. These initiatives span a wide spectrum of technologies, ranging from data analytics for predicting health outcomes to artificial intelligence for enhanced customer engagement. Through these investments, insurers gain valuable insights into new technologies and immerse themselves in more agile and forward-thinking work cultures. Collaborating with startups enables established insurance companies to cultivate a digital mindset and embrace the opportunities of the digital era.

Generali Global Corporate & Commercial (GC&C) has strengthened its capabilities by partnering with Descartes Underwriting, an innovative InsurTech company specializing in weather risk modelling and data-driven risk transfers. With cutting-edge technologies like image recognition, machine learning, and satellite data, Descartes Underwriting's parametric insurance solutions challenge the traditional insurance landscape by providing transparent and expedited claims management. This collaboration is particularly timely, considering the challenges posed by COVID-19 travel restrictions, as it allows GC&C to conduct digital and remote claim assessments seamlessly, ensuring uninterrupted services and swift payouts to policyholders.

Similarly, Liberty Mutual, a global insurance company, has established Liberty Mutual Strategic Ventures to actively invest in startups aligned with its strategic priorities and areas of expertise. Liberty Mutual aims to remain at the forefront of technological advancements and enhance its offerings by investing in early-stage and growth-stage companies. Notably, their partnership with Snapsheet, a digital claims management platform, empowers Liberty Mutual to streamline and modernize its claims processes through automation and data-driven insights.

Through these strategic investments and collaborations, insurers demonstrate their commitment to staying ahead of the curve, leveraging emerging technologies, and providing enhanced services to their policyholders. Insurance companies are pioneers in the ever-evolving digital landscape by embracing innovation and partnering with startups.

Internal Innovation Powerhouses

The recognition of the paramount importance of innovation has led some visionary companies to assert that it cannot be entirely outsourced. They understand the necessity of developing an exceptional ability to generate ideas internally, unravel their commercial potential, implement them on a grand scale, and seamlessly integrate them into existing processes, functions, and business lines. To fortify their in-house innovation prowess, organizations have established dedicated laboratories designed to coordinate idea development and propel the most promising concepts towards scalable success.

Among the pioneers who have launched their labs are AXA, MetLife, and Aviva. AXA's lab focuses on innovative advancements in data storage and analysis, while MetLife's esteemed LumenLab centres its endeavours around pioneering solutions for promoting healthy lifestyles.

Embracing the transformative potential of the digital era, Manulife, a global financial services provider, has established its groundbreaking LOFT innovation lab in Singapore. This visionary endeavour is a comprehensive, collaborative platform, assembling experts, technologists, and entrepreneurs to envision, prototype, and rigorously test novel solutions. By harnessing emerging technologies like artificial intelligence, Blockchain, and predictive analytics, Manulife aims to revolutionize the customer experience, streamline operations, and expand its range of products and services, elevating the industry into a new era of excellence.

Prudential, a renowned insurance company, has seized the opportunity presented by Singapore's propitious ecosystem for technological advancements, launching its innovation lab in the city-state. This lab catalyzes cutting-edge ideas and solutions, primarily focusing on digital customer experiences, personalized insurance products, and data-driven insights derived from advanced analytics.

Further exemplifying Prudential's commitment to innovation is its partnership with Nervotec, a digital health company based in Singapore. This collaboration aims to empower individuals to manage better and monitor their health and stress levels daily. Through the Pulse by Prudential app, users can effortlessly measure vital signs, such as heart rate, heart rate variability, respiration rate, and oxygen saturation levels, simply by scanning their faces with a mobile phone. These instant measurements enable individuals to assess their stress levels, emotional well-being, and overall fitness, thus enhancing their daily performance, particularly in physically demanding or customer-facing roles. Initially available to users in the Philippines and Singapore, this feature, named "My Pulse Daily," merges holistic health and technology to uplift the well-being of Prudential's valued customers and communities throughout Asia and Africa.

The momentum of digital disruption reverberates across industries as digitally enabled insurgent enterprises challenge the status quo and established business models. Incumbents are confronted with a pivotal choice: either succumb to disruption or embrace their role as disruptors.

1.5.2 Fully Decentralized Insurance

Fully decentralized insurance marks a significant departure from traditional insurance models, ushering in a new era of innovation and efficiency in the insurance sector. Platforms such as Etherisc, Teambrella, Guevara, Lemonade, Nexus Mutual, and Tidal Finance are at the forefront of this transformation, leveraging many cutting-edge technologies to reshape the landscape of insurance operations. These platforms harness diverse technologies, including big data analytics, artificial intelligence, Internet of Things, RPA, mobile apps, digital platforms, blockchain, and smart contracts to redefine how insurance is conducted. At the heart of fully decentralized insurance platforms is eliminating intermediaries, allowing for direct interactions between policyholders and insurers. This streamlined approach enhances efficiency and fosters transparency and trust within the insurance ecosystem. With its distributed ledger and cryptographic security features, blockchain technology ensures the transparency, immutability, and security of insurance transactions. Smart contracts are programmed to automatically execute predefined conditions and enable seamless policy issuance, claims processing, and payouts, reducing the need for manual intervention and minimizing the risk of errors or fraud (Alwis & Jinasena, 2022).

Moreover, big data analytics and artificial intelligence empower decentralized insurance platforms to analyse vast amounts of data in real-time. This data-driven approach enables insurers to accurately assess risks, personalize insurance offerings, and detect fraudulent activities more effectively. By leveraging the Internet of Things, insurers can gather real-time data from connected devices to inform risk assessment and underwriting processes. Robotic process automation streamlines administrative tasks, enhancing operational efficiency within decentralized insurance platforms. Mobile apps and digital platforms provide users with convenient access to insurance services, facilitating seamless interactions between policyholders and insurers. Together, these technologies form the foundation of fully decentralized insurance solutions, revolutionizing how insurance is delivered, managed, and experienced.

Despite the significant benefits of fully decentralized insurance solutions, they also face certain challenges that must be addressed. One key challenge is regulatory compliance, as decentralized insurance platforms operate relatively unregulated compared to traditional insurers. Ensuring compliance with existing insurance regulations while innovating in a decentralized context poses legal and regulatory hurdles that must be navigated carefully. Moreover, scalability and interoperability issues may arise as decentralized insurance platforms seek to accommodate growing users and integrate with existing insurance ecosystems. Addressing these challenges requires collaboration between industry stakeholders, regulators, and technology providers to establish standards, protocols, and best practices that foster the growth and sustainability of fully decentralized insurance solutions.

1.5.2.1 Some Notable Instances of Fully Decentralized Insurance Solutions

Etherisc's Blockchain-Powered Revolution

An exceptional illustration of the transformative potential of fully decentralized solutions in the insurance sector is Etherisc. Etherisc empowers individuals to partake in decentralized insurance markets, enabling parametric insurance transactions. Policyholders can directly engage with one another through smart contracts, eliminating the necessity for traditional insurance intermediaries. This approach automates the entire claims processing and payout system, ensuring unparalleled transparency and significantly reducing costs.

Etherisc, a decentralized insurance protocol, has introduced various innovative insurance products that revolutionize the industry. One unique offering is the USDC Depeg Protection, which safeguards investments in the USDC stablecoin market. This comprehensive coverage shields risk capital providers, ensuring resilience against abrupt instability in the USDC cryptocurrency. Etherisc has pioneered the development of travel delay protection, the world's first decentralized insurance solution for travel delays. Through automatic and nearly instant payouts, travellers can be promptly compensated for unexpected delays, providing peace of mind and ensuring a seamless travel experience. Another unique product by Etherisc is crop protection, which is designed to address agricultural stakeholders' risks. By allowing users to specify their field locations, this automated solution triggers payout mechanisms in response to drought or flood events reported by government agencies. This innovation offers farmers a vital safety net, mitigating the financial impacts of adverse weather conditions and promoting sustainability in the agricultural sector. The introduction of these revolutionary insurance products by Etherisc underscores the transformative power of blockchain technology. By leveraging decentralization, automation, and smart contracts, Etherisc is reshaping the insurance landscape, bringing transparency, efficiency, and resilience to policyholders worldwide.

Potential of Insurwave in Specialty Insurance

Insurwave is an awe-inspiring, fully decentralized insurance platform that has redefined insurance operations. Collaboratively developed by renowned industry leaders, including EY, Guardtime, Maersk, Willis Towers Watson, XL Catlin, MS Amlin, and Microsoft, Insurwave represents the pinnacle of innovation in the insurance industry.

This unique platform has ushered in a new era of efficiency and transparency by seamlessly integrating and securing diverse data sources to ensure shipments worldwide.

Traditionally, the marine insurance market has been plagued by information duplication, manual processes, and incomplete or unreliable asset data. Insurwave addresses these challenges head-on by connecting stakeholders, harmonizing data streams, and eradicating reconciliation errors. By leveraging distributed common ledgers, Insurwave creates an immutable audit trail that mitigates potential coverage gaps, ensures fair claim settlements, and minimizes billing discrepancies. This breakthrough platform fosters seamless collaboration among insurers, brokers, and clients, enabling cost optimization, enhanced capital efficiencies, and driving industry-wide growth. Insurwave's business operations extend beyond the marine insurance sector. It can be seamlessly applied to any commercial or speciality business line involving high-value assets. Organizations gain real-time access to critical client data, risk insights, exposure information, and claims data.

Lemonade with Cutting-Edge Mechanisms

Lemonade, Inc. offers renters', homeowners', car, pet, and term life insurance in the United States, contents and liability policies in Germany and the Netherlands, and renters insurance in France. The company is based in New York City. At the core of Lemonade's operations is its AI-powered platform, which enables swift and hassle-free insurance transactions. Customers can instantly purchase insurance policies and file claims through the platform, eliminating the need for lengthy paperwork and manual processes. Lemonade's use of artificial intelligence streamlines the entire claims processing and payout system, ensuring a prompt and efficient resolution for policyholders. Lemonade stands out among traditional insurance companies due to several inherent advantages. Lemonade offers policies with competitive pricing and flexible coverage options, catering to the evolving needs of modern consumers.

Moreover, their digital-first approach provides a seamless and intuitive user experience, making insurance more accessible and user-friendly. Furthermore, Lemonade and similar companies embrace a business model that aligns the interests of the insured and the insurer. Through their unique "Giveback" program, Lemonade commits to donating a portion of unclaimed premiums to charitable causes chosen by policyholders, fostering a sense of social responsibility and community engagement.

These types of innovative insurance companies are better equipped to meet the evolving demands of consumers, offering competitive pricing, user-friendly interfaces, and a commitment to social impact. As the industry continues to evolve, Lemonade and its counterparts pave the way for a new era of customer-centric and technologically advanced insurance solutions.

1.6 Traditional Model vs. Technology-enabled Decentralized Insurance Solutions—Which Prevails?

The traditional model empowers localized branches and agents within an insurance organization, endowing them with decision-making authority. Technology-enabled decentralized insurance solutions. These solutions use technology to construct a decentralized ecosystem for insurance transactions. Immersed in this ecosystem, transparency, security, and efficiency reign supreme as intermediaries are eliminated, allowing direct interactions between policyholders. By preserving transaction records on an immutable ledger and orchestrating automated processes through ingenious smart contracts, these solutions cultivate an unshakable foundation of trust among all participants.

While the traditional model heightens customer satisfaction and ensures internal harmony within an organization, technology-enabled decentralized insurance solutions embark on an audacious voyage, revolutionizing the insurance value chain. Boldly addressing pressing industry concerns such as fraud prevention, data security, and cost reduction, decentralized solutions artfully employ the distinctive characteristics of different technologies. Rather than waging fierce competition, these two approaches gracefully interweave to offer a symphony of complementary benefits. The traditional model amplifies customer contentment while flexing the organization's operational aspects. Simultaneously, technology-enabled decentralized insurance solutions fashion an unprecedented insurance landscape teeming with transparency, fortified security, and heightened efficiency.

The future of the insurance industry, it seems, shall witness a harmonious blend of these two approaches. Organizations may embrace hybrid models, adroitly melding the traditional model's strengths with technology-transformative prowess. This fusion shall propel customer satisfaction to new heights and direct the industry on the relentless path of progress (Gatteschi et al., 2018). In this epoch of digital metamorphosis, insurers must seize upon the intrinsic value of their existing customers, brands, data, and technical acumen, propelling them into the vanguard of the digital age.

Ultimately, the triumph of one path over the other lies enigmatically intertwined with a tapestry of diverse factors. Regulatory frameworks, technological advancements, industry-wide adoption, and the mercurial whims of customer preferences shall sway the scales. As the insurance industry evolves, stakeholders must embrace change with open arms, exploring uncharted possibilities and charting a course towards unyielding growth and resounding success.

1.7 Decentralized Insurance Market Opportunities

The decentralized insurance market is experiencing remarkable growth, fuelled by the increasing demand for transparent, cost-effective, and efficient insurance solutions. This surge in popularity can be attributed to several factors, including the widespread adoption of technologies, the emergence of self-executing smart contracts, the influential role of social media platforms like Discord and Twitter, and the widespread adoption of AI, ML, and Robotics (Alvin et al., 2022). As more people become aware of the benefits offered by decentralized insurance, the need for automated insurance operations such as underwriting, policy pricing, and claims settlement becomes evident.

The global decentralized insurance market has witnessed substantial growth, with a valuation of $1.4 billion in 2022. Experts project that this market will expand significantly, reaching $135.6 billion by 2032. This exponential growth is anticipated at a compound annual growth rate (CAGR) of 58.5% from 2023 to 2032 (Allied Market Research, 2023). These remarkable figures illustrate the immense potential and promising future of decentralized insurance. As the market continues to evolve and embrace innovative technologies, individuals and businesses alike are set to benefit from the transparency, efficiency, and accessibility offered by decentralized insurance solutions.

In an industry that constantly adapts to change, the fundamental goal remains unchanged: to deliver exceptional customer experiences, optimize cost-effectiveness, and drive sustainable growth. The digital revolution has significantly transformed customer expectations, and insurance businesses must adapt to meet these new demands. Customers now seek simplicity and convenience, desiring streamlined processes like one-click shopping. They crave round-the-clock access, swift service, and comprehensive and easily understandable information about insurance products, particularly pricing.

Blockchain technology and smart contracts play a pivotal role in achieving these goals. According to a report by McKinsey (2017), automation can reduce claims processing costs by up to 30%. This cost reduction benefits both insurers and customers, contributing to overall satisfaction. Furthermore, digital technology enables insurers to better understand their customers through rich data and its analysis.

Insurers can leverage this data to offer personalized products and services. For instance, they can provide auto insurance that charges based on the number of miles driven. Additionally, insurers can capitalize on timely opportunities by utilizing digital data. In a traditional setting, an insurer would be unaware when a customer with a home insurance policy puts their property up for sale. However, in a data-rich digital environment, this information becomes an opportunity to offer new coverage options such as home insurance for the buyer, auto insurance, or even life insurance to cover the mortgage on the new property.

Looking ahead, the insurance industry holds tremendous potential for revenue growth through innovative product offerings and protection services in new areas. Cybersecurity concerns demand products that safeguard against data breaches and associated damages for companies and households (Singh & Akhilesh, 2019). Furthermore, new insurance products tailored to homeowners acting as temporary hoteliers through platforms like Airbnb will likely emerge as the sharing economy expands.

The insurance industry has traditionally been perceived as slow to adopt digital advancements. However, the landscape is changing rapidly. Increased investments from venture capitalists signify a shift in mindset, as they injected $2.6 billion into insurtechs in 2015 and nearly $1.7 billion in 2016 (McKinsey, 2017). Although these newcomers primarily focus on distribution, particularly in property and casualty insurance, they gradually expand their presence across the entire value chain (International Association of Insurance Supervisors, 2017).

The insurance industry is undergoing a digital transformation driven by a commitment to meet customer expectations, optimize operations, and capitalize on growth opportunities. This shift towards customer-centricity and technological advancements sets the stage for an exciting and promising future. However, amidst this decentralized revolution, we must not overlook the ethical considerations that arise. Privacy protection, inclusivity, accountability, fairness, and non-discrimination are decentralized technology's ethical foundations to ensure a responsible and equitable ecosystem. By embracing these ethical principles, the insurance industry can chart a course towards technological innovation while upholding fairness, transparency, and sustainability values.

1.8 Traditional vs. Decentralized Insurance

The traditional insurance model has long been characterized by a centralized approach, where risk transfer takes place through bilateral contracts between the insured and insurance companies. Within this paradigm, a single insurance contract is often sold to many policyholders, with the insurance company acting as the central authority overseeing all aspects of the policies. These industry giants sway over the market, dictating the terms and conditions, leaving little room for individual negotiation or customization. Unfortunately, this rigidity often translates into limited coverage options and higher costs for policyholders, stifling their ability to tailor insurance to their unique needs.

There are several players within this centralized insurance system, each with distinct roles and responsibilities. The policyholders are at the heart of it all, driven by the desire for financial protection in the event of losses. They enter into insurance contracts with insurers, paying premiums in exchange for the promise of coverage. Insurers, in turn, serve as the underwriters, diligently assessing the risks associated with each policyholder's circumstances and determining the appropriate premiums. These insurers are responsible for processing and settling claims and ensuring policyholders receive the necessary support and financial assistance during distress.

The intermediaries facilitate the insurance journey, bridging the gap between policyholders and insurers. These skilled professionals, including insurance agents/brokers, underwriters, claims adjusters, insurance aggregators, and more, bring their expertise to guide policyholders through the complex insurance landscape. They help policyholders navigate their coverage needs, select suitable policies, assist with policy issuance, collect premiums, provide guidance on claims procedures, and meticulously evaluate the risks inherent in insurance policies. Intermediaries play a vital role in ensuring a seamless and informed experience for policyholders, acting as trusted allies throughout the insurance process.

Regulatory bodies and supervisory authorities are the guardians of policyholder interests and the market's integrity. These entities establish comprehensive guidelines, regulations, and licensing requirements that insurers, agents, and brokers must adhere to. They diligently monitor insurers' financial strength, enforce compliance with laws and regulations, and swiftly investigate consumer complaints to ensure fair and transparent practices. The tireless efforts of these regulatory bodies maintain the stability of the insurance landscape, fostering an environment of trust and protection for policyholders.

The reinsurers play a crucial role in the centralized insurance system. These entities offer insurance coverage to primary insurers, assuming a portion of the risk associated with the policies issued. By spreading and diversifying the risk across multiple entities, reinsurers assist primary insurers in managing their exposure to large and catastrophic losses. This collaboration provides financial stability and instils confidence in the insurance market, enabling insurers to offer broader coverage options and higher policy limits.

Hence, the traditional insurance model operates through a network of key players: policyholders, insurers, intermediaries, regulatory bodies, supervisory authorities, and reinsurers. Each entity contributes its specialized skills and functions to uphold the functioning of the centralized insurance system. Together, they work towards safeguarding the interests of policyholders, promoting transparency, and ensuring the resilience and longevity of the insurance industry. Figure 1.2 shows the functioning of the traditional insurance framework.

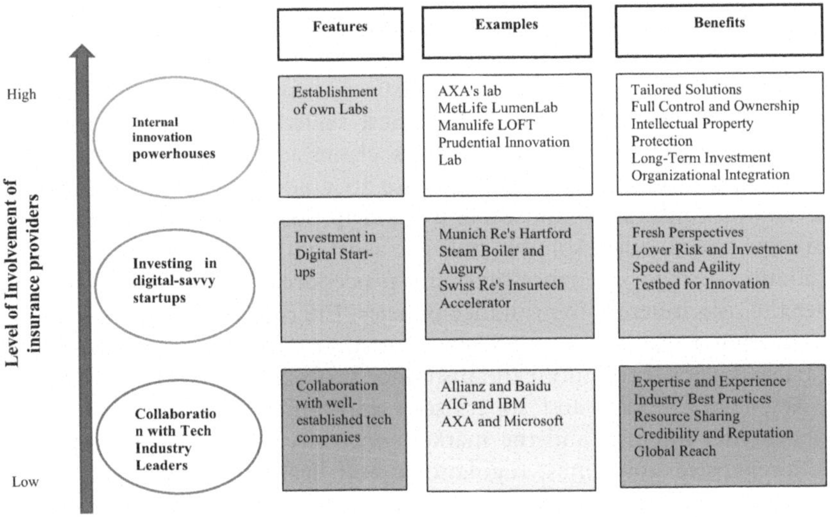

Fig. 1.2 Strategies for driving innovation in existing insurance landscape (*Source* Prepared by authors)

Decentralized insurance, on the other hand, operates on a different paradigm. It is based on a community-driven approach where participants come together to transfer and share risks instead of relying on a central authority to set the terms and conditions of financial arrangements. However, insurance decentralization can occur with and without the use of technology (see Fig. 1.1). Decentralized insurance schemes operate on transparency, trust, and consensus, eliminating the need for intermediaries and central authorities. Policyholders gain greater control over their insurance coverage, premiums, and claims processes through self-executing contracts. These contracts automate key insurance functions such as policy issuance, premium payments, claims settlement, and payouts, streamlining operations and enhancing efficiency.

Within the decentralized insurance framework, insurers and reinsurers can operate as decentralized entities or be integrated into the protocol. They play a vital role in underwriting policies, collecting and calculating premiums, developing contracts, and processing claims. Their participation ensures the smooth functioning of the insurance process and provides policyholders with the necessary financial protection. Capital providers also play a crucial role in decentralized insurance by contributing the funds needed to support coverage. These providers, whether individuals or institutions, contribute capital to the insurance pool, ensuring that sufficient funds are available to cover potential claims. For their contribution, they receive a part of the premium income. Their involvement strengthens the overall stability and sustainability of the decentralized insurance ecosystem. Decentralized insurance relies on a price oracle to determine accurate premiums, assess risks, and calculate claim payouts. This mechanism or external data source provides real-time information about insured risks, such as asset values or market prices. The price oracle ensures that insurance calculations are based on reliable and up-to-date data, enabling fair and accurate assessments. Protocol governance governs the decentralized insurance ecosystem, establishing rules, voting mechanisms, and community governance structures. This framework ensures transparency, fairness, and effective management of the decentralized insurance protocol. Protocol governance fosters a sense of ownership and collective responsibility within the decentralized insurance community by involving participants in decision-making processes. Figure 1.3 shows the fully decentralized insurance framework using blockchain technology.

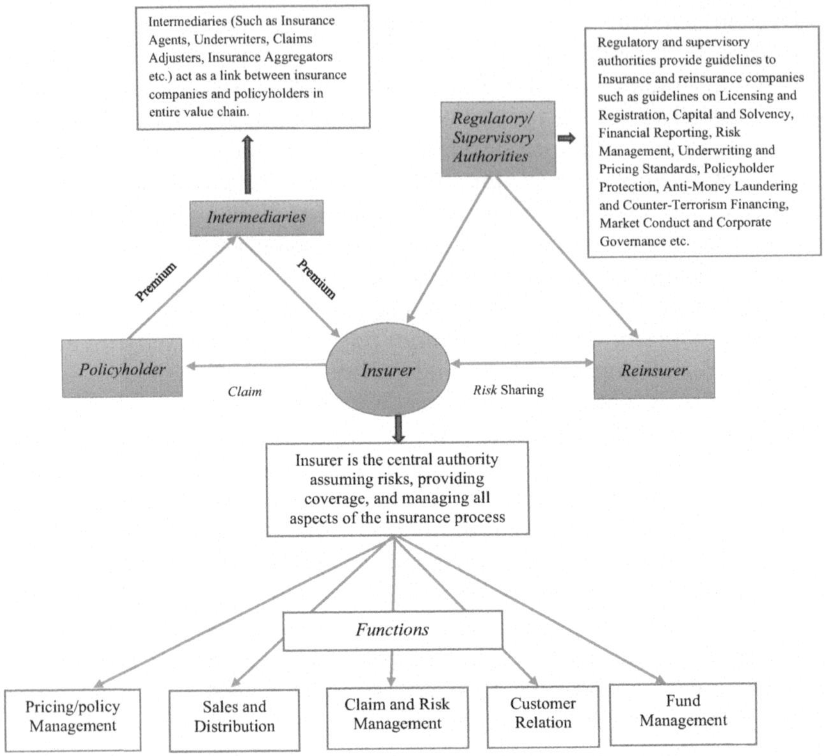

Fig. 1.3 Traditional insurance framework (*Source* Prepared by authors)

Decentralized insurance revamped the insurance landscape through blockchain technology, smart contracts, capital providers, price oracles, and protocol governance (see Fig. 1.4).

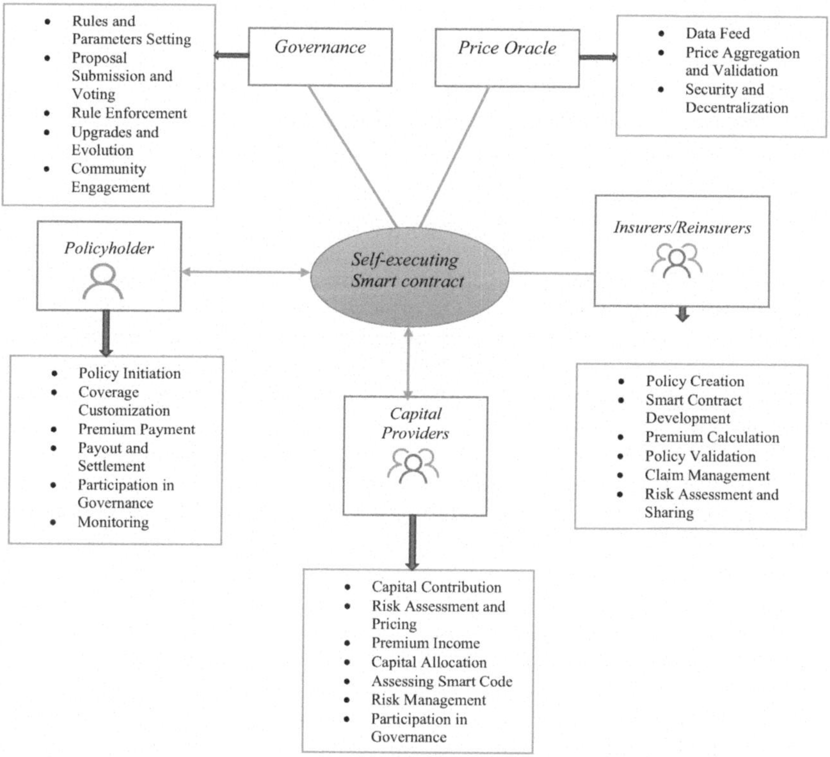

Fig. 1.4 Decentralized insurance framework (*Source* Prepared by authors)

1.9 Conclusion

Decentralized insurance offers unparalleled opportunities for improved business practices, enhanced customer experiences, and greater product innovation. Embracing decentralization in the traditional insurance model simplifies complex processes and introduces transparency and efficiency. Technology-based decentralized insurance platforms, such as Etherisc, Insurwave, and Teambrella, have emerged to eliminate intermediaries and facilitate direct interactions among policyholders. These solutions transcend the boundaries of the traditional model and establish a decentralized ecosystem for insurance transactions built on trust, transparency, and security. As the insurance industry continues to evolve, embracing ethical considerations with technology becomes even more critical because the historical development of insurance is deeply rooted in principles of solidarity, fairness, and social responsibility to protect policyholders. This necessitates responsible data management, algorithm fairness, transparency, and compliance with data protection regulations.

References

Abdikerimova, A., & Feng, R. (2022). Peer-to-peer multi-risk insurance and mutual aid. *European Journal of Operational Research, 299*(2), 735–749.

Allianz, S. E. (2016). *Insurers and reinsurers launch Blockchain initiative B3i.* Accessed on 18 August 2023 from https://www.allianz.com/en/press/news/commitment/sponsorship/161018-insurers-and-reinsurers-launch-blockchain-initiative-b3i.html

Allied Market Research. (2023). Decentralized Insurance Market Size, Share, Competitive Landscape and Trend Analysis Report, by Type, by End User: Global Opportunity Analysis and Industry Forecast, 2023–2032. Accessed 16 August 2024. https://www.alliedmarketresearch.com/decentralized-insurance-market-A74837

Alvin, K., Erik, L., Gwen, W., & Rex, Z. (2022). Decentralized insurance alternatives: Market landscape, opportunities and challenges. *The Society of Actuaries Research Institute*. Accessed on 18 August 2023 from https://www.soa.org/resources/research-reports/2022/decentralized-ins-alt/

Alwis, S., & Jinasena, T. M. K. K. (2022). A blockchain-based decentralized insurance platform. In *2022 International Research Conference on Smart Computing and Systems Engineering (SCSE), 5*, 137–142. IEEE.

Ankitha S. A. D. (2022). Block chain application in insurance services: A systematic review of the evidence. *SAGE Open*. Accessed on 18 August 2023 from https://doi.org/10.1177/21582440221079877

Bohnert, A., Fritzsche, A., & Gregor, S. (2019). Digital agendas in the insurance industry: The importance of comprehensive approaches. *The Geneva Papers on Risk and Insurance—Issues and Practice, 44*(1), 1–19. https://doi.org/10.1057/s41288-018-0109-0

Cousaert, S., Vadgama, N., & Xu, J. (2022). Token-based Insurance Solutions on Blockchain. In *Blockchains and the token economy: Theory and practice* (pp. 237–260). Springer International Publishing.

Deloitte. (2016). *Block chain applications in Insurance.* Accessed on 18 August 2023 from https://www2.deloitte.com/content/dam/Deloitte/ch/Documents/innovation/ch-en-innovation-deloitte-blockchain-app-in-insurance.pdf

Deloitte. (2017). *Artificial intelligence: From mystery to mastery—Unlocking the business value of AI in the insurance industry*. Accessed on 18 August

2023 from https://www2.deloitte.com/de/de/pages/innovation/contents/artificial-intelligence-insurance-industry.html

Fang, H., Qin, X., Wu, W., & Yu, T. (2023). *Mutual risk sharing and Fintech: The case of Xiang Hu Bao.* Accessed on 18 August 2023 https://www.aeaweb.org/conference/2023/program/paper/RFKByytf

Faulkner, M. (2017). *AIG claims industry first with blockchain insurance policy.* Accessed on 18 August 2023 from https://insuranceday.maritimeintelligence.informa.com/ID053839/AIG-claims-industry-first-with-blockchain-insurance-policy

Feng, R. (2023). *Decentralized insurance: Technical foundation of business models.* Springer

Gatteschi, V., Lamberti, F., Demartini, C., Pranteda, C., & Santamaría, V. (2018). Blockchain and smart contracts for insurance: Is the technology mature enough? *Future Internet, 10*(2), 20–35. https://doi.org/10.3390/fi10020020

Goodenough O., & Salkind, S. (2021). *Computable contracts and insurance: An introduction.* Accessed on 18 August 2023 from https://law.mit.edu/pub/computablecontractsandinsuranceanintroduction/release/1

Hirschfield, D., & Duric, M. (2022). *Why are smart contracts the smart choice for financial services?* Accessed on 18 August 2023 from https://www.taylorwessing.com/en/insights-and-events/insights/2022/02/why-are-smart-contracts-the-smart-choice-for-financial-services

International Association of Insurance Supervisors. (2017). *FinTech developments in the insurance industry.* Accessed on 18 August 2023 from https://www.iaisweb.org/page/news/other-papers-and-reports/file/65625/report-on-fintech-developments-in-the-insurance-industry

Kantur, H., & Bamuleseyo, C. (2018). *How smart contracts can change the insurance industry: Benefits and challenges of using Blockchain technology.* Accessed on 18 August 2023 from http://www.diva-portal.org/smash/record.jsf?pid=diva2%3A1214254&dswid=8446

McKinsey. (2017). *Digital disruption in Insurance: Cutting through the Noise.* Accessed on 18 August 2023 from https://www.mckinsey.com/~/media/mckinsey/industries/financial%20services/our%20insights/time%20for%20insurance%20companies%20to%20face%20digital%20reality/digital-disruption-in-insurance.ashx

Meeusen, P. (2017). B3i—Blockchain Insurance Industry Initiative Deutsche Bank. *InsurTech Conference.* Accessed on 18 August 2023 from https://www.swissre.com/dam/jcr:d560374e-d7ba-4472-a28c-1f53f932303b/2017_09_25_B3i_blockchain_insurance.pdf

Nath, I. (2016). Data exchange platform to fight insurance fraud on blockchain. In *2016 IEEE 16th international conference on data mining workshops*

(ICDMW) (pp. 821–825). IEEE Computer Society. https://doi.org/10.1109/ICDMW.2016.0121

Popovic, D., Avis, C., Byrne, M., Cheung, C., Donovan, M., Flynn, Y., Fothergill, C., Hosseinzadeh, Z., Lim, Z., & Shah, J. (2020). Understanding blockchain for insurance use cases. *British Actuarial Journal, 25*, e12.

PWC. (2023). *Revolutionising financial inclusion through Digital Insurance and Takaful Promoting inclusive insurance in Malaysia.* Accessed on 18 August 2023 from https://www.pwc.com/my/en/assets/publications/2023/20230416-revolutionising-financial-inclusion-through-digital-insurance-and-takaful.pdf

Ralph, O. (2017). *AIG sets up blockchain policy for Standard Chartered.* Accessed on 18 August 2023 from https://www.ft.com/content/03ea1b88-511b-11e7-a1f2-db19572361bb

Sheehan, M. (2022, July 28). B3i fails to raise new capital, enters insolvency. *Reinsurance News..* Accessed on 18 August 2023 from https://www.reinsurancene.ws/b3i-fails-to-raise-new-capital-enters-insolvency/

Singh A., & Akhilesh K. B. (2019). The insurance industry—Cyber security in the hyper-connected age. In K. Akhilesh & D. Möller D. (Eds.), *Smart technologies: Scope and applications* (pp. 201–219). Springer.

Stepanova, V., & Eriņš, I. (2021). Review of decentralized finance applications and their total value locked. *TEM Journal, 10*(1), 327.

Swiss Re. (2017a). *B3i—Blockchain Insurance Industry Initiative.* Accessed on 18 August 2023 from https://www.swissre.com/dam/jcr:d560374e-d7ba-4472-a28c-1f53f932303b/2017_09_25_B3i_blockchain_insurance.pdf

Swiss Re. (2017b). *A history of insurance.* Accessed on 18 August 2023 from https://www.swissre.com/dam/jcr:638f00a0-71b9-4d8e-a960-dddaf9ba57cb/150_history_of_insurance.pdf.

Terekhova, M. (2017). *AXA turns to smart contracts for flight-delay insurance.* Accessed on 18 August 2023 from https://www.businessinsider.com/axa-turns-to-smart-contracts-for-flight-delay-insurance-2017-9?IR=T

The Geneva Association. (2018). *Insurance in the digital age: A view on key implications for the economy and society.* Accessed on 18 August 2023 from. https://www.genevaassociation.org/sites/default/files/research-topics-document-type/pdf_public/insurance_in_the_digital_age_01.pdf.

The Geneva Association. (2023). *Assessing the potential of decentralised finance and blockchain technology in insurance.* Accessed on 18 August 2023 from https://www.genevaassociation.org/sites/default/files/2023-08/DeFi%20insurance_WEB.pdf

CHAPTER 2

Decentralized Insurance Business Models: Benefits and Ethical Dilemmas

2.1 Introduction of Decentralized Insurance Models

Decentralized insurance models offer a paradigm shift from traditional insurance system's centralized and rigid structures. They empower individuals and communities to participate actively in the insurance process, providing greater control and transparency in risk management. In recent years, these innovative models harness the power of distributed technology, decentralized governance, blockchain technology, smart contracts, AI and ML, robotics, big data analytics and IOT to transform the traditional insurance landscape, offering benefits beyond conventional insurance practices. By leveraging blockchain's immutability and transparency, these models create a trustless environment where policies are governed by smart contracts, reducing the need for intermediaries and increasing claims processing efficiency (Feng, 2023). The decentralized insurance models have gained attention, especially with the growing popularity of the sharing economy and changing consumer preferences.

Business models, in general, are diverse and encompass all the processes and policies a company adopts. They aim to answer questions about the target customers, the value the company can provide to them, and how it can do so cost-effectively. Essentially, a business model describes how a

N. Singhal et al., *Potential, Risks, and Ethical Implications of Decentralized Insurance*, Technology, Work and Globalization,
https://doi.org/10.1007/978-981-97-5894-4_2

company creates, delivers, and captures value for both the customer and itself.

In decentralized Insurance, business models vary across companies based on different criteria. However, they generally refer to an organization's framework and strategy to create, deliver, and capture value in the decentralized insurance ecosystem. A decentralized insurance business model outlines the key elements that define the organization's operations, revenue generation, and long-term sustainability. It offers a comprehensive view of how the organization intends to provide value to customers while ensuring profitability and sustainability within the decentralized insurance landscape. By defining and implementing a clear business model, decentralized insurance organizations can effectively address diverse technology's unique challenges and opportunities and the decentralized nature of insurance operations. A well-defined business model enables organizations to align their value proposition, revenue generation, cost structure, and key activities to offer competitive and sustainable decentralized insurance products and services.

It is worth noting that one insurance company may simultaneously implement different business models based on its specific strategies and objectives. One example of a company that has implemented several business models depending on the type of coverage provided is Etherisc. Etherisc operates on several models that differentiate it from traditional insurers, such as using artificial intelligence and blockchain technology to streamline processes and offering peer-to-peer and parametric Insurance. Etherisc is a blockchain-based insurance platform that has implemented a peer-to-peer insurance model. Etherisc's platform allows individuals to create or participate in peer-to-peer insurance pools. These pools are formed by individuals who collectively contribute funds to the pool. The funds are held in a smart contract on the blockchain, ensuring transparency and security. Peer-to-peer Insurance on the Etherisc platform allows individuals to interact with each other directly, pooling their resources to provide coverage and share risks. It promotes a sense of community and trust among participants. At the same time, Etherisc utilizes a parametric insurance model for certain types of coverage, such as crop insurance and flight delay insurance. Parametric Insurance is a type of coverage that pays out a predetermined amount based on predefined parameters or triggers rather than traditional claims assessment (Snape, 2023). In the case of crop insurance, Etherisc's parametric model works by establishing specific weather or yield conditions as triggers for compensation. For example, let's say a farmer purchases crop insurance through Etherisc. The policy may specify that farmers will receive a payout to cover their losses if the recorded rainfall during the growing season falls below a certain threshold. Instead of relying on individual claims and assessments, the parametric model uses weather data from reliable sources to determine if the trigger condition has been met. Regarding flight delay insurance, Etherisc's parametric model relies on predefined triggers related to flight delays. For instance, if a flight is delayed for a specified period beyond the scheduled departure time, the policyholder is automatically eligible for compensation according to the predetermined terms. This eliminates the need for time-consuming claims processing and allows for faster payouts to affected individuals.

Several business models in decentralized insurance can be implemented, and in Table 2.1, we have presented three widely used technologically diverse business models for decentralized insurance providers. This visual tool outlines the key components and structure of a decentralized insurance business model, highlighting essential elements such as key partners, resources, and channels crucial to success. From community builders to technology providers, each element is crucial in creating an ecosystem that fosters trust, efficiency, and innovation. The Table also illustrates the cost structures and revenue streams sustaining these decentralized insurance models, unravelling the financial mechanisms that underpin their viability, including premium payments and value-added services.

Acknowledging the diverse landscape of decentralized insurance models, it is crucial to recognize that not all rely on advanced technology. A notable category is community-based risk pools, encompassing various models such as Peer-to-Peer insurance, Mutual Aid Societies, Takaful or Islamic Insurance, Microinsurance Networks, Crowdsurance, and Community-Based Health Insurance. These community-based risk pool models share common features such as mutual assistance, trust, and a sense of community. They often operate on principles of solidarity, where members collectively share risks and support each other in times of need. The key distinction among them lies in the specific risks they address, the communities they serve, and the mechanisms through which they operate. These models exemplify innovative approaches to insurance that prioritize community engagement and mutual support.

Table 2.1 The Triptych of Technologically Diverse Decentralized Insurance Business Models

	Peer-to-Peer Insurance	*Parametric Insurance*	*Mutual Insurance*
Key activities	• Digital Platform Development • Risk pool management • Community Engagement and Governance through DAOs • Decentralized Identity and Verification • Reinsurance Arrangements • Customer Support • Compliance and Security	• Digital Platform Development • Data Oracles Integration • Parameter Definition • Decentralized Data Collection • Data Verification and Consensus • Policy Issuance and Premium Collection • Community Governance	• Collective Underwriting by Participants • Decentralized Decision-Making for Claim Settlements • Decentralized Risk Assessment and Diversification • Community-Driven Support and Dispute Resolution • Decentralized Governance Structures Ensuring Regulatory Adherence
Customer segment	• Like-Minded Individuals • Community-Centric Businesses • Collaborative Consumers • Specific Niche Markets	• Farmers and Agricultural Businesses • Travellers and Tourists • Event Organizers • Supply Chain and Logistics Companies • Micro and Small Businesses • Weather Dependent Industries	• Individual Policyholders • Small Businesses • Community Organizations • Farmers and Agricultural Producers • Local Government Entities • Industry Associations

(continued)

Table 2.1 (continued)

	Peer-to-Peer Insurance	*Parametric Insurance*	*Mutual Insurance*
Value Proposition	• Transparency • Lower Costs • Customization • Community Support • Fast and Automated Claims Processing • Participation in Risk Pooling	• Quick Payouts for Predefined Events • Reduced Administrative Costs • Accessible Coverage for Underserved Markets	• Community-Centred Coverage • Shared Risk and Responsibility • Tailored Policies for Members • Potential for Lower Premiums • Transparent and Member-Driven Operations • Collective Decision-Making
Key Partners	• Community Builders and Marketing Partners • Decentralized Autonomous Organizations • Technology Providers • Reinsurance Companies	• Data Providers on predefined triggers • Technology Providers • Risk Modelling Experts • Reinsurers	• Reinsurance Companies • Insurance Brokers/ Agents • Technology Providers (for digital platforms) • Legal and Compliance Advisors • Community Organizations (for outreach) • Financial Institutions (for investment management)
Customer relationship	• Empowering Policyholders • Responsive Support • Community Engagement • Reward Programs • User-Friendly Platforms • Feedback and Reviews	• Real-Time Data Access • Automated Claims Processing • Proactive Customer Support • Flexibility and Customization • User-Friendly Interface • Feedback Collection	• Personalized Member Support • Community Engagement Activities • Transparent Communication Channels • Responsive Claims Handling • Proactive Risk Management Advice • Continuous Feedback Loop

(continued)

Table 2.1 (continued)

	Peer-to-Peer Insurance	*Parametric Insurance*	*Mutual Insurance*
Key resources	• Digital Platforms for Member Interaction • Smart Contracts • Data Analytics and Underwriting Expertise • Risk Pool Management System • Decentralized Identity Verification • Reinsurance Partnerships • Financial Resources	• Smart Contracts • Data Oracles • Decentralized Identity Solutions • Network Nodes • Risk Modelling and Actuarial Expertise • Secure Wallets	• Financial Reserves • Risk Pools • Membership Base • Technology Infrastructure • Underwriting Guidelines • Regulatory Compliance Framework
Channel	• Online Platforms • Mobile Apps • Social Media • Peer Referrals • Collaboration • Online Forums and Discussion Platforms • Insurance Aggregators	• Online Platforms • Mobile Apps • Social Media • Referrals • Partnerships with Third-Party Platforms	• Digital Platforms and Mobile Apps • Insurance Company Websites • Third-Party Aggregators • Insurtech Partnerships • Digital Marketing and Social Media • Customer Referrals • Telematics and IoT Devices
Cost Structure	• Claims Payouts • Platform Development and Innovation • Reinsurance Premiums • Marketing and Customer Acquisition • Community Building and Engagement	• Claim Payout • Platform Development and Innovation • Data Oracles and External Data Sources Expenses • Index management fee • Reinsurance Premiums • Marketing and Promotion • Technology Integration	• Technology Infrastructure • Operational Expenses • Risk Pool Management • Compliance and Regulatory Costs • Member Acquisition and Engagement • Security and Cybersecurity • Technology Innovation

(continued)

Table 2.1 (continued)

	Peer-to-Peer Insurance	*Parametric Insurance*	*Mutual Insurance*
Revenue streams	• Premium Payments • Policy Fees • Investment Income • Partnerships and Referral Commissions • Community Growth and Membership Fees • Cross-Selling or Upselling	• Insurance Premiums • Transaction Fees • Reinsurance Premiums • Investment of Premiums • Data Sales or Access Fees • Revenue Sharing from Partnering Platforms	• Premiums from Policyholders • Investment Returns from Managed Funds • Transaction Fees for Smart Contract Execution • Membership Fees or Contributions • Revenue Sharing from Partnering Platforms • Tokenization and Cryptocurrency Revenue
Ethics	• Conflicts of Interest among Peers • Lack of Regulatory Oversight and Consumer Protection • Data Privacy and Security Concerns • Unequal Risk Pooling and Inclusivity • Trust and Reputation of Peer-to-Peer Platforms	• Trigger Parameter Accuracy and Reliability • Transparency in Parameter Definition and Changes • Data Integrity and Sources • Ethical Use of Data Analytics	• Transparency in Decision-Making • Equitable Distribution of Risk and Rewards • Community Empowerment and Participation • Privacy and Data Protection • Fairness in Claims Handling • Social Responsibility and Mutual Aid

Source Prepared by authors

Among community-based models, Mutual Aid Societies are interconnected communities that thrive on interpersonal relationships and mutual trust. Their operational structure is built upon transparent governance, where decision-making unfolds through open discussions and collective efforts, ensuring high transparency. This interconnectedness fosters a sense of communal responsibility, reflecting the ethos of mutual aid societies. In Takaful or Islamic Insurance, the emphasis is placed on cooperative principles rooted in Islamic tenets. Participants engage in a system that promotes mutual assistance, contributing to a communal pool where risks and responsibilities are shared collectively. This cooperative approach aligns with the principles of fairness and solidarity, making Takaful a distinctive decentralized insurance model that goes beyond technological frameworks to embody cooperative values.

Microinsurance networks target low-income communities, providing affordable insurance coverage. Members contribute small premiums, and payouts are designed to address specific risks faced by the community, such as health or agricultural risks. These networks often employ localized risk assessments to tailor coverage to the community's needs. Crowdsurance operates on a crowdfunding model where individuals pool their resources to cover each other's risks, similar to peer-to-peer insurance, but it involves a broader community. Trust among participants is crucial in crowdsurance, and social connections within the community play a significant role in building and maintaining this trust. Community-Based Health Insurance specifically addresses health-related risks within a community. Members contribute premiums to a communal pool, and the funds cover medical expenses for those in need. Some community-based health insurance models incorporate preventive measures and health education to reduce risk and healthcare costs.

While several decentralized insurance models operate without technology in different parts of the world, the increasing spread of technology has led many to incorporate it for scalability and efficiency. Integrating technology in decentralized insurance models has become imperative for staying competitive, streamlining processes, and reaching a broader audience by including improved data analytics for risk assessment, faster claims processing through automation, enhanced communication channels, and the ability to create innovative insurance products. These technological-driven solutions optimize internal operations and enhance the overall customer experience. In light of these advancements, this chapter delves into technologically driven decentralized insurance business models. It explores how these models leverage cutting-edge technologies to redefine the insurance landscape, providing insights into their key components, operational mechanisms, and the transformative impact they bring to the industry. By understanding the symbiotic relationship between technology and decentralized insurance, we can unravel the full potential of these innovative solutions in meeting the evolving needs of insurers and policyholders alike.

2.2 Peer-to-Peer (P2P) Insurance—Empowering Community Resilience

Peer-to-peer insurance is rooted in mutuality, trust, and collective responsibility. P2P insurance empowers policyholders to become insurers and insured, forming interconnected networks where risks are shared and managed collectively. Unlike conventional insurance setups where a centralized authority oversees policies and claims, P2P insurance thrives on the collective strength of its members, who unite to pool resources and offer mutual aid in times of crisis (Abdikerimova & Feng, 2022). This decentralized framework fosters transparency, fairness, and accountability, encouraging active decision-making and risk mitigation participation. P2P insurance platforms are designed with user-centric features, enabling seamless policy management and hassle-free claims reporting, thus empowering individuals to wield greater control over their insurance affairs. Furthermore, P2P insurance cultivates a culture of proactive risk prevention, incentivizing members to adopt prudent practices to safeguard against potential hazards. By championing community solidarity and shared responsibility, P2P insurance emerges as a compelling alternative, offering individuals enhanced financial security and a renewed sense of collective strength in navigating life's uncertainties.

This innovative model, bolstered by advancements in cutting-edge technologies, including blockchain, smart contracts, data analytics, robotic process automation, cloud computing, chatbots, predictive analytics, artificial intelligence, machine learning, and telematics and IoT devices, holds the potential to revolutionize the insurance landscape (Balasubramanian et al., 2021). These transformative technologies pave the way for a future where peer-to-peer insurance emerges as the standard practice (Capgemini, n.d.; The Geneva Association, 2023).

With innovative technologies, the P2P insurance model can operate with unprecedented efficiency and transparency (Ernest & Young, 2016). Claim processing, for instance, has become streamlined and automated. Rather than undergoing case-by-case approval through traditional underwriting, claims are assessed and validated automatically based on predefined conditions in smart contracts (NAIC, 2022). This accelerates the claims settlement process and eliminates the potential for bias or subjective decision-making. To facilitate premium payments and ensure the security of funds, P2P insurance platforms may employ digital wallets. These wallets act as digital escrow accounts, holding fixed-valued exchangeable tokens representing policyholders' premium contributions. Transactions within the P2P insurance ecosystem are conducted using platform-specific tokens, minimizing transaction costs and streamlining financial operations (Cousaert et al., 2022). This digital infrastructure ensures that each user's exposure is limited to the amount they have contributed to their digital wallet, providing financial security and risk control (Eling & Lehmann, 2018).

Communication and interaction within peer-to-peer insurance networks have been seamless with digital platforms and mobile apps. Members effortlessly connect with insurers, fellow policyholders, and community administrators through these technological channels via messaging systems, discussion forums, and social media integrations. Moreover, these platforms offer members the convenience of easily managing their insurance policies. From viewing policy details to changing coverage options, updating personal information, and renewing policies, members can perform these tasks swiftly with just a few taps or clicks. This accessibility enhances the convenience and flexibility of policy management and empowers members to take charge of their insurance coverage. Digital platforms and mobile apps have also streamlined the claims reporting and management process for P2P insurance members. Members can swiftly report claims through the app, providing relevant details and documentation electronically in case of loss or damage. Insurers can then process and track claims in real time, ensuring that members stay informed about the status and progress of their claims. These platforms foster community engagement among P2P insurance members by offering dedicated features for discussions, knowledge-sharing, and collaboration on risk management strategies. Members can participate actively, share insights, and build relationships within the insurance community. Clear visuals, concise messaging, and interactive elements enhance engagement and promote greater participation among members. Ultimately, seamless communication, convenient policy management, streamlined claims processing, and engaging community features enrich the overall experience for P2P insurance members, encouraging greater engagement and participation in the insurance community. Chatbots play a vital role in customer service, offering instant support and assistance powered by artificial intelligence (AI) and natural language processing (NLP), improving responsiveness, reducing costs, and enhancing overall satisfaction.

Data analytics and machine learning algorithms facilitate precise risk assessment and pricing by analysing vast datasets encompassing member demographics, claims history, and external risk factors in a peer-to-peer model. Proactive risk management by forecasting future events and trends, empowering insurers to anticipate risks, prevent losses, and adapt their strategies accordingly, and enhancing resilience and competitiveness is also enabled with predictive analytics. Furthermore, robotic process automation optimizes administrative tasks within P2P insurance operations, streamlining policy administration, claims processing, and customer support through the automation of repetitive processes. This improves operational efficiency and reduces costs, enabling insurers to allocate resources effectively and focus on value-added activities, ultimately enhancing operational agility and responsiveness. Augmented reality (AR) and virtual reality (VR) technologies further enrich P2P insurance services, providing immersive experiences for members through virtual property inspections, claims evaluations, and risk assessments. Telematics and IoT devices enable real-time monitoring of insured assets and behaviours, offering personalized services and incentivizing safer behaviours.

2.2.1 *P2P Insurance Models*

Typically, there are three P2P Decentralized insurance models: the self-organizing, broker, and carrier or collaborative (see Fig. 2.1).

2.2.1.1 *Self-organizing Peer-to-Peer Insurance*

The self-organizing peer-to-peer model is an approach to insurance where individuals come together to form a community or network to share risks and collectively manage their insurance needs. In this model, policyholders are both insurers and insured, contributing to a pool of funds used to cover claims within the community. In a self-organizing P2P insurance model, community members often have a say in how the insurance operates. They may participate in decision-making processes, such as setting premiums, determining coverage limits, and approving claims. The model typically leverages technology platforms that facilitate communication, administration, and the pooling of funds.

The first type of self-organizing P2P was launched in China in 2015 with TongJuBao. TongJuBao, a Chinese peer-to-peer insurance startup, has introduced a unique community risk-sharing platform that caters to

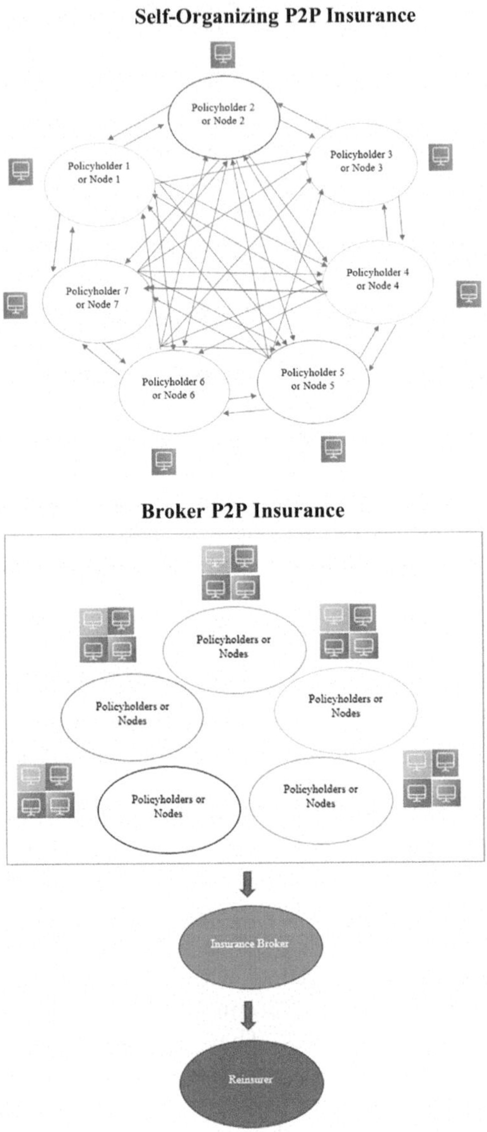

Fig. 2.1 Types of P2P Insurance (*Source* Prepared by authors)

Fig. 2.1 (continued)

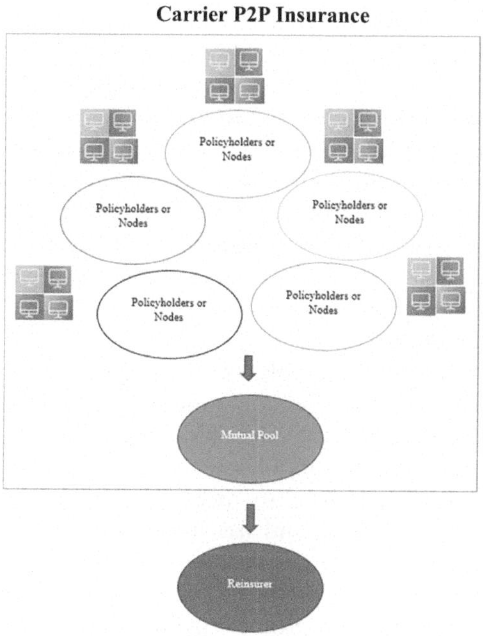

the Chinese market. Recognizing the significance of social risks in China, TongJuBao focuses on providing insurance solutions for marriage safety, child safety, and income protection. The platform operates by offering "Community Protection" to its members. When individuals seek coverage for specific life risks, they form communities of support within the platform. Members pool their premiums together and can withdraw from the communal pool in case of a claim. At the end of the year, if a substantial portion of the pool remains unclaimed, members can receive a refund of their premiums, potentially up to 75%, if no claims have been made. A distinguishing feature of TongJuBao's system is that the members can determine how the risk is shared. They can join existing communities or create their own, inviting family, friends, and colleagues to form a community of known contacts. Major decisions are made by a community vote, ensuring every member has a voice.

TongJuBao's role within the community is to maintain the administrative and technological platform, provide insurance expertise, and handle all claims. TongJuBao's experts carefully assess claims to ensure fairness and detect fraudulent activities (Levantesi & Piscopo, 2022). Notably, TongJuBao does not hold any stake in the outcome of claims. Instead, the company generates revenue solely from a percentage of the premiums paid into each community pool. As neither a broker nor an insurer, TongJuBao operates as a company licensed under Civil Law, providing the platform through which its community members enter into a contractual framework. Consequently, the startup currently operates outside traditional regulatory oversight, with the members shaping the direction of their insurance protection. However, regulatory measures will likely be imposed on TongJuBao as the model gains success and recognition in the industry.

Another example of a company that operates on a self-organizing peer-to-peer insurance model is Wrapbook, which offers specialized coverage for the film and entertainment industry. With its innovative approach, Wrapbook aims to simplify the insurance process and provide tailored solutions to meet the unique needs of production companies, crew members, and freelancers in the entertainment sector. Wrapbook's insurance offerings include coverage options, including general liability, workers' compensation, errors and omissions, and equipment coverage. These policies protect against various risks during film and television productions, including property damage, bodily injury, and legal claims. One of the key features of Wrapbook's insurance model is its use of technology. The company leverages digital platforms and automated processes to streamline the insurance experience. Customers can easily request quotes, manage their policies, and file claims through their online platform. The digitized workflow saves time and reduces paperwork, allowing production companies and crew members to focus more on their creative work. Other companies following the self-organizing P2P model include Vouch Insurance, Portabl, Wesura, InsurePal, and Versicherix. Each entity brings its unique spin to the concept, catering to different industries and niches. InsurePal stands out for its innovative blend of classical insurance principles with peer-to-peer endorsements on blockchain, underpinned by social proof. This hybrid model fosters a self-regulating ecosystem wherein the community plays a pivotal role in endorsing and validating insurance claims. To address scepticism surrounding P2P insurance, InsurePal offers a limited fee guarantee and many options to ensure competitive savings compared to traditional policies. By leveraging endorsements and guarantees, InsurePal cultivates a network that is increasingly risk-aware, thereby influencing behavioural changes among participants towards more prudent risk management practices (Sun et al., 2020).

2.2.1.2 *Broker Peer to Peer-to-Peer Insurance*

The broker peer-to-peer Insurance is characterized by the presence of an intermediary, typically an insurance broker, who facilitates the formation and management of peer groups. These groups are created through online networks or personal connections established by the broker, bringing together individuals with similar risk profiles and insurance needs. The participants in these groups contribute funds based on transparent and cooperative rules. A portion of the contributions is allocated to a common fund, while the remaining amount is transferred to a reinsurance company (Levantesi & Piscopo, 2022).

If the common fund sufficiently covers the claims, the members receive a share of the excess funds following a predetermined capital allocation rule. However, if the common fund falls short, the reinsurance coverage ensures claims are met. The broker model was the first peer-to-peer insurance model introduced with the launch of Friendsurance in Germany in 2010. Friendsurance connects individuals with similar risk characteristics, forms sharing groups, selects insurance products from partner insurance companies, and manages the collection and distribution of contributions. Friendsurance aims to reduce premiums by directly handling small claims compared to traditional insurance policies. The cooperative mechanisms employed, where fewer claims are settled, result in greater cashback redistribution to members and help mitigate moral hazard, adverse selection, fraud, and inefficiencies.

Another example of a company operating under the broker peer-to-peer insurance model is ManyPets, formerly known as Bought By Many. ManyPets aggregates individuals with similar Insurance needs into groups based on lifestyle, occupation, or specific interests. By leveraging the collective bargaining power of these groups, ManyPets negotiates with insurers to secure more favourable terms such as discounted premiums, enhanced coverage, or tailored policy features. For instance, ManyPets has created groups for pet owners and individuals seeking insurance coverage for specific dog breeds. By uniting many individuals with similar insurance requirements, Bought By Many demonstrates substantial demand for insurers, resulting in more competitive offers and customized policies (KPMG, 2017; Kulia, 2023).

Other examples of companies following the broker peer-to-peer insurance model include Inspeer, Peercover, and UVAMO. These companies play the broker intermediary role to connect like-minded individuals, negotiate with insurers, and provide innovative insurance solutions tailored to the needs of their peer groups.

2.2.1.3 *Carrier Peer-to-Peer Insurance*

The carrier or collaborative peer-to-peer insurance model unites individuals and groups to provide coverage for specific risks. In this model, participants assume the dual roles of insurers and insured, coming together to share the responsibility and pool their resources to manage risks collectively. Unlike traditional Insurance, where a centralized insurance company serves as the carrier, the carrier P2P model allows participants to take on the carrier function themselves and seek additional coverage from reinsurers in case of large claims.

Under the carrier P2P model, individuals with similar insurance needs and risk profiles form groups or communities based on shared interests, affiliations, or characteristics. Once a group is established, each participant contributes premiums or financial contributions to a common pool. This pool acts as the collective fund to cover potential claims and expenses. The group collectively assesses the claim when a participant experiences a covered loss or event. The assessment process can involve voting, consensus-based decision-making, or appointing trusted members within the group to manage claims. If the claim is deemed valid and approved by the group, funds from the pooled premiums compensate the participant or provide necessary support. Payments are made from the collective pool of funds contributed by the participants (Levantesi & Piscopo, 2022).

The carrier P2P model participants actively manage risks and ensure the group's financial stability. This can involve setting risk limits, establishing reserve funds, implementing risk mitigation strategies, and monitoring the overall financial health of the group. Technology platforms or applications are often utilized to facilitate communication, premium collection, claims management, and decision-making within the group, enhancing transparency and streamlining administrative processes.

Lemonade, launched in the United States in 2015, operates on the carrier model of decentralized Insurance. Policyholders unite to form a community, contributing premiums into a shared pool. Lemonade assumes the role of the reinsurer, managing claims and payouts from the pooled premiums. Any unclaimed premiums are donated to charitable causes through their Giveback program.

It's important to note that the self-organizing P2P model differs from the carrier model. In the carrier model, participants take on the primary role of insurers themselves, collectively assuming the carrier function. In contrast, in the self-organizing model, participants collaborate to manage the insurance process without assuming the carrier function.

2.2.2 *Benefits and Ethical Dilemmas in Peer-to-Peer Insurance*

P2P insurance fosters community by pooling risks and sharing responsibilities among like-minded individuals. It's personalized risk assessment and cost-effective premiums attract policyholders seeking more inclusive coverage. However, amidst the allure of its potential benefits, this disruptive paradigm also gives rise to a series of ethical dilemmas, notably concerning policy underwriting and pricing. Striking an intricate balance between the advantages of P2P insurance and the ethical implications it carries poses a formidable challenge for insurance providers.

Foremost among the ethical considerations in P2P insurance is ensuring fairness in policy underwriting and pricing. The very essence of this model rests on risk pooling and collective contributions based on shared characteristics or affiliations within the community. Yet, while this fosters a sense of solidarity, it must be vigilantly guarded against inadvertently leading to discrimination, whereby certain individuals or groups suffer unjust exclusions or higher premiums due to factors such as age, gender, or pre-existing conditions. Navigating this delicate territory necessitates deftly balancing personalized risk assessment and the unwavering avoidance of discriminatory practices.

Transparency constitutes yet another ethical dilemma that surfaces in the underwriting and pricing processes of P2P insurance. With individual members entrusted to assess the risks their peers bear, information asymmetry becomes a latent concern, casting doubt upon the integrity of risk evaluations and introducing the potential for unequal treatment of specific policyholders. Establishing transparent and standardized risk evaluation methodologies is a pivotal strategy to address and resolve these ethical challenges.

Further compounding the ethical landscape is moral hazard and adverse selection, which loom large in P2P insurance, beckoning insurers to traverse this treacherous terrain with utmost vigilance. As policyholders perceive the collective pool shouldering the financial burden, they may be less inclined to temper their risky behaviour, thus engendering moral hazard. Additionally, this groundbreaking model might unwittingly allure individuals with higher risks to actively seek P2P insurance, potentially unsettling the equilibrium of the risk pool and intensifying the spectre of adverse selection. Striking an equitable equilibrium involves deftly balancing the nurturing of community support while prudently avoiding circumstances that inadvertently incentivize hazardous behaviour.

Central to the efficacy of P2P insurance is the exhaustive reliance on data collection and analysis for precise risk assessment, which begets significant challenges concerning the privacy and security of policyholders' data. Prudent insurers understand the gravity of handling personal information responsibly and implement robust security measures to safeguard sensitive data from untoward breaches or misuse. Upholding the sacred trust bestowed upon them by policyholders mandates an unwavering commitment to ethical data management.

A cornerstone objective of P2P insurance rests upon promoting financial inclusion, setting its sights on empowering underserved or marginalized communities. However, the fulcrum of ethical consideration demands that these communities truly reap the benefits and that social equity is earnestly advocated. To that end, stringent measures must be enacted to prevent any form of exclusions or exploitation, fostering equal insurance coverage opportunities and cementing this transformative paradigm's ethical foundation.

Yet, in this novel landscape, cultivating trust and effectual governance within the P2P insurance community is paramount, necessitating open and transparent communication between insurers and policyholders. Embracing ethical governance mechanisms, such as DAOs, empowers policyholders as active participants in decision-making, endowing the process with transparency and imbuing it with an aura of fairness.

To address these multifaceted ethical dilemmas, P2P insurers must exalt fairness, transparency, and inclusivity within their underwriting and pricing practices. Implementing clear policies and guidelines for risk assessment, the vigilant preservation of data privacy, and active engagement with the community constitute the critical stepping stones to fostering trust and ameliorating ethical challenges. Regular reviews of underwriting and pricing practices further fortify the ethical fortitude of the P2P insurance ecosystem, detecting and remedying potential biases and elevating the model to a more sustainable and ethically responsible realm. In unison, insurers, regulators, policymakers, and industry stakeholders forge a formidable alliance to create ethical frameworks that safeguard the interests of policyholders while preserving the integrity of the P2P insurance model. In threading this delicate balance, P2P insurance stands committed to its journey as an ethical and potent alternative, poised to redefine the contours of the insurance industry.

2.3 Parametric Insurance—Revolutionizing Risk Coverage

Parametric insurance solutions have emerged as new to risk management, offering an alternative to traditional insurance models. Unlike conventional policies that assess physical damage, parametric Insurance revolves around a measurable index and predefined triggers or payout mechanisms. This innovative insurance model has gained significant traction due to its ability to cover complex and unpredictable risks, such as pandemics, cyberattacks, terrorism, flight delays, business interruption, natural catastrophes, and climate-related weather risks.

Parametric Insurance relies on specific physical or natural parameters to determine payout eligibility. For example, a parametric insurance policy might trigger a payout when the magnitude of an earthquake reaches a certain Richter scale measurement or when a hurricane's wind speed surpasses a predefined threshold in a defined location. By setting these triggers, parametric Insurance allows for faster claims processing without the need for extensive assessment of physical damage. Insurers and insured parties establish the payout amount, trigger data source, and underlying calculations for the trigger in advance (Capgemini, n.d.; Brettler & Gosnear, 2020).

Technological advancements have played a pivotal role in enabling the adoption of parametric insurance by enhancing data collection, processing capabilities, and risk modelling techniques. Parametric insurance relies on predefined parameters or triggers to determine policy payouts rather than traditional claims assessment based on individual losses. The proliferation of data sources, including satellite imagery, weather sensors, and IoT devices, has provided insurers with real-time and high-resolution data on various perils, such as natural disasters, weather events, and market fluctuations. This abundant availability of data ensures accurate and timely assessment of risks, a critical component in parametric insurance where payouts are contingent upon specific events or conditions.

Moreover, technological advancements have empowered insurers with advanced analytics and modelling capabilities, enabling them to analyse vast datasets and develop sophisticated risk models for parametric insurance. These models leverage historical data, predictive analytics, and probabilistic algorithms to precisely quantify risks and calibrate parametric triggers to align with actual exposures. This analytical prowess enhances risk assessment accuracy and enables insurers to offer parametric insurance products that accurately reflect the underlying risks. In addition to advanced analytics, automation technologies such as smart contracts powered by blockchain play a pivotal role in streamlining policy administration and claims processing in parametric insurance. Smart contracts automatically execute policy terms and trigger payouts when predefined conditions are met, eliminating the need for manual intervention and reducing administrative overhead. This automation ensures transparency, efficiency, and timely payouts, enhancing the appeal of parametric insurance for both insurers and policyholders.

Several companies have emerged as prominent providers of parametric insurance solutions. Global Parametrics, founded in 2016, aims to leverage advances in climate science, data modelling, and financial engineering to manage and mitigate the risks of extreme weather and natural hazards worldwide. Their innovative products cover a range of sectors, including renewables, agribusiness, financial services, and humanitarian organizations. Global Parametrics provides several customized products for clients, such as drought and crop stress forecasts, protection against energy-production shortages, flood forecasts, anticipatory financing for impending hazards from wind, precipitation, and surge, and protection against wildfires, volcanic ash, sand storm, etc. (Sullivan, 2023). Arbol, another industry player, utilizes data, blockchain, and AI-powered platforms to offer climate risk management solutions. Arbol demonstrates the versatility and potential of parametric insurance solutions by providing coverage for various risks, such as business interruption and travel-related issues. Descartes Underwriting utilizes machine learning and real-time monitoring from satellite imagery and IoT to provide coverage against natural catastrophes and emerging risks. Their comprehensive parametric insurance offerings cover risks such as cyclones, floods, earthquakes, wildfires, and supply chain disruptions.

2.3.1 *Parametric Solution Implementation: An Overview of Key Steps*

When implementing parametric insurance solutions, companies typically follow a systematic approach. This process involves analysing a client's risk and exposure, constructing a customized index, designing a financial solution, and providing underwriting capacity (Swiss Re, 2023). By adhering to these steps, companies can effectively offer parametric coverage to clients, ensuring prompt payment during a triggered event. Figure 2.2 shows the steps involved in parametric Insurance in the decentralized world.

Step 1: Risk and Exposure Analysis.

Understanding and assessing risks is fundamental to designing effective insurance solutions that provide adequate coverage and protection to clients. Risk and exposure analysis, the first step in the insurance underwriting process, thoroughly examines external data sources and the client's portfolio data. This detailed analysis enables insurers to gain insights into the client's vulnerabilities and potential risks, paving the way for developing tailored insurance products. Risk and exposure analysis methodology involves several key steps, each aimed at gathering, analysing, and interpreting relevant data to assess the client's risk profile comprehensively. The first step in risk and exposure analysis is gathering external data sources and the client's portfolio data. External data sources may include historical data on natural disasters, weather patterns, economic indicators, and industry trends. The client's portfolio data, on the other hand, provides insights into their assets, operations, geographic locations, and risk exposures. Once the data is collected, insurers integrate and consolidate the external data sources with the client's portfolio data. This integration process involves matching and correlating datasets to identify patterns, trends, and potential risk factors that may impact the client's business or assets. After integrating the data, insurers identify and assess the client's various risks. This involves analysing the data to identify potential threats, vulnerabilities, and exposures that may risk the client's operations or financial stability. Based on the analysis, insurers identify relevant parameters and triggers that align with the client's needs and risk profile. These parameters serve as the basis for designing the insurance coverage and defining the conditions under which policy payouts will be triggered. Once the parameters are identified, insurers assess the severity

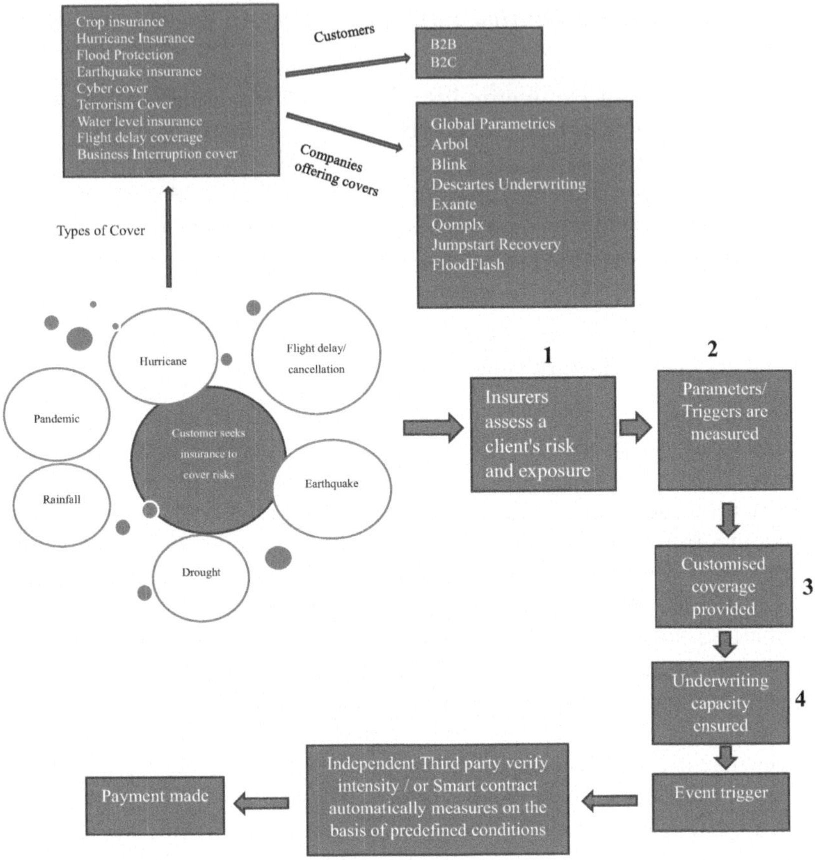

Fig. 2.2 Steps involved in the Parametric Insurance (*Source* Prepared by authors)

and likelihood of each risk scenario. This involves evaluating the potential impact of each risk scenario on the client's business or assets and the probability of occurrence.

Step 2: Customized Index Construction.

Following the comprehensive risk and exposure analysis, the subsequent step in the insurance underwriting process is constructing a customized index for the client. This index is the cornerstone for determining trigger events and subsequent payouts in the insurance policy. By tailoring the index to the client's specific needs and risk profile, insurers can ensure a precise and relevant assessment of events that may impact the client's business or assets. The methodology of customized index construction involves several key steps, each aimed at designing an index that accurately reflects the client's risk profile and insurance needs. Firstly, building upon the parameters identified during the risk and exposure analysis, insurers further refine and specify the parameters that will form the basis of the customized index. These parameters should be relevant to the client's business or assets and reflect the risks identified during the analysis. Once the parameters are identified, insurers define trigger events that activate policy payouts. These trigger events are based on specific thresholds or conditions associated with each parameter. For example, a trigger event in property insurance may be defined as a certain wind speed threshold during a hurricane. In crop insurance, a trigger event may be defined as a certain level of rainfall deficiency during a drought. Using the identified parameters and trigger events, insurers calculate the index formula that will be used to assess the occurrence of trigger events. The index formula may involve weighting different parameters based on their relative importance or risk contribution. Before finalizing the customized index, insurers validate and test the index formula to ensure its accuracy and effectiveness in assessing trigger events. This may involve back-testing the index formula using historical data or conducting sensitivity analysis to assess its robustness across different scenarios. Throughout the index construction process, insurers dialogue with the client to ensure that the index design aligns with their risk tolerance and insurance needs. Client feedback and input are invaluable in fine-tuning the index parameters and trigger events to reflect the client's specific circumstances accurately.

Step 3: Financial Solution Design.

Once the customized index is constructed, the subsequent step in the insurance underwriting process is designing a financial solution that aligns with the client's risk profile and objectives. Financial solution design encompasses several key considerations, each aimed at developing a parametric policy that meets the client's requirements and objectives. One of the primary considerations in financial solution design is determining the payout structure of the parametric policy. This involves defining how payouts will be calculated and disbursed in the event of a trigger event. Payouts may be structured as a lump sum payment or distributed over a specified period, depending on the client's preferences and risk exposure. Insurers must also consider whether payouts will be fixed or variable based on the severity of the trigger event. Another critical aspect of financial solution design is calculating the premiums for the parametric policy. Premiums are typically based on the level of risk exposure, the probability of trigger events, and the desired level of coverage. Insurers may use actuarial models, risk assessments, and historical data to calculate premiums accurately. Insurers must consider factors such as the client's risk tolerance, budget constraints, and desired level of financial protection when determining premium amounts. Financial solution design also involves defining the coverage limits of the parametric policy. Coverage limits specify the maximum amount paid during a trigger event, protecting the client against potential losses. Insurers must carefully evaluate the client's risk exposure and financial position to determine appropriate coverage limits that provide sufficient protection without being overly burdensome. In addition to payout structure, premium calculations, and coverage limits, financial solution design includes defining the terms and conditions of the parametric policy. This includes outlining the eligibility criteria for triggering a claim, the documentation required to support a claim, and any exclusions or limitations that may apply. Clear and transparent policy terms and conditions ensure that the insurer and the client understand their respective rights and obligations under the policy.

Step 4: Underwriting Capacity Provision.

Underwriting capacity provision is a critical component of parametric insurance, as it safeguards the financial stability and integrity of the insurance contract. In parametric insurance, where payouts are triggered by predefined events rather than individual claims assessment, the availability of underwriting capacity ensures that insurers can honour their commitments promptly and efficiently. Insurers instil confidence in clients by maintaining adequate underwriting capacity and demonstrating their ability to provide timely financial assistance during a covered loss. The methodology of underwriting capacity provision involves several key steps, each aimed at ensuring that the insurer possesses the financial resources necessary to fulfil its obligations under the parametric insurance contract. The first step in underwriting capacity provision is conducting a comprehensive financial analysis to assess the insurer's solvency and liquidity position. This analysis evaluates the insurer's assets, liabilities, cash reserves, and capital adequacy to determine its ability to absorb potential losses and meet its obligations under the parametric insurance contract. Once the financial analysis is complete, insurers implement robust risk management practices to mitigate potential risks and exposures that could impact their underwriting capacity. This may include diversifying the insurer's investment portfolio, purchasing reinsurance coverage, and implementing risk transfer mechanisms to minimize the impact of catastrophic events on the insurer's financial position.

Insurers often secure additional underwriting capacity through reinsurance arrangements with other insurers or reinsurers. Reinsurance protects against large or unexpected losses, allowing insurers to share risk with other market participants and enhance their underwriting capacity. Reinsurance arrangements may take various forms, including excess loss treaties, quota share agreements, and catastrophe bonds. Insurers must comply with regulatory capital adequacy requirements to maintain sufficient capital reserves to support their underwriting activities. Regulatory authorities set minimum capital requirements based on the insurer's risk profile and business activities to safeguard policyholder interests and maintain the insurance industry's stability.

2.3.2 *Advantages and Ethical Challenges of Parametric Insurance*

Parametric Insurance offers several advantages over traditional models. One of the primary benefits lies in its ability to effectively cover complex and unpredictable risks that often defy conventional insurance frameworks (Nasdaq, 2021). Risks like pandemics, cyberattacks, and climate-related weather events present formidable challenges to traditional underwriting and claim assessment methods. However, parametric Insurance's reliance on predetermined triggers and objective data enables it to respond swiftly and accurately to such unprecedented risks, providing policyholders with much-needed protection.

Moreover, parametric Insurance exhibits exceptional scalability as a microinsurance product, addressing the coverage gaps faced by underserved communities, particularly smallholder farmers. In regions where agriculture predominantly consists of small-scale farms, these farmers often lack access to affordable and relevant insurance coverage. Parametric Insurance, when integrated with microinsurance principles, can cater to the specific needs of these vulnerable populations. This enhances their financial resilience and promotes economic development in these regions, fostering a sense of security among small-scale farmers (Ernst & Young, 2022).

Despite its advantages, parametric Insurance poses several ethical challenges, necessitating careful consideration and responsible governance. One of the fundamental ethical concerns is the fairness and transparency of policy underwriting (Cohn et al., 2017). The reliance on objective triggers and risk pooling can inadvertently lead to discriminatory practices if certain policyholders are unfairly excluded or charged higher premiums based on personal characteristics or affiliations within the community. Striking a balance between personalized risk assessment and equitable policyholder treatment becomes paramount to maintaining ethical integrity.

Another ethical dilemma arises from the potential lack of transparency in the underwriting and pricing processes. As individual members within the community often assess the risks of their peers, information asymmetry can occur, raising questions about the accuracy and objectivity of risk evaluations. Policyholders must clearly understand the triggers that activate their coverage and the potential outcomes to ensure a fair and informed claims process. Transparent communication and standardized risk evaluation methodologies are essential in addressing these concerns and ensuring ethical practices within parametric Insurance.

Furthermore, parametric insurance can be susceptible to moral hazards and adverse selection. The streamlined and automated claims process might incentivize policyholders to engage in risky behaviour, knowing that the collective pool will absorb the costs without traditional claims investigation. Similarly, individuals with higher risks may be more motivated to seek parametric coverage, potentially skewing the risk pool and impacting the overall sustainability of the insurance model. Ethical considerations entail finding the right balance between promoting community support and discouraging actions that could compromise the financial health of the risk pool.

Parametric Insurance presents promising solutions for covering complex risks and promoting financial inclusion. However, ethical challenges demand robust and transparent practices to ensure fairness, equity, and accountability within the insurance model. Striving for a delicate equilibrium between parametric Insurance's advantages and ethical implications is pivotal to developing an ethically responsible and sustainable insurance landscape.

2.4 Mutual Insurance Models

Mutual insurance offers alternative frameworks to conventional ones, prioritizing collective ownership and cooperative principles. Within a mutual insurance framework, policyholders transcend their roles as mere customers; they become proprietors of the insurance enterprise itself. This distinctive ownership structure endows members with collective ownership and control over the organization, typically manifested through voting rights and active participation in strategic decision-making processes. The crux of mutual insurance lies in its democratic governance structure, where policyholders have a stake in shaping the company's policies, objectives, and operations. This participatory approach fosters a sense of community and mutual trust among members as they work together to safeguard their shared interests and financial well-being. This foundational ethos permeates every aspect of mutual insurance's operational mechanisms, shaping how premiums are collected, claims are processed, and surplus funds are distributed.

Premiums serve as the lifeblood of mutual insurance, constituting the primary funding source for the company's operations and claims payments. However, collecting premiums in mutual insurance is not merely transactional but imbued with a sense of communal responsibility and shared risk. Policyholders contribute premiums based on their risk profiles, pooling their resources to mitigate the financial impact of potential losses. Moreover, collecting premiums in mutual insurance reflects a commitment to fairness and transparency. Unlike traditional insurers that may adjust premiums based on profit considerations, mutual insurers strive to balance affordability and sustainability. Premiums are determined through a collaborative process that considers the collective interests of policyholders, ensuring that financial contributions are equitable and accessible to all members.

One of the hallmarks of mutual insurance is its commitment to the equitable redistribution of surplus funds. Mutual insurers operate on the principle that financial benefits should be shared fairly and transparently among members. Any surplus funds generated by the company, whether through investment returns or underwriting profits, are not siphoned off for private gain; instead, they are returned to policyholders in the form of dividends or reduced premiums. This equitable distribution mechanism underscores the cooperative ethos of mutual insurance, fostering a sense of ownership and shared prosperity among members. By reinvesting surplus funds into the community, mutual insurers empower policyholders to participate in the company's financial success, reinforcing that mutual insurance is a collective endeavour to serve the common good.

In addition to promoting mutual aid and solidarity, the operational mechanisms of mutual insurance are also characterized by a focus on operational efficiency and customer-centricity. Unlike large corporate insurers burdened by bureaucratic processes and profit-driven agendas, mutual insurers are agile and responsive to the needs of their members. Claims processing in mutual insurance is streamlined and expedited, emphasizing delivering prompt and personalized service to policyholders. Decisions regarding claims settlements are made with members' best interests in mind, prioritizing fairness, transparency, and compassion.

Nowadays, mutual insurance is popularized due to the use of technologies in every aspect of insurance operations. Mutual insurance platforms often utilize websites or mobile applications for enrolment and policy management. These platforms allow members to register for insurance coverage, submit necessary documentation, and manage their policies online. Digital enrolment streamlines the process, reduces paperwork, and increases accessibility for community members, especially those in remote or underserved areas. Mobile technology, including SMS messaging and mobile apps, is used for outreach and communication with members. Mutual insurance schemes can send alerts, reminders, and important updates regarding insurance coverage, premium payments, and claims processing via mobile devices. Mobile communication enhances engagement and ensures community members stay informed about their insurance benefits and responsibilities. Mutual insurance schemes leverage data analytics to assess the risks faced by members and determine appropriate insurance coverage and pricing. By analysing demographic data, historical claims information, and other relevant variables, insurers can identify risks specific to the community and tailor insurance products accordingly. Data analytics also enable insurers to monitor trends, anticipate emerging risks, and adjust insurance offerings in response to changing needs. In agricultural-based mutual insurance schemes, remote sensing technologies and satellite imagery are used to assess crop health, monitor weather patterns, and detect potential risks such as droughts or floods. This data helps insurers and organizers make informed decisions about insurance coverage, crop management practices, and disaster preparedness measures. Remote sensing technology enhances risk assessment and improves the accuracy of insurance payouts in agricultural communities.

Blockchain technology is utilized in mutual insurance schemes to enhance transparency, security, and trust in insurance transactions. By recording insurance contracts, premium payments, and claims data on a decentralized ledger, blockchain ensures transparency and immutability of records. This reduces the risk of fraud, enhances trust between insurers and members, and simplifies claims processing and verification. Technology enables monitoring and feedback systems where members can provide input and feedback on insurance services and processes. Online surveys, feedback forms, and forums allow members to voice their concerns, suggest improvements, and participate in decision-making processes. This participatory approach strengthens member engagement, fosters trust, and ensures that insurance products meet members' needs.

Several insurance platforms operate under the mutual insurance model, exemplifying a cooperative approach where policyholders are also company owners. Among these platforms, notable examples include Achmea, Guardian Life Insurance Company of America, MassMutual, Takadao, and Al-Rajhi Takaful. Guardian Life Insurance Company of America recognized as one of the largest mutual insurance companies globally, stands out for its pioneering efforts in digital transformation. In 2016, Guardian embarked on a comprehensive digital transformation initiative, breaking away from the traditional stereotypes prevalent in the insurance industry. Digital transformation was still a nascent concept at the time, particularly within the insurance sector. However, Guardian recognized the evolving landscape and the imperative to adapt to the digital age. Six years later, the insurance industry has shifted profoundly, with digital innovation at its forefront. Businesses are embracing new technologies, reimagining business models, and enhancing operational capabilities through digital tools and platforms. Before 2016, Guardian Life faced challenges in scaling its operations due to legacy systems and outdated mainframe technologies. These legacy systems impeded the development of new features and products, resulting in lengthy, cumbersome, and costly processes. Essentially, Guardian's technical infrastructure posed limitations that hindered its growth potential. Recognizing the need for flexibility, agility, and innovation to address evolving market demands, Guardian's leadership determined that transitioning to a cloud-based model was essential. By leveraging cloud technology, Guardian aimed to achieve greater scalability, agility, and efficiency in its operations. API integrations with real-time connectivity emerged as a key strategy, offering the potential to streamline administrative tasks and reduce errors significantly. According to Guardianlife, API integrations could save companies up to 200 hours per year in managing administrative tasks, highlighting the transformative impact of digitalization on operational efficiency and effectiveness (Guardianlife, n.d.).

Achmea, a distinguished insurance cooperative and mutual holding company established in the Netherlands in 1811, has evolved into the largest insurance provider in the country. Operating under the mutual insurance model, Achmea exemplifies the cooperative spirit of mutual insurance, wherein policyholders assume dual roles as insured individuals and company owners. This unique structure empowers policyholders, also called members, to actively engage in Achmea's governance and decision-making processes, fostering a customer-centric approach centred on addressing the needs and preferences of its membership base rather than solely focusing on profit maximization. Through the fundamental principle of risk pooling, Achmea ensures that financial risks associated with insurance coverage are collectively shared among policyholders/members, thereby cultivating a sense of security and community within its membership (ICMIF, 2021). Achmea has embraced various digital technologies to enhance operational efficiency and adapt to the evolving digital landscape. For instance, the company has implemented advanced data analytics tools to assess and manage risks more effectively, enabling data-driven decision-making processes. Achmea has leveraged cloud computing technologies to modernize its infrastructure, facilitating greater scalability, flexibility, and accessibility of its services. Moreover, Achmea has integrated digital platforms into its operations, providing policyholders with convenient and user-friendly interfaces for managing their insurance policies, reporting claims, and engaging with the company. Through these digital initiatives, Achmea aims to optimize its operations, enhance customer experiences, and maintain its position as a leader in the insurance industry (Achmea, 2018).

MassMutual, as a mutual company, operates with a distinct focus on benefiting its members, policy owners, and customers rather than serving external shareholders. This unique structure allows MassMutual to prioritize the needs and interests of its stakeholders, driving decisions that align with their long-term financial well-being. MassMutual has embarked on a digital transformation journey in recent years, leveraging cloud technology to enhance its operational capabilities and optimize data utilization. By transitioning to the cloud, MassMutual has unlocked new opportunities to leverage advanced technologies such as machine learning and data analytics. These technologies enable MassMutual to extract valuable insights from its data, empowering the company to make informed decisions and deliver personalized experiences to its stakeholders. The adoption of cloud technology has streamlined data consumption and integration processes within MassMutual's operations. With enhanced data accessibility and integration capabilities, the company can leverage its data more effectively across various applications and digital systems of engagement. This seamless integration facilitates real-time notifications and responses to critical events, such as payments, ensuring prompt and proactive customer communication. Rather than waiting for batch processing cycles, MassMutual can now provide immediate notifications and services, enhancing customer satisfaction and overall operational efficiency (DXC Technology, 2012).

2.4.1 Models of Mutual Insurance

2.4.1.1 Mutual Insurance Companies

Mutual insurance companies represent a traditional yet enduring model in the insurance industry, characterized by a cooperative ownership structure where policyholders are also the organization's owners. This unique ownership arrangement distinguishes mutual insurers from publicly traded insurance companies, as they do not have external shareholders. Instead, policyholders collectively own the mutual insurance company and play a central role in its governance and decision-making processes. The essence of mutual insurance lies in the principle of mutuality, which emphasizes the collective pooling of resources and risks among policyholders. Members of a mutual insurance company share the profits and losses generated by the company, reflecting a commitment to equitable distribution and shared responsibility. This cooperative ethos fosters a sense of community and solidarity among policyholders, who have a vested interest in the success and stability of the mutual insurer. Mutual insurance companies offer their members a diverse range of insurance products, spanning various lines of coverage such as life insurance, property insurance, liability insurance, and more. These products are designed to meet policyholders' diverse needs and preferences, providing financial protection against risks and uncertainties in their personal and business lives.

Mutual insurance companies offer a multitude of benefits rooted in their customer-centric approach, setting them apart from profit-driven corporations. Central to their ethos is a steadfast commitment to prioritizing the interests and satisfaction of policyholders above all else. Unlike traditional insurers solely focused on maximizing shareholder returns, mutual insurers place a premium on the well-being of their members. This ethos permeates every aspect of their operations, from decision-making processes to product offerings and customer service standards. By aligning their strategies with the needs and preferences of policyholders, mutual insurers foster a culture of cooperation, mutual aid, and shared responsibility within their membership base. In addition to promoting a customer-centric ethos, mutual insurers play a vital role in providing financial security and peace of mind to individuals and businesses alike. By pooling resources and spreading risks among members, mutual insurance companies offer a safety net that protects against unforeseen events and unexpected losses. This collaborative approach not only enhances the affordability and accessibility of insurance coverage but also fosters a sense of trust and loyalty among policyholders.

Moreover, the cooperative ownership structure inherent in mutual insurance companies underscores their dedication to serving the collective interests of policyholders. As company owners, policyholders have a direct stake in its success and governance, empowering them to actively participate in decision-making processes and shape the organization's direction. This democratic approach ensures that the voices of policyholders are heard and their needs are met, reinforcing a sense of community and solidarity among members.

Mutual insurance companies are stalwarts of cooperation, mutual aid, and shared responsibility, embodying an enduring commitment to fulfilling the needs of policyholders while nurturing a profound sense of community and solidarity. Their customer-centric ethos and cooperative ownership structure distinguish them as pillars of stability and support within the dynamic insurance landscape, ensuring that policyholders' interests remain paramount. An example of mutual insurance companies is The Penn Mutual Life Insurance Company. Founded in 1847, The Penn Mutual Life Insurance Company has carved out a storied legacy in Philadelphia, Pennsylvania, spanning over 175 years. As a mutual company, Penn Mutual has steadfastly committed to policyholders, navigating through evolving economic landscapes while consistently fulfilling its promises. In 2023 alone, Penn Mutual demonstrated its unwavering dedication by disbursing a remarkable \$2.8 billion benefits, marking a record dividend payout to policyholders. With a total adjusted surplus reaching $3.3 billion, the company achieved its highest surplus level in its illustrious history. Life insurance and annuity sales surged to $386 million and $945 million, respectively, underscoring Penn Mutual's resilience and market relevance. The company's impressive financial performance has garnered recognition from rating agencies, with reaffirmed ratings and stable outlooks attributed to its robust product offerings, well-diversified investment portfolio, and consistent operational results. Penn Mutual's enduring commitment to excellence is further evidenced by its unparalleled track record, having maintained A or better ratings from AM Best for an astounding 97 years, a testament to its financial strength and stability. Beyond financial metrics, Penn Mutual's legacy extends to its profound impact on individuals, families, and businesses, empowering them on their journey towards financial prosperity. Through strategic partnerships with Financial Professionals nationwide, Penn Mutual fosters resilience and confidence, enabling generations to achieve their financial aspirations with assurance. With a comprehensive suite of competitive solutions encompassing life insurance, annuities, wealth management, and institutional asset management, Penn Mutual and its affiliates stand as trusted allies dedicated to safeguarding the financial well-being of its clients and their families (The Penn Mutual Life Insurance Company, 2023).

2.4.1.2 Cooperative Insurance

Cooperative insurance operates similarly to mutual insurance but is structured as a cooperative organization. Policyholders are also members and owners of the cooperative, with each member having equal voting rights, thereby ensuring democratic governance and collective decision-making. Cooperative insurers often specialize in specific types of insurance coverage or cater to particular communities or industries, tailoring their services to meet the unique needs of their membership base. Introducing cooperative insurance heralds a departure from traditional insurance models by emphasizing cooperation, collective ownership, and democratic participation. By transforming policyholders into active stakeholders, cooperative insurers foster a sense of ownership and empowerment among members, encouraging them to engage in the governance and management of the organization actively. This participatory approach enhances transparency, accountability, and trust within the cooperative, reinforcing its commitment to serving the best interests of its members.

The features of cooperative insurance extend beyond its organizational structure to encompass its focus on community building, risk-sharing, and mutual support. Unlike conventional insurers driven by profit motives, cooperative insurers prioritize the welfare of their members, striving to provide affordable, accessible, and tailored insurance solutions that address their membership base's specific needs and preferences. Through collaborative risk-sharing mechanisms and collective bargaining power, cooperative insurers empower members to mitigate risks effectively and navigate uncertainties with greater confidence and resilience.

Cooperative insurance presents numerous advantages for its members, contributing to their financial stability, empowerment, and community solidarity. Firstly, by pooling resources, cooperative insurers can enhance the financial stability of their members. Through collective contributions from all members, the insurer accumulates a larger pool of funds, which can be used to cover claims and other operational expenses. This shared financial burden spreads risks across a larger group, reducing the impact of individual losses and providing greater overall stability to the membership base. Cooperative insurance empowers its members by granting them greater control over insurance decisions. As owners of the cooperative, policyholders have a direct stake in the governance and management of the organization. They can participate in decision-making processes, such as voting on key policies, electing board members, and providing feedback on insurance offerings. This democratic approach ensures that members' voices are heard and their interests are prioritized in decision-making. Cooperative insurers also leverage collective bargaining power to negotiate favourable terms with service providers, resulting in lower premiums and higher coverage limits for their members. By representing a large and unified group of policyholders, cooperative insurers can secure better deals and more competitive rates from reinsurers, vendors, and other industry partners. This translates into cost savings for members and broader access to comprehensive insurance coverage at affordable prices.

Cooperative insurance also fosters a culture of mutual aid and support within the community. Members benefit from the financial protection provided by their insurance coverage and the solidarity and assistance of fellow members in times of need. In the event of a loss or hardship, members come together to offer support, guidance, and practical assistance to those affected, reinforcing the bonds of community and cooperation. This collective ethos of mutual aid strengthens the resilience of the membership base and fosters a sense of belonging and solidarity among members. An example of a cooperative insurance company is

Co-operators Group Limited, a prominent figure in the Canadian insurance and financial services landscape, boasting assets under administration exceeding $62 billion. Founded in 1945 in Regina, Saskatchewan, on Treaty 4 territory, The Co-operators embodies the cooperative ethos, recognizing the traditional land of the Cree, Saulteaux, Dakota, Lakota, and Nakoda peoples, as well as the Métis peoples. With a comprehensive suite of financial solutions, including multi-line insurance, wealth management products, institutional asset management, and brokerage operations, The Co-operators is committed to providing its members financial security and peace of mind (The Co-operators Group Limited, 2022).

Offering a wide range of insurance products such as auto, home, life, farm, travel, and commercial insurance, The Co-operators serves the diverse needs of its members across Canada. With a firm belief in the strength of collective action, The Co-operators operates as a financial services cooperative, emphasizing the idea that together, individuals are stronger, safer, and more resilient. Supported by a dedicated team of nearly 7,000 employees and a network of over 2,800 licensed insurance representatives, The Co-operators is deeply rooted in its commitment to serving its members and communities. In 2019, The Co-operators embarked on a transformative journey to digitize auto insurance, exceeding initial ambitions by enabling clients to receive quotes and complete insurance transactions online for home and auto insurance products. Building on this success, the company accelerated its digital transformation efforts in 2022, enhancing the digital experience for clients across various points of interaction. This milestone strengthens The Co-operators' core business lines. It opens doors to more holistic financial planning conversations with its clientele, further solidifying its position as a trusted financial security and wealth management partner (The Co-operators Group Limited, 2022).

2.4.1.3 *Takaful Insurance*

Takaful insurance, rooted in Islamic principles, represents a unique form of cooperative risk-sharing among participants. Unlike conventional insurance, which involves transferring risk from policyholders to the insurer in exchange for premiums, Takaful operates based on mutual assistance and shared responsibility. At the heart of Takaful is cooperation and solidarity, where participants collectively pool their resources to bear the financial burdens of unexpected events. Unlike conventional insurance, which relies on transferring risk to the insurer, Takaful embodies the principle of mutual assistance, ensuring that the community shares risks and rewards. Central to Takaful operations is adherence to Sharia principles, ensuring that all transactions and contracts follow Islamic law. This entails avoiding elements such as interest (riba), uncertainty (gharar), and gambling (maysir), which are prohibited in Islam. Takaful contracts must adhere to Sharia guidelines to maintain validity and ethical integrity. Takaful operates through separate funds: the participant fund and the operator (or shareholders') fund. Contributions from participants are pooled into the participant fund, which is solely dedicated to paying claims and covering administrative expenses. The operator fund belongs to the shareholders or operators of the Takaful company and is used to generate profits through investments. In Takaful, participants mutually share the scheme's risks and profits. Any surplus generated from the participant fund after covering claims and expenses is distributed among the participants as dividends or contributions to a charitable fund. This profit-sharing mechanism aligns with Islamic principles of equitable distribution and social responsibility. Takaful funds are invested following Islamic investment principles, which prohibit investments in businesses involved in activities deemed unethical or non-compliant with Sharia law. Investments must adhere to principles such as avoiding interest-based transactions (riba), speculative trading (gharar), and investments in businesses deemed harmful to society. Transparency and accountability are fundamental principles in Takaful operations.

Participants have the right to access information about the financial performance of the Takaful fund, including its assets, liabilities, and investment activities. Regular reporting and audits ensure Takaful operators adhere to ethical standards and fulfil their participant obligations. Takaful operates through various models, including Mudarabah, Wakalah, and Wakalah-Yad Damanah. In the Mudarabah model, the Takaful operator acts as a Mudarib (investment manager), while participants provide the capital (contributions). According to pre-agreed ratios, profit generated from investments is shared between participants and the operator. In the Wakalah model, the operator charges a fee for managing the Takaful fund on behalf of participants, with any surplus being returned to participants. The Wakalah-Yad Damanah model combines elements of Mudarabah and Wakalah, where the operator acts as an investment manager and an underwriter, sharing profits and losses with participants.

Takaful Insurance operates on a set of fundamental principles that underpin its ethical and cooperative framework. Firstly, the Principle of Cooperation (Ta'awun) underscores the essence of mutual assistance and community support within the Takaful system. Participants unite to provide aid in times of need, fostering a sense of solidarity reflective of Islamic values. Secondly, the Principle of Shared Responsibility (Kafalah) emphasizes the collective burden-sharing of financial risks among participants. Rather than individuals bearing losses alone, Takaful distributes these burdens across the community, promoting a culture of shared accountability. Thirdly, the Principle of Ethical Conduct (Adl and Ihsan) mandates integrity, transparency, and fairness in all Takaful dealings. Operators must uphold ethical standards in line with Islamic teachings, promoting trust and integrity within the system. Sharia Compliance (Shariah) is a foundational principle ensuring that Takaful operations align with Islamic law. Sharia scholars oversee compliance and ethical adherence in contracts, investments, and transactions. Additionally, the Principle of Risk Sharing (Mudharabah) emphasizes collective risk pooling, where participants collectively unite resources to bear financial risks. Lastly, the Principle of Profit and Loss Sharing (Mudarabah) dictates that participants share the risks and rewards of the Takaful scheme, promoting equitable distribution of gains and losses within the community. These principles collectively define the ethical and cooperative framework of Takaful Insurance, distinguishing it from conventional insurance models and reinforcing its alignment with Islamic values and principles.

TAKADAO pioneers a groundbreaking paradigm in Takaful insurance, seamlessly merging blockchain technology with the principles of Shariah-compliant finance. At its core, TAKADAO embodies a synergy of decentralized autonomous organizations, cryptocurrencies, smart contracts, and tokenization, offering participants a robust and transparent platform. DAOs, or Decentralized Autonomous Organizations, serve as the backbone of TAKADAO. Unlike traditional corporate structures, DAOs are governed by immutable smart contracts, eliminating the need for intermediaries and ensuring a democratic decision-making process. Through DAO tokens, participants assert their membership and ownership rights within the organization, with each token representing a vote in governance matters. The fusion of blockchain technology with Takaful insurance principles is evident in TAKADAO's dual-entity structure. Firstly, a Takaful operator oversees the management of funds generated from management fees, adhering to regulatory frameworks and providing essential technical expertise. Secondly, the DAO entity manages funds sourced from participants' contributions, fostering a community-driven approach to risk-sharing. Transparency and accountability are paramount within TAKADAO. Participants actively engage in DAO governance through democratic voting mechanisms, ensuring their interests are represented by a board of directors elected from within the community. This distinct governance model distinguishes TAKADAO from conventional insurance structures, empowering participants and fostering trust. Central to TAKADAO's ethos is its innovative benefit multiplier system, tailored to each participant's unique circumstances. Through real-time tracking of contributions and fund performance, participants enjoy dynamic benefit amounts reflective of the DAO fund's performance. In times of surplus, benefits increase, while the fund's deficit is mitigated through interest-free loans from the Takaful operator, reinforcing the ethos of mutual support and cooperation. TAKADAO's commitment to Shariah compliance extends beyond technological innovation. Regulatory oversight ensures that both the Takaful operator and the DAO fund operate within the bounds of ethical finance, safeguarding participants from personal liability and upholding principles of financial integrity. TAKADAO redefines the landscape of Takaful insurance, marrying cutting-edge blockchain technology with the principles of Shariah-compliant finance. Through transparency, community governance, and dynamic risk-sharing mechanisms, TAKADAO embodies the future of ethical insurance solutions, paving the way for a more inclusive and sustainable financial ecosystem (TAKADAO, n.d.).

2.4.1.4 Community-based Insurance

Community-based insurance (CBI) is a form of insurance that operates within a specific community or social group, often in underserved or marginalized areas with limited access to traditional insurance products. Unlike conventional insurance models, which are profit-driven and centralized, CBI is designed to meet local communities' unique needs and circumstances. One of the defining features of Community-Based Insurance is its emphasis on community participation and ownership. In CBI schemes, community members actively participate in designing, implementing, and managing insurance programs, ensuring that solutions are tailored to local needs and preferences. This participatory approach increases community engagement and empowerment and fosters a sense of ownership and accountability among participants. CBI schemes often leverage social capital and traditional community networks to facilitate risk-sharing and mutual assistance. Community members pool their resources and share risks collectively, providing financial protection against common perils such as crop failure, livestock loss, or natural disasters. By harnessing the strength of collective action, CBI enhances the resilience of communities and reduces their vulnerability to shocks and crises. Community-based insurance promotes financial inclusion by extending insurance coverage to underserved populations who may otherwise be excluded from formal insurance markets. By offering affordable and accessible insurance products tailored to local needs, CBI helps bridge the insurance gap and promotes socioeconomic stability and development within communities. Another key aspect of CBI is its focus on sustainability and long-term resilience. Rather than relying solely on external aid or interventions, CBI schemes empower communities to build their capacity to manage risks and withstand adversity independently. This includes investing in risk-reduction measures, building local infrastructure, and fostering economic diversification to reduce dependence on vulnerable livelihoods. Community-based insurance represents a bottom-up approach to insurance that prioritizes community empowerment, participation, and resilience. By harnessing local knowledge, social capital, and solidarity, CBI schemes offer a promising avenue for expanding insurance coverage, promoting financial inclusion, and building stronger, more resilient communities.

Tontine Insurance, also known as "tontine," represents a traditional form of community-based insurance deeply rooted in West African culture. In this system, individuals contribute regular payments into a collective fund, understanding that the accumulated savings will be used to provide financial assistance to members during times of need, such as illness, death, or emergencies. Typically organized based on kinship or social ties, tontine groups foster solidarity and mutual aid among participants, who actively engage in decision-making and risk-sharing processes. While not conforming to traditional insurance models, tontines embody the principles of mutual support and community resilience inherent in Community-Based Insurance. The operational mechanics of tontines vary across regions and communities, each implementing its variations while adhering to the fundamental concept of collective savings and support. Members contribute fixed sums to a communal pot, with distribution cycles occurring on a weekly or monthly basis until every member has received their share. In Nigeria and Senegal, tontines are commonly used to finance businesses or large-scale projects, while in Ethiopia, the "Idir" functions as insurance against unforeseen emergencies. Although often favoured by female traders, tontines attract participants from diverse backgrounds, offering a practical alternative for those not engaging with formal financial systems. Recognizing the potential of tontines to address financial inclusion challenges, MaTontine, a pioneering start-up, has digitized this age-old practice using mobile technology in Senegal. With an estimated annual value of $200 million in Senegal alone, tontines represent a significant financial resource. Yet, their traditional format limits their capacity to deliver value-added services that could uplift participants from poverty. By automating tontine processes and introducing mobile-based banking solutions, MaTontine aims to leverage technology to unlock the full potential of tontines, offering a range of financial services, including micro-loans and micro-insurance products. Despite the innovative strides taken by MaTontine, the company acknowledges the enduring social cohesion fostered by traditional tontines, which has tempered its efforts to establish new groups. Instead, MaTontine focuses on digitizing existing tontines, employing a credit scoring methodology to assess members' creditworthiness and group dynamics. With a bold vision to provide financial services to a million women across Africa within five years, MaTontine seeks to harness the collective strength of tontines while advancing financial inclusion and empowerment on the continent (Akande & Turner, 2018).

2.4.1.5 Mutual Aid Societies

Mutual Aid Societies, also known as fraternal benefit societies or friendly societies, are voluntary organizations formed by individuals who share common interests or backgrounds, with the primary aim of providing mutual assistance and support to their members in times of need. These societies typically operate cooperatively, where members pool their resources to create a safety net offering financial, social, and emotional assistance during hardship or crisis. The origins of Mutual Aid Societies can be traced back to early human history, where communities banded together to support and protect their members. In the modern context, Mutual Aid Societies emerged as a response to the social and economic challenges faced by individuals and communities, particularly during industrialization and urbanization. These societies flourished in the nineteenth and early twentieth centuries, providing vital support to members through insurance coverage, healthcare services, funeral benefits, and social activities. One of the defining features of Mutual Aid Societies is their democratic and participatory governance structure. Members of these societies typically have equal voting rights and participate in decision-making processes related to managing funds, allocating resources, and eligibility criteria for receiving assistance. This democratic ethos fosters a sense of ownership and accountability among members, ensuring that the society operates in the best interests of its members. Mutual Aid Societies offer their members a wide range of benefits, including financial security, social belonging, and access to essential services. By pooling resources and spreading risks across a larger group, members can access insurance coverage and other benefits at lower costs than individual arrangements. Mutual Aid Societies often provide a sense of community and belonging, offering opportunities for social interaction, networking, and support among members. In recent years, Mutual Aid Societies have experienced a resurgence of interest, driven by a growing recognition of their potential to address contemporary social and economic challenges. These societies are seen as a grassroots response to gaps in traditional social welfare systems, offering an alternative model based on solidarity, cooperation, and mutual support. With the rise of digital technology and online platforms, Mutual Aid Societies have adapted to new organization and outreach forms, making them more accessible and inclusive to diverse communities. Mutual Aid Societies continue to play a vital role in supporting and assisting individuals and communities facing adversity. Through their cooperative ethos and commitment to mutual aid, these societies embody the principles of solidarity, resilience, and community empowerment, offering a beacon of hope and support in an uncertain world.

2.4.2 Advantages and Ethical Challenges of Mutual Insurance

Mutual insurance companies exemplify a customer-centric approach by prioritizing the interests of policyholders over shareholder profits. This commitment to policyholder satisfaction often translates into superior service, customized products, and competitive pricing. Unlike traditional insurers focused solely on maximizing shareholder returns, mutual insurers place a premium on meeting the needs and expectations of their policyholders, thereby fostering long-term relationships built on trust and mutual benefit. Policyholder ownership is a fundamental aspect of mutual insurance, distinguishing it from shareholder-driven models. In mutual insurance companies, policyholders are also owners, giving them a direct stake in the organization's success. This ownership structure promotes transparency, accountability, and member engagement, as policyholders have a voice in the company's governance and decision-making processes. By empowering policyholders to participate in key decisions, mutual insurers build a culture of trust and collaboration that strengthens the bond between the company and its members. Mutual insurance operates on shared risk and responsibility, where policyholders collectively pool their resources to cover potential losses. Risk pooling spreads the financial risks associated with insurance coverage across the entire membership base, reducing the burden on individual policyholders in the event of a claim. This collective approach to risk management promotes fairness and equity, ensuring that all members contribute and benefit proportionally based on their exposure to risk. Financial stability is a cornerstone of mutual insurance, prioritizing long-term sustainability over short-term profits. By adopting prudent underwriting practices, conservative investment strategies, and effective risk management, mutual insurers build robust financial reserves to withstand economic volatility and unforeseen events. Focusing on financial strength and stability instils confidence among policyholders, assuring them that their insurance needs will be met reliably and responsibly over the long term. Mutual insurance fosters a sense of community and solidarity among policyholders, reinforcing social bonds and promoting mutual support in times of need. As members of a mutual insurance company, policyholders come together to provide assistance and comfort to fellow members facing adversity, embodying the spirit of mutual aid and cooperation. This sense of community extends beyond insurance, strengthening social ties, and promoting social cohesion within communities served by mutual insurers.

Ethical challenges loom large for mutual insurance companies as they navigate the intricacies of their operations while upholding core values of integrity, transparency, and fairness. At the heart of these challenges lies the delicate balance between serving policyholders' best interests and ensuring the organization's financial stability. Conflicts of interest often emerge in this balancing act, requiring mutual insurers to ethically manage decisions that prioritize policyholder welfare without compromising the company's long-term viability. By adhering to ethical principles and aligning incentives with policyholder interests, mutual insurers can effectively navigate these conflicts while upholding their commitment to serving the needs of their members. Transparency and accountability serve as pillars of trust within mutual insurance companies. Upholding high standards of transparency entails providing clear and accurate information regarding products, pricing, and financial performance. Policyholders should have meaningful representation in the company's governance, ensuring that decision-making processes remain inclusive and reflect their interests. Through fostering transparency and accountability, mutual insurers can cultivate strong relationships with policyholders and reinforce their dedication to ethical business practices. Fairness and equity form essential ethical considerations for mutual insurers. Insurance products and services must be accessible and equitable, catering to the diverse needs of policyholders across socioeconomic backgrounds and risk profiles. Consequently, mutual insurers must meticulously evaluate pricing strategies, underwriting practices, and claims handling procedures to uphold fairness and avoid instances of discrimination. By prioritizing fairness and equity, mutual insurers uphold the principle of mutual aid and solidarity, fostering an environment of inclusivity and trust among policyholders. Social responsibility emerges as a critical ethical imperative for mutual insurers. These companies are responsible for contributing positively to their communities by promoting financial literacy, supporting philanthropic endeavours, and adhering to ethical guidelines and industry regulations. By embracing their role as responsible corporate citizens, mutual insurers can make meaningful contributions to society while enhancing their reputation as ethical and trustworthy institutions. Sustainability and innovation pose ethical challenges for mutual insurers. While ensuring financial stability and risk management remains paramount, mutual insurers must also embrace innovation to meet the evolving needs of policyholders. This entails responsible resource management, strategic investments in technology and talent, and a steadfast commitment to continuous improvement. By striking a delicate balance between stability and innovation, mutual insurers can uphold ethical standards while driving positive change and delivering lasting value to their policyholders and communities.

2.5 Conclusion

Decentralized insurance models represent a paradigm shift in the insurance industry, driven by innovative technologies and a customer-centric approach. Peer-to-peer, parametric, and mutual insurance models offer unique advantages and ethical challenges, catering to diverse customer needs and preferences. P2P insurance fosters community resilience and empowerment by enabling individuals to pool resources and share risks collectively. However, it also raises concerns about data privacy and fairness in risk pooling. Parametric insurance streamlines claims processing and offers rapid payouts, particularly suitable for weather-related events and travel insurance. Yet, accurate parameter definition and transparency in risk assessment are required to ensure reliability and trustworthiness. Mutual insurance models prioritize policyholder interests and community support, promoting solidarity and shared responsibility. Nevertheless, they must navigate conflicts of interest and ensure equitable treatment of members to maintain trust and transparency.

Decentralized insurance models offer unparalleled control, transparency, and efficiency benefits, revolutionizing traditional insurance practices. By leveraging innovative technologies and ethical business practices, these models empower consumers, promote financial inclusion, and foster resilience in insurance markets. However, addressing ethical dilemmas and regulatory concerns is essential to ensure decentralized insurance models' long-term sustainability and trustworthiness. Moving forward, continued innovation, collaboration, and regulatory oversight will be crucial in realizing the full potential of decentralized insurance models to meet the evolving needs of policyholders and stakeholders in the insurance industry.

References

Abdikerimova, A., & Feng, R. (2022). Peer-to-peer multi-risk insurance and mutual aid. *European Journal of Operational Research, 299*(2), 735–749.

Achmea. (2018). *Achmea supports Zurich Insurance Group accelerating its digital operations*. Accessed on 2 May 2024 from https://news.achmea.nl/achmea-supports-zurich-insurance-group-accelerating-its-digital-operations/

Akande, S., & Turner, L. (2018, September 11). *Bringing an ancient African savings system into the digital age*. Accessed on 2 May 2024 from https://edition.cnn.com/2018/09/11/africa/ancient-african-savings-tontine/index.html

Balasubramanian, R., Libarikian, A., & McElhaney, D. 2021. *Insurance 2030—The impact of AI on the future of insurance*. Accessed on 19 August 2023. https://www.mckinsey.com/industries/financial-services/our-insights/insurance-2030-the-impact-of-ai-on-the-future-of-insurance

Brettler, D., and Gosnear, T. 2020. *Parametric Insurance Fills Gaps Where Traditional Insurance Falls Short.* Accessed on 19 August 2023. https://www.insurancejournal.com/news/international/2020/01/09/553850.htm

Capgemini. (n.d.). *Towards smarter, efficient and trusted insurance marketplaces through computable contracts.* Accessed 19 August 2023. https://www.capgemini.com/insights/research-library/towards-smarter-efficient-and-trusted-insurance-marketplaces-through-computable-contracts/

Cohn, A., West, T., & Parker, C. (2017). Smart after all: Blockchain, smart contracts, parametric insurance, and smart energy grids. *Georgetown Law Technology Review, 1*(2), 273–304.

Cousaert, S., Vadgama, N., & Xu, J. (2022). Token-based insurance solutions on blockchain. In *Blockchains and the Token Economy: Theory and Practice* (pp. 237–260). Springer International Publishing.

DXC Technology. (2012). *MassMutual gains speed and agility by moving existing insurance applications from mainframe to the AWS cloud.* Accessed on 2 May 2024 from https://dxc.com/content/dam/dxc/projects/dxc-com/us/pdfs/insights/customer-stories/MassMutual%20Customer%20Story.pdf

Eling, M., & Lehmann, M. (2018). The impact of digitalization on the insurance value chain and the insurability of risks. *The Geneva Papers on Risk and Insurance—Issues and Practice,* (43), 359–396.

Ernest & Young. (2016). *Blockchain technology as a platform for digitization: Implications for the insurance industry.* Accessed 19 August 2023 from https://assets.ey.com/content/dam/ey-sites/ey-com/en_gl/topics/advisory/EY-blockchain-technology-as-a-platform-for-digitization.pdf?download

Ernst & Young. (2022). *2022 Global Insurance Outlook Achieving growth through people, purpose and technology.* Accessed on 19 August 2023. https://assets.ey.com/content/dam/ey-sites/ey-com/en_gl/topics/insurance/ey-2022-global-insurance-outlook-report.pdf

Feng, R. (2023). *Decentralized insurance technical foundation of business models.* Springer.

Guardianlife. (n.d.). *Leading through change How the technology industry and Guardian can win together.* Accessed on 2 May 2024 from https://www.guardianlife.com/tech-wins

ICMIF. (2021). *Case study: Achmea (Netherlands).* Accessed on 2 May 2024 from https://www.icmif.org/icmif-undrr/achmea-netherlands/

KPMG. (2017). *Will on-demand insurance become mainstream?* Accessed on 19 August 2023. https://assets.kpmg.com/content/dam/kpmg/uk/pdf/2017/09/will-on-demand-insurance-become-mainstream.pdf

Kulia, S. (2023). On-demand insurance: The rise of customizable, usage-based coverage. *The Times of India.* Accessed 19 August 2023. https://timesofindia.indiatimes.com/blogs/voices/on-demand-insurance-the-rise-of-customizable-usage-based-coverage/

Levantesi, S., & Piscopo, G. (2022). Mutual peer-to-peer insurance: The allocation of risk. *Journal of Co-Operative Organisation and Management, 10*(1), 100154.

NAIC. (2022). *Peer-To-Peer (P2P) Insurance*. Accessed on 19 August 2023 from https://content.naic.org/cipr-topics/peer-peer-p2p-insurance

Nasdaq. (2021). *How blockchain smart contracts are reinventing the insurance industry.* Accessed on 19 August 2023. https://www.nasdaq.com/articles/how-blockchain-smart-contracts-are-reinventing-the-insurance-industry-2021-01-29

Snape, G. (2023). *Is blockchain finally coming for the insurance industry?* Accessed on 19 August 2023 from https://www.insurancebusinessmag.com/us/news/technology/is-blockchain-finally-coming-for-the-insurance-industry-433879.aspx

Sullivan, K. J. (2023). *Insuring for climate change: The role of parametric insurance*. Accessed on 19 August 2023. https://www.lexisnexis.com/community/insights/legal/practical-guidance-journal/b/pa/posts/insuring-for-climate-change-the-role-of-parametric-insurance

Sun, R. T., Garimella, A., Han, W., Chang, H. L., & Shaw, M. J. (2020). Transformation of the transaction cost and the agency cost in an organization and the applicability of blockchain—A case study of peer-to-peer insurance. *Front Blockchain, 3*, 1–24. https://doi.org/10.3389/fbloc.2020.00024

Swiss Re. (2023). *Comprehensive guide to parametric insurance*. Accessed on 19 August 2023. https://corporatesolutions.swissre.com/dam/jcr:0cd24f12-ebfb-425a-ab42-0187c241bf4a/2023-01-corso-guide-of-parametric-insurance.pdf

TAKADAO. (n.d.). *TAKADAO Whitepaper*. Accessed on 2 May 2024 from https://www.takadao.io/Takadao_Whitepaper.pdf

The Co-operators Group Limited. (2022). *Integrated Annual Report 2022*. Accessed 19 August 2023 from https://www.cooperators.ca/en/about-us/corporate-overview/annual-reports

The Geneva Association. (2023). *Assessing the potential of decentralised finance and blockchain technology in insurance*. Accessed on 19 August 2023 from https://www.genevaassociation.org/sites/default/files/2023-08/DeFi%20insurance_WEB.pdf

The Penn Mutual Life Insurance Company. (2023). *2023 Annual Report*. Accessed on 2 May 2024 from https://www.pennmutual.com/static-assets/annual-report/annual-report.pdf

Decentralized Insurance Platforms: Innovation and Technology for Trust and Efficiency

3.1 Introduction

The rise of decentralized insurance platforms marks a fundamental shift from the traditional centralized insurance model towards a more transparent, efficient, and trustless system. At the core of these platforms lies a digital ecosystem where all aspects of insurance, from policy issuance to premium payments, claims processing, and risk management, occur seamlessly without the need for a central authority or traditional insurance company. Several pioneering decentralized insurance platforms, such as Etherisc, Guevara, Teambrella, and TongJuBao, have emerged in recent years, representing a transformative shift in the insurance industry landscape. These platforms operate as fully decentralized entities, leveraging cutting-edge technologies like blockchain, smart contracts, and peer-to-peer networking to revolutionize the insurance experience. Eliminating the need for a central authority empowers users to participate directly in insurance transactions and decision-making processes. Among these platforms, Etherisc shines as a beacon of innovation, leveraging blockchain technology and smart contracts to ensure transparent and efficient claims processing while fostering trust and reliability within the insurance ecosystem. Guevara offers collective car insurance through an online peer-to-peer platform, employing digital platforms and mobile apps to provide users with a seamless insurance experience. Teambrella adopts

N. Singhal et al., *Potential, Risks, and Ethical Implications of Decentralized Insurance*, Technology, Work and Globalization,
https://doi.org/10.1007/978-981-97-5894-4_3

a unique approach by offering a peer-to-peer smart contract based on cryptocurrencies like Bitcoin or Ethereum, promoting transparency and accountability within the community. TongJuBao leverages digital platforms and mobile apps to facilitate peer-to-peer Insurance, assisting users in managing risks and sharing financial burdens during challenging times. Lemonade harnesses advanced technologies such as big data analytics, AI, IoT, and robotic process automation to disrupt the insurance landscape further. Lemonade offers a diverse range of insurance products, catering to individuals' specific needs through mobile apps and digital platforms. Together, these decentralized insurance platforms and innovative Insurtech companies stand at the forefront of a new era in Insurance. Through the amalgamation of decentralization and technology, they are reshaping the very essence of Insurance, rendering it more accessible, transparent, and user-centric than ever before.

Continuing the narrative of innovation, traditional insurance entities are also actively embracing the tenets of decentralized Insurance through strategic alliances with pioneering technology firms, highlighting the pivotal role that technology and decentralization play in reshaping the insurance sector. For example, American International Group, Inc. has collaborated with IBM and Standard Chartered Bank to initiate a groundbreaking multinational insurance policy utilizing blockchain technology's "smart contract" feature. This landmark initiative eliminates the logistical complexities associated with multinational policies, providing a swift and cost-effective solution facilitated by smart contracts. Likewise, AXA has partnered with blockchain startup Fizzy to introduce innovative flight delay insurance products, harnessing the power of smart contracts on the Ethereum blockchain. This pioneering approach streamlines the compensation process for flight delays, instilling greater confidence and transparency in the insurer-customer relationship.

Several forward-thinking companies, including Ensuro, iChain, Ethos, and Asteya, leverage blockchain technology and smart contracts to offer disruptive insurance solutions. Ensuro, for instance, operates as a decentralized underwriting platform, utilizing blockchain and smart contracts to streamline underwriting processes while enhancing transparency and trust among policyholders. iChain leverages blockchain to provide the IChain Hoken Wallet, a comprehensive repository of insurance product information that ensures the integrity and immutability of insurance-related data, thus fostering greater trust within the insurance ecosystem. Ethos harnesses the power of big data analytics, predictive analytics, and mobile applications to offer innovative life insurance solutions tailored to individual needs. Ethos' utilization of predictive analytics and data science technologies enables the provision of life insurance policies covering a wide range of expenses, from home mortgages to college tuition, thereby enhancing accessibility and affordability for consumers. Digital platform-based enterprises like Penni and Kin have also made significant strides in revolutionizing insurance distribution and service delivery. Penni offers digital distribution solutions for insurance companies and brokers, facilitating the establishment of robust online sales channels. Kin's digital insurance service platform empowers consumers to seamlessly purchase home insurance over the phone, simplifying insurance procurement and enhancing overall customer satisfaction and experience. These decentralized insurance platforms streamline the insurance purchasing process and improve customer experience and satisfaction.

The emergence of decentralized insurance platforms has profound implications for the insurance industry, disrupting traditional business models and reshaping the competitive landscape. By eliminating intermediaries and reducing administrative overhead, these platforms can significantly lower costs for insurers and policyholders, making Insurance more accessible and affordable for a wider range of individuals and businesses. Decentralized insurance platforms promote innovation and competition by fostering an environment where new entrants can easily enter the market and experiment with novel insurance products and services. This increased competition drives greater efficiency and innovation across the insurance value chain, benefiting consumers through improved coverage options, pricing, and customer service. Automating insurance processes through smart contracts is at the core of decentralized insurance platforms. This automation reduces administrative overheads and minimizes delays and errors, leading to faster and more efficient insurance services. Transparency and trust are fundamental pillars of decentralized insurance platforms. By recording insurance policies, claims, and transactions on immutable and transparent blockchain ledgers, these platforms ensure that all interactions are verifiable and tamper-proof. Policyholders, insurers, and other stakeholders can access real-time information about insurance activities, fostering greater trust and confidence in the insurance process. One key advantage of decentralized platforms is the reduced fees and costs associated with insurance coverage. By eliminating intermediaries and streamlining processes, these platforms can offer insurance coverage at lower premiums and with reduced fees compared to traditional insurance providers. This cost-effectiveness makes Insurance more accessible to a broader range of individuals and businesses, promoting financial inclusion.

Decentralized governance mechanisms empower users to participate in decision-making processes that shape insurance coverage policies, premiums, and parameters. Through decentralized governance models, policyholders and other stakeholders can vote on proposals, influence platform policies, and contribute to the design of innovative insurance products. This democratic approach increases transparency, accountability, and responsiveness to user needs.

Global accessibility is another significant advantage of decentralized insurance platforms. Operating on networks that are accessible globally, these platforms enable anyone with internet access to purchase insurance coverage without the need for intermediaries or geographic restrictions. This democratization of access to insurance services ensures that individuals and businesses worldwide can protect themselves against risks effectively.

However, the widespread adoption of decentralized insurance platforms also presents challenges and regulatory considerations, particularly concerning data privacy, security, and compliance with existing insurance regulations. As these platforms mature and scale, policymakers, and regulators must adapt to the evolving regulatory landscape to ensure consumer protection and market stability.

3.2 Decentralized Insurance Platforms: Mapping the Categories

3.2.1 Decentralized Insurance platform for On-Chain Risks

A decentralized insurance platform for on-chain risks provides insurance coverage specifically tailored to risks associated with activities conducted directly on the blockchain or DeFi ecosystem. On-chain risks refer to potential hazards or vulnerabilities within the blockchain network, transactions, smart contracts, or other on-chain activities. These risks could include smart contract bugs, protocol vulnerabilities, hacking incidents, or even losses due to unexpected changes in blockchain consensus mechanisms. Such a platform typically uses smart contracts and decentralized governance mechanisms to pool funds from participants and automatically execute insurance payouts when predefined conditions, such as a verified on-chain incident, are met. The decentralized nature of these platforms ensures transparency, immutability, and trustlessness in the insurance process, allowing users to mitigate on-chain risks confidently. Examples of decentralized insurance platforms for on-chain risks are Nexus Mutual, Tidal Finance, Unslashed, and InsurAce.

Nexus Mutual is a provider of on-chain protection in the cryptocurrency insurance sector. The company offers comprehensive cover products designed to protect against various risks associated with digital assets and protocols. Nexus Mutual primarily serves the cryptocurrency industry by enabling members to share risks and providing a platform for covering products, handling claims, and assessing risks. Founded in 2017 in London, United Kingdom, Nexus Mutual is a peer-to-peer insurance platform that raised 2.7 million USD in funding. Tidal Finance is a decentralized discretionary mutual cover protocol that offers the DeFi community the ability to hedge against the failure of any DeFi protocol or asset. Founded in 2016 in Texas, United States, Tidal Finance operates on the Polygon blockchain and has raised a total of 1.95 million USD in funding. Similarly, Unslashed is a decentralized insurance protocol designed to cover major DeFi protocols, utilizing blockchain technology, smart contracts, artificial intelligence, machine learning, and predictive analytics. Unslashed was founded in 2020 in London, United Kingdom, and has raised 2 million USD in funding. InsurAce, another prominent player in the decentralized insurance space, offers reliable, robust, and secure insurance services to DeFi users. Founded in 2020 in Hamilton, Bermuda, InsurAce operates across multiple blockchains, including Polygon, BSC, Ethereum, and Avalanche. The company provides comprehensive coverage for various risks within the decentralized finance (DeFi) space, allowing users to secure their investment funds against potential threats and vulnerabilities. InsurAce has raised a total of 1 million USD in funding.

InsureDAO, established in 2021 in Singapore, is a decentralized insurance protocol that manages risks associated with smart contract vulnerabilities in the DeFi industry. InsureDAO offers a range of insurance products with dynamic pricing tailored to users' needs. The platform primarily serves the DeFi community, offering protection against various risks to ensure the security and stability of decentralized financial protocols. InsureDAO has raised a total of 1 million USD in funding. Uno Re, founded in 2020 in Tallinn, Estonia, focuses on providing comprehensive Insurance and security services within the cryptocurrency and blockchain industry. The company offers a range of products, including exploit protection coverage, stablecoin de-peg insurance, bridge protection, and market maker coverage, all designed to safeguard digital assets and protocols against various risks. Uno Re has raised a total of 2.1 million USD in funding.

As a part of the decentralized insurance platform, all the insurance platforms provided in Table 1 cover risks unique to the decentralized financial landscape, such as smart contract vulnerabilities, protocol hacks, or asset loss due to platform failures and unstable stablecoins. The necessity for insurance coverage in the realm of on-chain risk is underscored by the intricate and rapidly evolving nature of decentralized financial systems. We need Insurance for on-chain risk, even though several insurance policies, such as IT or cyber insurance, cover digital risks related to information technologies. The reason is that traditional insurance policies, such as cyber insurance policies that cover digital risks related to information technologies, currently do not or cannot consider the newly identified risk vectors (Neale, Drake & Konstantopoulos, 2020). Cyber insurance policies rely on centralized actuarial/statistical assessment by the insurer i.e., considering extreme value theory models such as in Eling and Wirfs (2021). In contrast, the decentralized insurance platform has Decentralized premium determination (judgement-rated, prediction markets). Moreover, cyber insurance policies have established insurance distribution channels and centralized marketplaces, whereas decentralized insurance platforms facilitate decentralized marketplaces through different insurance protocols. Insurance policies offered by a decentralized insurance platform that covers on-chain risk also differ from those of insurable objects because cyber insurance covers hard- and software-related risks and associated processual or human components (Biener, Eling & Wirfs, 2014).On-chain risk insurance covers the risk of Assets stored in (self)custodial wallets and assets operationalized through or locked in smart contracts (Table 3.1).

3.2.2 Decentralized Insurance Platform for Off-Chain Risks

Decentralized insurance platforms represent a groundbreaking approach to mitigating off-chain risks. These platforms cater to events, incidents, or risks beyond blockchain networks or cryptocurrency ecosystems, offering coverage for various real-world occurrences. Off-chain risks encompass a

Table 3.1 Decentralized insurance platforms covering on-chain risk

Platform	*Blockchain*	*Technology*	*Description*	*Founding year*	*Location*	*Company stage*	*Model*	*Product/services*	*Total fund raised*	*TVL*	*Token*	*Website*
Nexus Mutual	Ethereum	Blockchain Technology Smart Contracts	Nexus Mutual offers comprehensive on-chain protection for cryptocurrencies, enabling members to share risks and access cover products tailored to the digital asset landscape	2017	London United Kingdom	Unattributed VC	Peer-to-Peer Insurance	Digital Asset Protection Protocol Cover	2.7	264.13	NXM	nexusmutual.io
Tidal Finance	Polygon	Blockchain Technology Smart Contracts	Tidal Finance provides a decentralized mutual cover protocol empowering the DeFi community to hedge against any DeFi protocol or asset failure	2016	Texas, United States	Seed VC	Parametric Insurance	Decentralized Mutual Cover Customized Risk Contracts Smart Contract Protection	1.95	0.22	TIDAL	tidal.finance/
Unslashed	Ethereum	Blockchain Technology Smart Contracts Artificial Intelligence and Machine Learning Predictive Analytics	Unslashed is a decentralized insurance protocol safeguarding major DeFi protocols. It shields users from risks like smart contract failures, wallet exploits, and exchange hacks in the DeFi realm	2020	London, United Kingdom	Seed VC	Parametric Insurance	Defi Protocol Insurance Comprehensive coverage against smart contract failures, wallet exploits, and exchange hacks	2	60.07	USF	unslashed.finance

(continued)

Table 3.1 (continued)

Platform	*Blockchain*	*Technology*	*Description*	*Founding year*	*Location*	*Company stage*	*Model*	*Product/services*	*Total fund raised*	*TVL*	*Token*	*Website*
InsurAce	Polygon BSC Ethereum Avalanche	Blockchain Technology Smart Contracts	InsurAce offers comprehensive DeFi insurance, pioneering cross-chain portfolio-based covers for low-premium protection. With robust security and sustainable returns, it rewards users through its mining program	2020	Hamilton, Bermuda	Incubator/ Accelerator	Peer-to-Peer Insurance	Protocols Cover CEX and IDO platform cover Investment Portal	1	1.48	INSUR	insurace.io
InsureDAO	Ethereum Arbitrum Astar Optimism	Blockchain Technology Smart Contracts	InsureDAO offers dynamic-priced Insurance tailored for DeFi, addressing smart contract risks. It serves the DeFi community, ensuring protocol security and stability	2021	Singapore	Other Investors	Peer-to-Peer Insurance	Smart Contract vulnerability risks	1	0.123	SURE	insuredao.fi
Ease.org	Ethereum	Blockchain Technology Smart Contracts Artificial Intelligence and Machine Learning Predictive Analytics	Ease offers a decentralized coverage protocol, allowing users to safeguard their DeFi tokens without paying premiums, all while accruing compounding yield	2016			Peer-to-Peer Insurance Parametric Insurance	Defi Asset Protection	8.29		EASE	https://ease.org/

Platform	*Blockchain*	*Technology*	*Description*	*Founding year*	*Location*	*Company stage*	*Model*	*Product/services*	*Total fund raised*	*TVL*	*Token*	*Website*
Neptune Mutual	Arbitrum Ethereum BSC	Blockchain Technology Smart Contracts Artificial Intelligence and Machine Learning Predictive Analytics	Neptune Mutual uses a parametric insurance model, offering payouts based on preset parameters instead of individual assessments. This approach ensures quick and reliable payouts for all policyholders affected by an incident, simplifying the claiming process	2021	Tortola, Virgin Islands	Series A | Alive	Parametric Insurance	Defi Asset Protection	10.05	0.639	NPM	neptunemutual.com
Cozy V2	Ethereum Optimism	Blockchain Technology Smart Contracts Mobile Apps and Digital Platforms	Cozy V2 provides decentralized Insurance for DeFi, guarding against risks like smart contract hacks and depegs. It utilizes blockchain and smart contracts, allowing users to hedge risks while earning yields. Users can buy protection or earn yields by backing markets enhancing DeFi security	2017	Paris, France	Series A	Peer-to-Peer Insurance	Defi Protection Smart Contract Coverage Customizable Coverage	4.51	0.962	COZY	https://www.cozy.finance/

(continued)

Table 3.1 (continued)

Platform	*Blockchain Technology*		*Description*	*Founding year*	*Location*	*Company stage*	*Model*	*Product/services*	*Total TVL fund raised*	*Token*	*Website*
Takadao	Ethereum	Block Chain Technology	Takadao is an insurance firm using the takaful model, where participants pool funds to protect each other mutually. It invests these funds, paying claims and redistributing surpluses among members. Takadao also develops Web3 infrastructure, enabling community-owned Insurance with reliable, inclusive, and affordable innovations	2022	Riyadh, Saudi Arabia	Seed	Mutual Insurance	Community-owned Insurance Takaful Model Implementation Innovative Web3 Infrastructure	1.75	TAKA	takadao.io

Platform	*Blockchain*	*Technology*	*Description*	*Founding year*	*Location*	*Company stage*	*Model*	*Product/services*	*Total fund raised*	*TVL*	*Token*	*Website*
Uno Re	Ethereum BSC Kava	Block Chain Technology	Uno Re provides comprehensive insurance and security services for the cryptocurrency and blockchain industry, offering exploit protection, stablecoin de-peg insurance, bridge protection, and market maker coverage. Serving both institutional and retail clients, Uno Re aims to safeguard digital assets and protocols from various risks	2020	Tallinn, Estonia	Acquired/ Merged	Peer-to-Peer Insurance	Exploit protection coverage Stablecoin de-peg insurance Bridge protection Market Maker coverage	2.1	0.154	UNO	unore.io

Note Total Raised (In Million USD) TVL (In Million USD)
Source https://defillama.com/protocols/Insurance as of 15 April 2024
https://www.cbinsights.com/company/friendsurance/alternatives-competitors as of 15 April 2024

broad spectrum, including natural disasters like earthquakes, floods, hurricanes and travel-related incidents, health-related issues, property damage, and liability claims.

Several decentralized insurance platforms have emerged to address off-chain risk, each employing unique technologies and approaches to decentralization such as Teambrella, TongJuBao, Guevara, and Lemonade. For instance, Teambrella utilizes blockchain technology to provide a peer-to-peer smart contract system based on cryptocurrencies like Bitcoin or Ethereum. This platform enables users to collectively insure against various risks, promoting transparency and autonomy in the insurance process. Lemonade offers coverage for renters, homeowners, cars, pets, and life insurance, targeting individuals seeking comprehensive insurance solutions, emphasizing user-friendly digital platforms and innovative technologies. Decentralized insurance platforms transcend traditional insurance models by offering greater transparency, lower costs, and expanded coverage options. By decentralizing the insurance process, these platforms eliminate the need for central intermediaries, fostering trust and collaboration within the insurance ecosystem. With their emphasis on innovation and inclusivity, decentralized insurance platforms have the potential to reshape the future of Insurance, offering individuals and businesses worldwide greater control over their insurance needs (Table 3.2).

3.2.3 Technological-enabled Insurance Platforms for Decentralizing Traditional Insurance Models

Technology-enabled insurance platforms refer to insurance companies or entities that leverage advanced technological solutions and principles of decentralization to enhance their operations while retaining the core principles of traditional insurance models. These platforms incorporate various technologies to streamline processes, improve customer experience, and remain competitive in the evolving insurance landscape. These platforms can be categorized into Blockchain-Based Insurtechs, Digital Insurance Platforms, Data-Driven Insurance Solutions, and Insurance Technology Providers.

Blockchain-Based Insurtechs leverages blockchain technology for insurance solutions. These companies include Nsure, Ensuro, CyStellar, and YAS MicroInsurance. Nsure is an online insurance agency that utilizes blockchain technology to recommend the coverage consumers need. It employs proprietary algorithms and data analytics to analyse risks

Table 3.2 Decentralized insurance platforms covering off-chain risk

Platform	*Technology*	*Description*	*Founding year*	*Location*	*Company stage*	*Model*	*Product/ services*	*Total raised*	*Website*
Teambrella	Blockchain Technology	Teambrella offers a peer-to-peer insurance platform utilizing smart contracts powered by cryptocurrencies like bitcoin or Ethereum	2015	St. Peters-burg Russian Federa-tion	Seed | Alive	Peer-to-Peer Insurance	Collision deductible Insurance pet insurance	0.84	teambr ella. com
TongJuBao	Digital Platforms and Mobile Apps	TongJuBao is a P2P insurance platform designed to assist users in managing various social risks. Through its digital platforms and mobile apps, TongJuBao enables individuals to participate in peer-to-peer Insurance, focusing on mitigating social risks effectively	2015	Shanghai China	Convertible Note | Alive	Peer-to-Peer Insurance	Social risks	0.03	tongju bao. com
Guevara	Digital Platforms and Mobile Apps	Guevara offers an online peer-to-peer platform where individuals can join groups to insure their cars collectively. Through this platform, users can share insurance costs and benefits with others, fostering a community-based approach to car insurance	2013	England United Kingdoms	Dead	Peer-to-Peer Insurance	Motor insurance	2.3	heygue vara. com

(continued)

Table 3.2 (continued)

Platform	*Technology*	*Description*	*Founding year*	*Location*	*Company stage*	*Model*	*Product/ services*	*Total raised*	*Website*
Etherisc	Blockchain Technology Smart Contracts	Etherisc offers various parametric insurance options covering various risks, including crop protection, train delay protection, health insurance, and more. It uses blockchain technology for transparent and efficient claims processing	2016	Munich Germany	Incubator/ Accelerator - II | Alive	Parametric Insurance	Crop protection Train delay protection Carbon credit protection Flight delay Health insurance Rain/Travel Weather protection Hurricane insurance Natural disaster insurance Life insurance	220	eth erisc. com
Lemonade	Big Data Analytics Artificial Intelligence Internet of Things Robotic Process Automation Mobile Apps and Digital Platforms	Lemonade provides comprehensive insurance solutions for renters, homeowners, cars, pets, and life insurance. Leveraging big data analytics, AI, IoT, RPA, and mobile apps, Lemonade offers innovative and user-friendly insurance products tailored to individuals seeking comprehensive coverage	2015	New York United States	IPO	Peer-to-Peer Insurance	Renters Insurance Homeowners Insurance Cars Insurance Pets Insurance Life insurance	467	lem onade. com

Note Total Raised (In Million USD)
Source https://defillama.com/protocols/Insurance as of 15 April 2024
https://www.cbinsights.com/company/friendsurance/alternatives-competitors as of 15 April 2024

and provide personalized insurance recommendations. Formerly known as Finturo, Nsure focuses on home, automobile, and other sectors to enhance transparency and efficiency in insurance transactions. Ensuro operates as a decentralized underwriting platform, offering underwriting services through smart contracts and cryptocurrency funds. It enables retail and professional investors to participate in underwriting activities using stablecoins. Ensuro aims to facilitate transparent and efficient underwriting processes by leveraging blockchain technology while minimizing counterparty risks. CyStellar primarily serves industries such as Insurance, agriculture, and logistics with its blockchain-based solutions. It provides risk management solutions by leveraging blockchain technology to enhance transparency and traceability in Insurance, agriculture, and supply chain operations. CyStellar aims to optimize risk assessment and management processes while improving stakeholder trust and collaboration. YAS MicroInsurance is a blockchain-based insurtech company operating in the insurance industry. It offers on-demand microinsurance products covering various activities and situations such as travel, outdoor sports, and pet care. By leveraging blockchain technology, YAS MicroInsurance aims to offer simple, affordable, and efficient insurance solutions that are accessible through its mobile application.

Digital Insurance Platforms provide digital distribution solutions and online insurance services. Examples of these companies are Friendsurance, Penni, Kin, and Openly. Friendsurance is a prominent player in the digital insurance platform space. It focuses on digitizing insurance services and operates within the insurance and banking sectors. Friendsurance offers user-friendly insurance solutions, utilizing digital platforms and mobile apps to provide insurance products and services to banks and insurance companies. It is known for its peer-to-peer insurance model, which encourages groups of friends to pool their premiums together to lower costs and receive cashback rewards for claims-free periods. Penni specializes in providing digital distribution solutions for insurance companies and brokers. It offers a white-label distribution solution that enables insurers, brokers, and distribution partners to establish online sales channels for insurance products. Penni's platform facilitates the digitization of insurance sales processes, allowing for efficient online transactions and customer interactions. Founded in 2017 and based in Copenhagen, Denmark, Penni focuses on enhancing the digital presence of insurance providers and improving the accessibility of insurance products to consumers.

Kin is another notable player in the digital insurance platform sector. It provides a digital insurance service platform offering various insurance plans, primarily homeowners insurance. Kin enables users to purchase insurance plans over the phone without needing physical visits, streamlining the insurance purchasing process and making it more convenient for consumers. Formerly known as Bright Policy, Kin emphasizes simplicity and accessibility in its digital insurance offerings. Openly operates as a homeowner insurance platform, offering home insurance coverage to consumers through independent agents. It provides a digital platform allowing consumers to easily access and purchase insurance products, leveraging digital distribution solutions to streamline the buying process. Openly aims to provide transparent and flexible home insurance options, catering to the needs of modern homeowners.

Data-driven insurance solutions utilize big data analytics, predictive analytics, and AI for insurance products and services. These companies are Skyline Partners, Ethos, and Slice Labs. Skyline Partners is a leading player in the realm of data-driven insurance solutions. The company specializes in utilizing big data analytics to develop custom insurance products tailored to the specific needs of its clients. By analysing vast amounts of data, including demographic information, market trends, and historical claims data, Skyline Partners aims to identify emerging risks and opportunities in the insurance market. The company leverages predictive analytics and AI algorithms to forecast trends and anticipate potential risks, allowing insurers to mitigate risks and optimize their insurance portfolios proactively. Skyline Partners' data-driven approach empowers insurers to make informed decisions, enhance underwriting accuracy, and improve overall business performance. Ethos is another prominent player in the data-driven insurance solutions space. The company provides life insurance solutions powered by predictive analytics and data science technologies. Ethos utilizes advanced algorithms to analyse vast amounts of data, including medical history, lifestyle factors, and financial information, to assess the risk profile of potential policyholders and determine appropriate coverage levels. By leveraging predictive analytics, Ethos can accurately predict life expectancy and mortality rates, enabling it to offer competitive premiums and tailored insurance policies to its customers. Ethos' data-driven approach enables it to streamline the underwriting process, reduce administrative overhead, and expedite policy issuance, enhancing customer experience and driving business growth. Slice Labs is a leading innovator in data-driven insurance solutions, focusing on providing digital insurance products designed to protect small businesses. The company leverages big data analytics, predictive analytics, and AI to develop customized insurance solutions that address small businesses' unique needs and challenges. By analysing data from various sources, including business operations, industry trends, and customer behaviour, Slice Labs can accurately assess risk factors and tailor insurance coverage to specific business needs. Additionally, the company's data-driven approach enables it to automate claims processing, detect fraudulent activities, and optimize pricing strategies, thereby improving operational efficiency and reducing costs for insurers and policyholders. Slice Labs' commitment to data-driven innovation has positioned it as a leader in the insurtech industry, driving the adoption of digital insurance solutions and revolutionizing how insurance is bought and sold.

Insurance technology providers play a vital role in the insurance industry by offering innovative technology solutions to streamline various aspects of insurance operations. These companies specialize in developing software platforms, applications, and tools that enhance policy administration, claims management, and data analysis processes. By leveraging cutting-edge technology, Insurance technology providers enable insurers to improve operational efficiency, reduce costs, enhance customer experiences, and gain actionable insights into their business operations. The examples of these companies are ChainThat and Qover. ChainThat is a leading provider of technology solutions tailored for the insurance industry. The company offers a comprehensive suite of software products and services aimed at addressing key challenges faced by insurers in policy administration, claims management, and data analysis. ChainThat's technology solutions enable insurers to streamline policy administration processes, including policy issuance, underwriting, billing, and document management. The company's platform facilitates efficient claims management by automating claims processing, facilitating stakeholder communication, and detecting fraudulent activities. ChainThat provides advanced data analysis tools that enable insurers to gain actionable insights from their data, identify trends, and make data-driven decisions to optimize business performance. With its innovative technology solutions, ChainThat empowers insurers to enhance operational efficiency, improve customer satisfaction, and drive business growth. Qover is another notable insurance technology provider specializing in offering technology solutions for policy administration, claims management, and data analysis in the insurance industry. The company provides a range of software products and services designed to streamline insurance operations and improve the overall efficiency of insurers. Qover's platform offers advanced features for policy administration, including policy issuance, policy management, and document generation, enabling insurers to automate repetitive tasks and reduce manual errors. Qover's claims management solutions facilitate the efficient processing of insurance claims by automating claims intake, adjudication, and settlement processes. The company offers powerful data analysis tools that enable insurers to extract valuable insights from their data, monitor key performance indicators, and make data-driven decisions to optimize business outcomes. With its innovative technology solutions, Qover empowers insurers to stay competitive in a rapidly evolving market by enhancing operational efficiency, reducing costs, and improving customer satisfaction (Table 3.3).

3.3 Technologies Used by Decentralized Insurance Platforms

Insurance platforms are at the forefront of technological innovation, leveraging a comprehensive suite of advanced technologies to revolutionize insurance operations and enhance customer experiences. Each of these technologies plays a unique role in reshaping the insurance industry landscape and driving digital transformation. Blockchain and distributed ledger technology are revolutionizing insurance operations by automating contract execution and verification. Digital platforms and mobile apps allow insurers to deliver seamless user experiences and engage customers more effectively. These platforms provide policyholders convenient access to insurance services, allowing them to purchase policies, submit claims, and manage their accounts from any device. By embracing digital platforms and mobile apps, insurers can enhance customer satisfaction, improve retention rates, and differentiate themselves in a competitive market.

IoT devices play a crucial role in insurance risk assessment by enabling real-time data collection and analysis. These devices gather information from various sources, such as connected vehicles, wearable devices, and smart home systems, to assess risks accurately and adjust insurance premiums accordingly. By leveraging IoT devices, insurers can offer personalized insurance products, mitigate risks more effectively,

Table 3.3 Technological-enabled insurance platforms for decentralizing traditional insurance models

Platform	*Technology*	*Description*	*Founding year*	*Location*	*Company stage*	*Product/services*	*Total raised*	*Website*
Nsure	Blockchain Technology Big Data Analytics Predictive Analytics	Nsure, formerly Finturo, is a digital insurance agency utilizing a proprietary algorithm and data analytics to advise consumers on optimal coverage for various sectors like home and automobile insurance	2018	Florida, United States	Private Equity - II | Alive	Home Insurance Automobiles	20.12	nsure.com
Ensuro	Blockchain Technology Smart Contracts	Ensuro functions as a decentralized underwriting platform, providing underwriting services through contracts backed by a cryptocurrency fund composed of stablecoin deposits from retail and professional investors	2021	Singapore	Seed VC - III | Alive	Decentralized Capital Provider for Insurance Risk	5	ensuro.co
iChain	Blockchain Technology	Chain is an insurance technology company. The company offers IChain Hoken Wallet that provides information such as the product name, insurance money, insurance period, the insurance policy image, and more	2016	Tokyo, Japan	Incubator/ Accelerator | Alive	Insurance Policy Management	1.87	ichain.co.jp

(continued)

Table 3.3 (continued)

Platform	*Technology*	*Description*	*Founding year*	*Location*	*Company stage*	*Product/services*	*Total raised*	*Website*
CyStellar	Blockchain Technology	CyStellar primarily serves sectors such as the insurance industry with risk management solutions, the agriculture industry with precision agriculture solutions, and the logistics industry with supply chain optimization	2017	London, United Kingdom	Incubator/ Accelerator - II | Alive	Risk Management Solutions	0.04	cystel lar.com
Skyline Partners	Big data	Skyline specializes in creating custom, data-driven insurance solutions for stakeholders, including re/insurers, brokers, underwriting agents, distribution agents, affinity partners, and government agencies. With cutting-edge technology and robust relationships, we transform data streams into transparent, responsive protection, minimizing costs, reducing basis risk, and eliminating surprises	2017	London, United Kingdom	Seed VC | Alive	Event-Driven Insurance Data Sourcing Policy Design and Structuring Calculation Services Underwriting Management Claims Notification and Management	1.75	skyline. par tners

Platform	*Technology*	*Description*	*Founding year*	*Location*	*Company stage*	*Product/services*	*Total raised*	*Website*
ChainThat	Blockchain DLT Smart Contracts	ChainThat is a technology solutions provider focused on the insurance industry. The company offers products that assist with policy administration, management of multinational programs, and claims management, all aimed at enhancing the efficiency and potential of insurance businesses. ChainThat primarily serves brokers, carriers, and MGAs in the insurance sector. It is based in London, England		London, United Kingdom	Series A | Alive	Policy Administration Management of Multinational Programs Claims Management	2.61	chainthat.com
Friendsurance	Digital platforms and Mobile apps	Friendsurance is a company that focuses on the digitization of insurance services, operating within the insurance and banking sectors. The company provides user-friendly insurance solutions, offering banks and insurance companies digital insurance products and services. Primarily, Friendsurance sells to the banking and insurance industries. It worked on a peer-to-peer insurance model	2010	Berlin, Germany	Loan | Alive	Third-Party Liability Household Insurance	16.98	friendsurance.com

(continued)

Table 3.3 (continued)

Platform	*Technology*	*Description*	*Founding year*	*Location*	*Company stage*	*Product/services*	*Total raised*	*Website*
Penni	Digital platforms and Mobile apps	Penni provides digital distribution solutions for insurance companies and insurance brokers. It provides a white-label distribution solution that helps insurers, brokers, and distribution partners establish online insurance sales channels. The company was founded in 2017 and is based in Copenhagen, Denmark	2017	Copenhagen, Denmark	Incubator/Accelerator - II | Alive	Digital Distribution Solutions for Insurance Companies and Insurance Brokers	8.91	
Omocom	Blockchain Technology Smart Contracts	Omocom specializes in digital and embedded insurance solutions within the insurance industry. The company develops and distributes insurance products through platform partners, managing everything from claims adjustment to local compensation across Europe. Omocom's unique API is tailored for various rental models, including purchases, subscriptions, leasing, and short-term and long-term rentals, facilitating seamless transactions and user experiences	2017	Stockholm, Sweden	Series A | Alive	Digital And Embedded Insurance Solutions Insurance Products Distribution Through Platform Partners Claims Adjustment and Compensation Management	9.25	omocom.insurance

Platform	*Technology*	*Description*	*Founding year*	*Location*	*Company stage*	*Product/services*	*Total raised*	*Website*
Crowdheroes	Digital platforms and Mobile apps	Crowdheroes provides cloud-based broker management software for the insurance and real estate sectors. The company offers tools for customer relationship management, document storage, contract management, and insurance comparisons through an integrated platform. These services are designed to streamline the workflow of insurance and real estate professionals by offering a user-friendly interface and customizable features. It is based in Berlin, Germany	2017	Berlin, Germany	Incubator/ Accelerator | Alive	Customer Relationship Management Document Storage Contract Management	0.01	crowdheroes.de
Ethos	Big Data Analytics Mobile Apps and Digital Platforms Predictive Analytics	Ethos provides life insurance solutions. It offers predictive analytics and data science technologies for life insurance policies. It covers home mortgages, debt, college tuition, and more expenses	2016	Texas, United States	Series D - III | Alive	Life Insurance Solutions Home Mortgage Solutions Debt Solutions College Tuition Solutions	413.96	ethoslife.com

(continued)

Table 3.3 (continued)

<table>
<tr><th>Platform</th><th>Technology</th><th>Description</th><th>Founding year</th><th>Location</th><th>Company stage</th><th>Product/services</th><th>Total raised</th><th>Website</th></tr>
<tr><td>Ladder</td><td>Digital Platform</td><td>Ladder is a company that specializes in providing term life insurance through a digital platform within the insurtech industry. The company offers affordable term life insurance policies with the flexibility to adjust coverage as the policyholder's life circumstances change. Ladder's services are designed to be accessible online, with a paperless application process and tools like an insurance calculator to help customers determine their coverage needs</td><td>2015</td><td>California, United States</td><td>Series D | Alive</td><td>Life Insurance</td><td>203.55</td><td>ladder life. com</td></tr>
<tr><td>Slice Labs</td><td>Big Data Analytics
Internet of Things
Robotic Process Automation
Mobile Apps and Digital Platforms
Cloud Computing</td><td>Slice Labs operates as a technology company in insurance. The company offers digital insurance products that protect small businesses, all accessible via its cloud-based platform. Its products primarily cater to the small business sector</td><td>2015</td><td>New York, United States</td><td>Series A - II | Alive</td><td>Insurance Products Designed to Protect Small Businesses
On-Demand Insurance</td><td>35.5</td><td>slice.is</td></tr>
</table>

Platform	*Technology*	*Description*	*Founding year*	*Location*	*Company stage*	*Product/services*	*Total raised*	*Website*
Asteya	Blockchain AI algorithms Mobile Apps and Digital Platforms Cloud Computing	Asteya offers diverse income insurance solutions, including accidental death, permanent disability, and term life insurance products	2020	Florida, United States	Incubator/ Accelerator | Alive	Accidental Death Insurance Permanent Disability Income Insurance Term Life Insurance	18.53	asteya.world
Openly	Digital platforms and proprietary software	Openly operates as a platform for homeowner insurance, providing coverage directly to consumers via independent agents	2017	Massachusetts, United States	Series D | Alive	Homeowner Insurance	237.77	openly.com
Kin	Digital Platform	Kin provides a digital insurance service platform. It offers various insurance plans to buy homeowners insurance over the phone without any physical visits. Kin was formerly known as Bright Policy	2016	Illinois, United States	Series D - IV | Alive	Homeowner Insurance	453.09	kin.com

(continued)

Table 3.3 (continued)

Platform	*Technology*	*Description*	*Founding year*	*Location*	*Company stage*	*Product/services*	*Total raised*	*Website*
Qover	Digital Platform API	Qover is an insurance technology company. It provides claims management, insurance solutions, data analysis and reports, and more. The company offers accident, health, mobility, purchase, travel, and property insurance	2016	Brussels, Belgium	Series C | Alive	Claims Management Insurance Solutions Data Analysis and Reports	69.93	qover.com
YAS MicroInsurance	BlockChain	YAS MicroInsurance is a blockchain-based insurtech company operating in the insurance industry. The company offers on-demand microinsurance products covering various activities and situations, such as travel, outdoor sports, and pet care. These insurance products are designed to be simple, affordable, and efficient and can be accessed and managed through the YAS app	2019	Wanchai, Hong Kong	Seed VC - II | Alive	On-Demand Microinsurance Products For Travel Outdoor Sports Pet Care	4.5	yas.io

Note Total Raised (In Million USD)
Source https://defillama.com/protocols/Insurance as of 15 April 2024
https://www.cbinsights.com/company/friendsurance/alternatives-competitors as of 15 April 2024

and improve underwriting accuracy. Robotic process automation streamlines backend operations by automating repetitive tasks and workflows. With minimal human intervention, RPA solutions can handle various administrative tasks, such as data entry, document processing, and claims processing. By deploying RPA, insurers can improve operational efficiency, reduce costs, and free up human resources to focus on more value-added activities. Cloud computing infrastructure provides insurers with scalable and reliable computing resources on-demand. Cloud-based solutions offer flexibility, agility, and cost-effectiveness, allowing insurers to adapt quickly to changing business needs and scale their operations as required. By leveraging cloud computing, insurers can enhance agility, improve collaboration, and accelerate innovation in a rapidly evolving market. Augmented reality and virtual reality technologies transform insurance customer engagement and risk assessment processes. These immersive technologies enable insurers to create interactive experiences for policyholders, such as virtual property inspections and simulated risk scenarios. By incorporating AR and VR into their operations, insurers can enhance customer satisfaction, improve risk assessment accuracy, and differentiate their offerings in the market. Chatbots provide insurers with instant customer support and assistance through natural language processing and machine learning algorithms. These AI-powered chatbots can answer customer queries, provide policy information, and assist with real-time claims processing. By deploying chatbots, insurers can enhance customer service, reduce response times, and increase operational efficiency. Predictive analytics algorithms enable insurers to analyse vast data sets and extract actionable insights for personalized insurance products and pricing. These algorithms use machine learning and statistical techniques to identify trends, patterns, and correlations in data, allowing insurers to anticipate customer needs and behaviours more accurately. By leveraging predictive analytics, insurers can optimize pricing strategies, mitigate risks, and improve underwriting decisions. Application programming interfaces (APIs) facilitate seamless integration with external systems and enable insurers to leverage third-party services and data sources. These APIs allow insurers to connect with various platforms, such as payment gateways, data providers, and analytics tools, to enhance their capabilities and expand their offerings. By embracing APIs, insurers can improve interoperability, accelerate innovation, and create new revenue streams.

Adopting advanced technologies is transforming the insurance industry, enabling insurers to enhance transparency, efficiency, and accessibility globally. By embracing a multifaceted approach to technology adoption, decentralized insurance platforms can disrupt the industry and deliver innovative solutions that meet customers' evolving needs in today's digital age. The selection of technologies insurance platforms use depends on several factors, including business objectives, customer needs, regulatory requirements, and technological capabilities. As insurers continue to embrace digital transformation, integrating advanced technologies will play a crucial role in shaping the insurance industry's future.

3.3.1 Blockchain Technology

Blockchain technology is the cornerstone of smart contracts, providing a decentralized database structure that securely captures and records all network transactions, past and future. Resembling a timestamped linked list, this distributed ledger continually expands with each new node, containing detailed transaction data and the cryptographic hash of the preceding block (Crawford etal., 2016). Unlike conventional databases, blockchain operates on a peer-to-peer network, enabling multiple copies of the ledger to be shared across diverse network participants' devices and locations. This decentralized approach ensures transparency, irreversibility, and security without needing a centralized server for coordination. Smart contracts leverage blockchain for verification, validation, and enforcement of contractual terms, ensuring the integrity of agreements between parties (Deloitte, 2016a, 2016b). Transactions within the blockchain include sender and recipient addresses, along with transaction value/data, all cryptographically secured for confidentiality. Once validated, transactions become immutable, fostering trust and transparency among participants. Smart contract data is encrypted and stored in the blockchain ledger, safeguarding it from loss, modification, or deletion. The storage structure of blockchain revolves around "blocks" that house transactional data, each block linked to the previous one via a unique cryptographic hash. This creates an ordered list of blocks constituting the blockchain, where validated transactions are appended to the network, ensuring their integrity and immutability. Participants in the network maintain identical replicas of the ledger, ensuring universal transparency and accessibility. Mining, a critical aspect of blockchain, involves validating transactions by participants known as miners. Miners select new transactions, include them in a new block, and perform mathematical calculations to solve functions and determine a "nonce" value for the block. This process, known as proof of work, validates transactions and prevents malicious activities, with miners rewarded for their efforts. Validated blocks are added to the blockchain, where other miners update their ledger copies (Chekriy & Mukhin, 2018).

In the insurance industry, blockchain technology operates through seven key components: Transaction, Verification, Structure, Validation, Blockchain Mining, Built-in Defense, and The Chain. These components synergistically enhance efficiency, reduce costs, and foster stakeholder trust. By leveraging blockchain, insurers streamline operations, automate claims settlement processes, and enhance data security, ultimately improving customer experiences and driving industry-wide innovation. Blockchain technology operates within insurance by leveraging seven key components, ensuring secure and transparent transactions. A blockchain transaction involves the transfer of assets or information between parties, securely recorded on the blockchain network for transparency and immutability. Before a transaction is added to the blockchain, it undergoes verification to ensure its validity through cryptographic techniques, authenticating the sender's identity and ensuring data integrity. The blockchain's structure consists of a chain of blocks, each containing verified transactions linked in chronological order. Validation of transactions is crucial, ensuring only legitimate transactions are added to the ledger, with validators performing complex calculations to reach a consensus on validity. Blockchain mining adds new blocks to the blockchain by validating transactions and rewarding miners who solve cryptographic puzzles. Built-in defense mechanisms protect against fraudulent activities and cyberattacks, leveraging decentralization, cryptographic hashing, and consensus mechanisms for security. The blockchain stores a complete record of all transactions across the network, with each block containing a unique cryptographic hash of the previous block, ensuring a tamper-proof and auditable trail of transactions. When a block is validated, the miner solving the puzzle is rewarded, and the block is distributed through the network, with each node adding it to the majority chain, contributing to the network's immutable and auditable blockchain (Fig. 3.1).

Blockchain technology has catalyzed a transformative shift in the insurance industry, with various organizations harnessing its potential to streamline processes and enhance transparency (Daley, 2020). Etherisc,

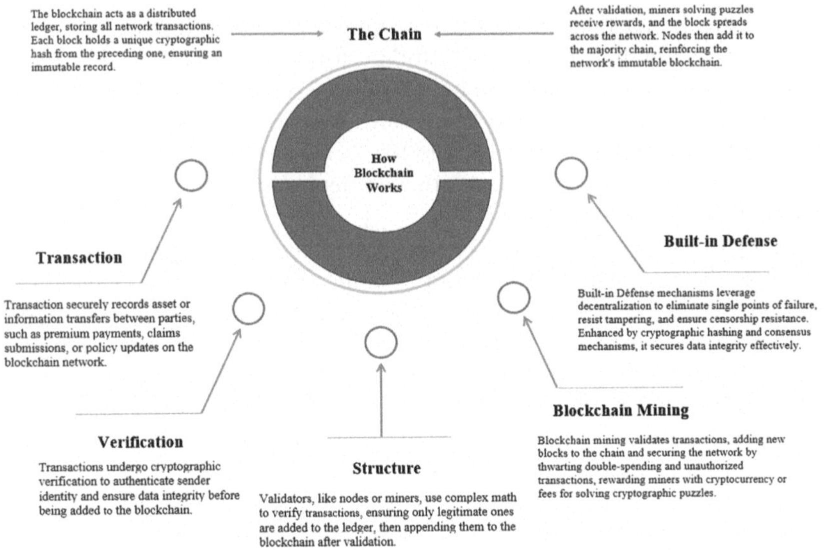

Fig. 3.1 How Blockchain works in insurance operations (*Source* Prepared by authors)

based in Munich, Germany, pioneers decentralized insurance applications, reducing inefficiencies like high transaction fees and lengthy claim-processing times using blockchain. They've developed decentralized insurance applications spanning diverse sectors, including crop insurance for farmers and protection against crypto wallet hacking. Meanwhile, Guardtime, headquartered in Irvine, California, collaborates with logistics giant Maersk to create a maritime insurance network based on blockchain. Their Insurwave framework manages insurance processes for over 1,000 vessels, handling more than 500,000 maritime insurance data ledger transactions. Etherisc has developed solutions to cover the risk of crypto wallet theft in case of attacks. Etherisc, by understanding the need for decentralized insurance where wallets are insured, provides crypto wallet insurance covering a large sum. This is a great use case of decentralized finance. In a typical case of Crypto loans, the insurance policy pays off the loan if the collateral the borrower provides is destroyed or stolen. Etherisc and several other companies like Sweetbridge, Celsius, Nexo, Libra Credit, and others established a consortium that safeguarded and secured collateralized crypto-backed loans, an amazing decentralized insurance application. Fidentiax in Singapore operates the world's first tradeable insurance policy marketplace, where users can buy, sell, or store policies securely on the blockchain. Their blockchain-powered digital ledger, ISLEY, provides clients with comprehensive summaries of their policies and notifications for premium due dates. Fizzy, an insurance tool for flight delays, is a subsidiary of the multinational insurance giant AXA. Fizzy uses blockchain to guarantee instant coverage and compensation for members whose flights are delayed for more than 2 hours. The company's blockchain supplements travel insurance, which typically does not cover financial losses incurred due to flight delays. The tool uses smart contracts to lock-in terms of payments and policy details. Users have to enter their flight details, configure their coverage, and make a payment. Blockchain can then aid Fizzy to check flight delay data immutably and reimburse customers. Fizzy's instant blockchain-based flight delay payments covered 80% of all worldwide flights by December 2018. Teambrella is an insurance marketplace whereby the team co-insures claims, rather than being a centralized insurance provider. For example, a member of Teambrella in the United States will inform the team that their dog needs emergency surgery. The rest of the team will vote on whether to pay for the operation of the pup and how much of the cost they can cover.

To execute insurance payments, Teambrella uses blockchain and smart contracts. Members of one Teambrella group are locked in a smart contract and use these contracts to vote for each claim transparently and execute the payment. The organization currently has four insurance pilot groups in Peru, the Netherlands, Argentina, and Germany that are concerned with bicycle damage and pets. They are expanding their operations to include pet insurance in the United States. and automobile insurance in Russia. (Daley, 2020; Shetty et al., 2022). Teambrella is also a self-governing insurance tech organization; the company uses Ethereum smart contracts for claim and policy management. They allow for transparency and self-regulation. Participants discuss each claim and vote to meet a consensus on claim coverage. If the claim is approved, each participant shares a part of their premium with a claimant peer. Box 3.1 displayed the use case where blockchain technology is used in various operations of the insurance sector.

Box 3.1: Use Cases of Blockchain for the Insurance Sector

Insurance Policy Offering

Blockchain technology revolutionizes the creation and management of insurance policies through smart contracts, establishing a secure and transparent framework. This innovative approach allows participants to either create new insurance policies or join existing ones on a blockchain-based platform. When initiating a new policy, the creator outlines specific coverage details, which may include the coverage amount, premium amount, and policy duration. Existing policies are open for participation, enabling individuals to join based on their insurance needs.

Whether seeking to join an existing policy or create a new one, applicants must provide personal information and specific details crucial for accurately assessing risk and determining appropriate coverage levels (Grima, et al., 2020). Once the applicant submits their details, the insurance network participants collectively assess whether the proposed coverage amount and premium align with the policy's objectives and risk factors. This consensus mechanism ensures that policy terms are fair and equitable for all participants. Upon acceptance, the applicant makes the premium payment securely recorded on the blockchain. The decentralized nature of blockchain technology ensures the integrity and immutability of these transactions, providing a tamper-proof record of premium payments. The pre-agreed policy terms and conditions, including coverage details, premium amounts, and policy duration, are encoded into a smart contract and stored on the blockchain. These smart contracts act as self-executing agreements, automatically enforcing the agreed upon terms once specific conditions are met.

In this decentralized insurance system, premium amounts are securely collected and stored using blockchain technology. This process involves the creation of a common fund known as premium pooling, which aggregates the premiums contributed by each policyholder within the network. A dedicated smart contract for claim processing is automatically activated when a claim event occurs. After verification, the smart contract releases the claim amount to the policyholder, utilizing the premium pool to provide financial compensation.

A minimum number of policyholders is required to activate a policy to ensure the adequacy of funds to cover claims. Once this minimum requirement is met, the predetermined policy period begins, extending coverage to all participating members. After the policy period ends, any remaining funds in the premium pool can be redistributed among policyholders or carried forward to the next policy cycle. This approach contrasts with the conventional insurance model, where such surplus typically accrues to the intermediary company as profit. Instead, the decentralized system reinvests these surplus funds into the community.

A reinsurance structure is implemented to further safeguard against unexpected claim events that exceed the available premium pool. This reinsurance pool comprises contributions from various insurance policies within the platform, ensuring reimbursement to the premium pool in shortfall cases. This additional layer of financial security and stability enhances the resilience of the decentralized insurance ecosystem.

Incident Reporting and Assessment

Blockchain ensures that incident data, including location, time, and involved parties, is recorded tamper-proof, reducing the risk of fraud and manipulation. This transparent ledger allows for streamlined verification processes, eliminating the need for intermediaries and expediting claims processing. Blockchain facilitates community-based consensus mechanisms for assessing claims, enabling network participants to determine claims' validity collectively. Integration with trusted entities, such as law enforcement agencies or repair agents, further enhances the reliability of incident data. Moreover, blockchain prioritizes privacy and security, encrypting personal data related to incident reports while allowing authorized access.

Fraud detection in blockchain technology predominantly relies on smart contracts. These are specialized protocols designed to automate the validation and enforcement of contracts. Smart contracts facilitate secure, traceable, and permanent transactions without the need for intermediaries. They contain all transaction details and execute procedures only when specified conditions are met. Unlike traditional paper contracts, smart contracts are generated by computers, ensuring precision, and efficiency.

An example of this application is the "Anti-Moth" project by Taikang Online, which utilized blockchain-based insurance fraud detection. The company's smart contracting system can determine if a client meets the insurance criteria and intends to proceed with insurance, thus preserving privacy while preventing fraud (Wang & Kogan, 2018).

Storage Structure

The storage structure within a blockchain system is integral to maintaining the integrity and security of data while ensuring efficient management. In the context of the insurance platform, the storage mechanism must balance between security, accessibility, and cost-effectiveness. While data stored on the blockchain benefit from inherent security features like tamper-proofing and irreversibility due to cryptographic hashing, they lack privacy as they are accessible to all participants (Zhao, 2020). Moreover, storing large volumes of data directly on-chain can incur significant costs. To mitigate these challenges, a hybrid approach to data storage is proposed, utilizing both on-chain and off-chain storage solutions. Sensitive or infrequently accessed data, such as confidential information or large files, can be stored off-chain, reducing the burden on the blockchain and preserving privacy. Critical transactional data and smart contracts, which govern the interactions within the insurance platform, remain stored on-chain. This hybrid storage model ensures that essential data is securely managed while minimizing costs and maintaining efficiency within the blockchain network. Smart contracts are crucial in managing various aspects of the insurance platform's operations. These self-executing contracts are encoded with predefined rules and conditions, enabling automated and transparent execution of processes. In the insurance platform, several key smart contracts can be utilized. The Premium Pool Smart Contract facilitates the collection and secure storage of premium amounts contributed by policyholders, ensuring transparency and trust in premium payments.

The Insurance Policy Smart Contract stores and enforces the terms and conditions of insurance policies, including coverage details and premium amounts. It may incorporate reputation details of policyholders, enabling transparent assessment of risk profiles and claim eligibility. The Claim Processes Smart Contract automates the claims process, allowing for the submission, verification, and settlement of claims through transparent and auditable procedures. The proposed insurance platform can achieve robust data management, security, and operational efficiency within the blockchain ecosystem by leveraging smart contracts and a hybrid storage structure.

Claim Assessment and Claim Payment

Accepting or denying claim requests and assessing claim amounts in the platform uses a community voting mechanism. A verified incident is forwarded for community voting, as well as the claim request and file proof. The policyholder involved in the incident can request a claim amount that can be covered according to his policy (Kar & Navin, 2021). The community can view the verified incident report and the policyholder's claim request. The community can then vote to either accept or deny the claim. For a claim request to be accepted, a majority acceptance percentage, such as at least 70%, for the claim request is required. The community can also decide the compensation claim amount through the voting mechanism. If a request is approved, the claim processing smart contract checks for the validity of voting, the reputation of the policyholder, and whether the policy covers the agreed claim amount. After verification of terms and conditions, the approved claim amount is released to the policyholder instantly from the premium pool via the smart contract. To address the practical applicability of the voting mechanism, claim requests, and member voting are proposed to be held periodically within a specified time window such that members of a policy are encouraged to vote according to a convenient schedule. For Example, a scheduled 8-hour voting period can be enforced on requests submitted 16 hours before the start of voting.

Sustainability

The sustainability of the insurance platform is intricately woven into its design, with a multifaceted approach aimed at ensuring the long-term viability and prosperity of the system while nurturing a thriving community of participants. Central to this endeavour is the management of the premium pool fund, which serves as the financial backbone of the platform. A strategic portion of the premium pool is reinvested to safeguard its sustainability, with the returns channelled back into the fund. This prudent reinvestment strategy not only helps to grow the fund over time but also allows for the rewarding of loyal policyholders who contribute to its stability. A pivotal aspect of sustainability lies in cultivating trust and accountability within the community. To this end, each policyholder has a reputation token meticulously managed by the platform's smart contract. This token is a tangible reflection of a policyholder's reliability and commitment to the community. Factors such as claims history, adherence to policy terms, and platform tenure all contribute to this reputation token's value. As a policyholder's reputation grows, so does their standing within the community, affording them access to enhanced coverage options and potential returns on investments.

Furthermore, the platform fosters a culture of proactive engagement and investment among its members. Beyond fulfilling their premium obligations, members are encouraged to invest additional funds into the platform, bolstering its financial resilience. These contributions are channelled into the overall fund and offer attractive interest rates, providing members with a pathway to financial growth while fortifying the platform against unforeseen challenges. In addition to these proactive measures, the platform implements a robust reinsurance mechanism to mitigate risks and ensure the prompt and adequate compensation of claims. By maintaining a dedicated reinsurance pool, the platform can effectively manage risks and safeguard the interests of its members, even in scenarios where the premium pool may fall short. Through these comprehensive sustainability measures, the platform endeavours to thrive in the ever-evolving insurance landscape and foster a sense of collective prosperity and resilience among its community members. By prioritizing transparency, accountability, and proactive engagement, the platform aims to create a sustainable ecosystem where all stakeholders' needs are met and trust and confidence reign supreme.

3.3.2 *Digital Platforms and Mobile Apps*

Gone are the days when clients were required to directly contact insurance agents or make in-person visits to procure a policy. With the advent of the internet, individuals are now more informed about the range of offerings available in the market. Today, anyone can effortlessly compare insurance products, peruse testimonials, and discover specialized plans tailored to their needs. This shift has been facilitated by the emergence of insurance platforms such as Ladder, Lemonade, Al-Rajhi Takaful, Weecover, Qover Insurify, CoverHound, and Friendsurance, which are actively reshaping distribution models within the industry. By leveraging these platforms, clients can articulate their requirements more precisely, enabling service providers to enhance their visibility by aligning with consumer demand.

Insurers also benefit from reduced distribution costs, as these platforms streamline consumers' connection with suitable insurance products. Moreover, the targeted nature of leads generated through these marketplaces enhances the efficiency of insurers' marketing efforts, resulting in a more effective allocation of resources. Thus, these insurance shopping platforms facilitate a more streamlined and accessible insurance purchasing experience but also contribute to optimizing insurers' marketing strategies in the digital age. Decentralized insurance platforms operate independently, untethered from centralized systems, databases, or protocols to manage insurance policies, claims, and customer interactions. Take, for instance, Friendsurance, a dynamic provider offering a comprehensive suite of insurance solutions spanning home, auto, liability, and pet coverage, all accessible through intuitive digital platforms. At the heart of Friendsurance lies a groundbreaking peer-to-peer insurance model. Here, small cohorts of policyholders band together, pooling their premiums to form a collective safety net against potential claims. This unique approach fosters a strong sense of community and mutual assistance among members, setting Friendsurance apart as a beacon of innovation in the insurance landscape. Friendsurance is committed to pioneering features designed to incentivize responsible behaviour and enhance the customer experience. From rewarding claim-free periods to leveraging state-of-the-art technologies such as digital platforms, mobile applications, and advanced data analytics, Friendsurance continuously pushes the boundaries of what's possible in insurance service delivery.

The proliferation of mobile phones and the development of applications (commonly known as "apps") have enabled numerous companies to extend their reach to a broader audience beyond previously feasible. The impact of mobile technology on insurance platforms varies depending on factors such as the generation of mobile networks in use and the prevalent types of mobile devices. Smartphones, coupled with internet access, facilitate innovative solutions that leverage the functionality of apps. Mobile networks supporting short messages and high-capacity data transfers are indispensable to achieve this. This becomes especially pertinent in emerging markets with low insurance penetration and a lack of well-established distribution channels. For example, Friendsurance leverages a mobile app to connect small groups of individuals (typically 10–16 insured). In the event of an insured occurrence, an insured can report a claim via the Friendsurance app and receive coverage accordingly. Upon contract expiration, customers receive pre-agreed cashback from the funds pooled within the group. Friendsurance primarily focuses on mitigating small risks associated with property, such as a broken window in a house.

Another notable example is Besurance, an innovative peer-to-peer insurance carrier. Besurance operates as an Insuretech risk-sharing platform aggregating insured based on risk profiles. Utilizing actuarial software, the platform generates tailored quotations for respective risk groups. Community members then evaluate and approve claims, fostering a collaborative and transparent insurance process. Digital platforms and mobile applications have emerged as indispensable tools, orchestrating seamless interactions among insurers, policyholders, and other stakeholders within the insurance ecosystem. These sophisticated platforms and apps serve as the primary conduit through which users access, manage, and navigate their insurance policies, facilitating various activities ranging from policy inquiries to claim submissions and communications with insurers. The significance of these digital platforms and mobile apps lies in their ability to deliver a convenient and user-centric experience. Empowering policyholders with accessibility at their fingertips, these platforms enable individuals to effortlessly view policy details, execute premium payments, and monitor claims status, all from the comfort and convenience of their smartphones or computers. Such accessibility enhances user satisfaction and fosters a culture of transparency and empowerment within the insurance process. Integrating digital platforms and mobile apps into insurance operations offers insurers many opportunities to optimize efficiency and elevate customer engagement. By deploying advanced analytics and artificial intelligence, insurers can tailor insurance offerings to match individual customers' unique needs and preferences on digital platforms, enhancing the relevance and resonance of their products.

Additionally, incorporating chatbots and virtual assistants with digital platforms empowers insurers to provide real-time support and assistance to policyholders, bolstering overall customer satisfaction and loyalty. Digital platforms and mobile apps also serve as conduits for integrating cutting-edge technologies such as the Internet of Things (IoT) and wearable devices into insurance products. By leveraging data generated by IoT devices, insurers can pioneer usage-based insurance policies that dynamically adjust premiums based on real-time usage patterns and behaviour, thus aligning premiums more closely with risk exposure.

3.3.3 *Machine Intelligence (MI) and Robotic Process Automation (RPA)*

Machine Intelligence (MI), encompassing both Artificial Intelligence (AI) and Machine Learning (ML), stands as a transformative force poised to revolutionize the insurance industry at every level, from distribution and underwriting to pricing and claims processing (Anchen, 2022; IAIS, 2023). The influence of advanced technologies and data in this realm is already palpable, with notable shifts observed in distribution and underwriting practices. Today, policies are increasingly priced, purchased, and bound in near real-time, reflecting the swift integration of MI-driven solutions into traditional insurance processes (Kumar, et al., 2023). As MI continues to evolve and increase, its impact on the insurance landscape is expected to be seismic, driving efficiency, enhancing decision-making capabilities, and ultimately reshaping the industry as we know it.

Purchasing insurance has undergone a significant transformation, characterized by swifter transactions and reduced involvement from insurers and customers. Thanks to advancements in AI algorithms, a wealth of individual behaviour data is readily available, enabling the creation of precise risk profiles (Gatteschi et al., 2018). Consequently, the time required to purchase auto, commercial, or life insurance policies has been slashed to mere minutes or even seconds. While instant quotes have been commonplace in auto and home insurance, advancements in telematics and the proliferation of in-home IoT devices are poised to enhance further insurers' ability to issue policies immediately to a broader customer base as pricing algorithms mature. In life insurance, although many carriers have experimented with simplified issue products primarily catering to the healthiest applicants, these offerings often come at a higher price than fully underwritten alternatives. However, with the increasing integration of AI into life underwriting processes, coupled with the ability of carriers to pinpoint risk in a more nuanced and sophisticated manner, a new wave of mass-market instant issue products is on the horizon, promising greater accessibility and affordability for consumers (NAIC, 2024).

AI-based cognitive models have accelerated the purchase of commercial insurance. By leveraging the data generated by these sources, insurers can promptly generate bindable quotes, expediting the insurance purchasing process and enhancing overall operational efficiency.

Nowadays, underwriting for most personal and small business products within life, property, and casualty insurance has evolved significantly. The underwriting process, which historically involved extensive manual assessment, has now been streamlined to a matter of seconds through extensive automation. This automation is facilitated by a sophisticated combination of machine and deep learning models integrated into the technological infrastructure of insurers (Ladva & Grasso, 2023). These advanced models utilize internal data and various external data sources, accessed through application programming interfaces and partnerships with external data and analytics providers. Information gathered from devices supplied by mainline carriers, reinsurers, product manufacturers, and distributors is aggregated into diverse data repositories and streams. This rich pool of data empowers insurers to make proactive decisions regarding underwriting and pricing, enabling them to reach out to customers with bindable quotes for product bundles tailored to their individual risk profiles and coverage needs (Balasubramanian, et al., 2021). Regulators undertake the crucial task of reviewing AI-enabled, machine learning-based models, ensuring transparency in determining the traceability of scores akin to the derivation of rating factors employed in current regression-based coefficients. To ascertain the appropriateness of data usage for marketing and underwriting purposes, regulators evaluate a combination of inputs incorporated into these models.

Moreover, they develop test policies for providers engaged in rate determination for online plans, aiming to verify that algorithmic outcomes fall within approved boundaries. Public policy considerations impose restrictions on accessing sensitive and predictive data, such as health and genetic information, to mitigate underwriting and pricing flexibility reduction and the escalation of anti-selection risks in specific segments.

While price remains a pivotal factor in consumer decision-making, insurers are actively innovating to mitigate competition solely based on pricing. Advanced proprietary platforms serve as conduits connecting customers and insurers, offering differentiated experiences, features, and value propositions. In certain segments, intensified price competition leads to razor-thin margins becoming the norm, whereas in others, distinctive insurance offerings foster margin expansion and differentiation. In jurisdictions embracing change, the pace of pricing innovation accelerates significantly. Real-time pricing, grounded in usage-based and dynamically assessed risk evaluations rich in data, empowers consumers to make informed decisions regarding the influence of their actions on coverage, insurability, and pricing.

Claims processing continues to be a core function for insurance carriers, albeit with a significant shift towards automation, where over half of claims activities are now automated. Advanced algorithms play a pivotal role in streamlining initial claims routing and enhancing efficiency and accuracy in the process (Yong, 2023). The advent of Internet of Things sensors and various data-capture technologies, such as drones, has largely replaced conventional manual methods for reporting initial loss incidents. Moreover, automated claims triage and repair services are frequently initiated immediately following a loss event. For instance, in the event of an auto accident, policyholders capture streaming video of the damage, which is then translated into detailed loss descriptions and estimated amounts. Vehicles with autonomous features that sustain minor damage can autonomously navigate to repair shops for servicing while another autonomous vehicle is dispatched in the interim. In homeowners' insurance, IoT devices are increasingly utilized to proactively monitor water levels, temperature, and other critical risk factors, promptly alerting occupants and insurers of potential issues before they escalate.

Automated customer service applications now manage most interactions with policyholders, utilizing both voice and text-based interfaces. These applications follow self-learning scripts tailored to interface seamlessly with various systems, including claims, fraud detection, medical services, policy management, and repair systems. As a result, many claims are resolved within minutes, a stark departure from the previous norm of days or weeks. Human involvement in claims management is primarily focused on specific areas: addressing complex and uncommon claims, handling contested claims where human interaction and negotiation play a crucial role supported by analytics and data-driven insights, addressing claims associated with systemic issues and risks stemming from emerging technologies (such as cybersecurity threats targeting critical IoT systems), and conducting random manual reviews of claims to ensure adequate oversight of algorithmic decision-making processes.

Claims organizations are intensifying their efforts towards risk monitoring, prevention, and mitigation, leveraging IoT technology and emerging data sources to oversee risk levels and initiate interventions when certain factors surpass predefined thresholds determined by AI algorithms. Interactions between customers and insurance claims departments aim to preempt potential losses. Individuals receive instantaneous alerts, often linked with automatic inspection, maintenance, and repair interventions. In large-scale catastrophe claims scenarios, insurers employ real-time monitoring of properties and vehicles through an integrated network of IoT devices, telematics systems, and mobile phone data, assuming that mobile service and power remain uninterrupted in the affected areas. In power outages, insurers can proactively file claims using data aggregators that consolidate information from satellites, networked drones, weather services, and policyholder data in real time. This system has undergone rigorous testing by major carriers across various catastrophe scenarios, ensuring that highly accurate loss estimations are promptly submitted during actual emergencies. Detailed reports are automatically furnished to reinsurers, expediting the flow of reinsurance capital.

In understanding the future trajectory of the re/insurance industry, the widespread anticipation revolves around the transformative potential of artificial intelligence in refining coverage and pricing adjustments. This vision underscores the allure of leveraging advanced AI algorithms to enhance the precision and granularity of insurance offerings, ultimately optimizing risk assessment and pricing strategies. By harnessing AI-driven insights, insurers aim to understand individual risks better, thereby tailoring coverage to meet policyholders' unique needs and preferences more accurately. This long-term objective promises increased efficiency and effectiveness within the insurance value chain and holds the potential to foster greater customer satisfaction and loyalty through personalized insurance solutions. However, while the future possibilities of AI in re/insurance are undoubtedly promising, it is essential to acknowledge the tangible benefits that AI is already delivering in the present landscape. From claims processing automation to underwriting optimization and fraud detection, AI technologies are already revolutionizing various facets of the insurance industry, driving efficiency gains and cost savings. In the near term, insurers increasingly focus on leveraging AI to augment decision-making processes, enhance customer experiences, and mitigate risks more effectively. Moreover, as AI evolves, new opportunities emerge across the insurance value chain, including enhanced predictive analytics, dynamic pricing models, and proactive risk management strategies. This ongoing integration of AI-driven solutions is poised to reshape the re/insurance industry, unlocking new avenues for growth, innovation, and value creation.

Several pioneering companies have emerged as frontrunners in leveraging MI to enhance various aspects of insurance processes. These companies include Clover, Fabric, GetSafe, Trov, and Lemonade, each employing AI-driven solutions to address specific challenges within the industry. Clover, headquartered in San Francisco, CA, United States, has secured substantial funding of $285 million, positioning itself as a prominent player in the health insurance sector. Utilizing MI, Clover focuses on constructing detailed clinical profiles of individuals to identify gaps in care and preemptively address potential health issues. By offering personalized visits and allowing customers the freedom to select their preferred healthcare providers, Clover aims to minimize the occurrence of costly hospital stays, ultimately improving overall healthcare outcomes. Fabric, with a funding of $2.5 million, stands out in the life insurance landscape by streamlining the signup process through AI-generated quotes for accidental death claims. The company's emphasis on simplicity and speed enables users to obtain life insurance coverage in just two minutes, facilitated through a user-friendly interface accessible across multiple devices. Fabric's innovative approach exemplifies how MI can streamline traditionally complex processes, making insurance more accessible and user-friendly. Based in Heidelberg, Germany, GetSafe is another notable player harnessing the power of AI in insurance operations. By leveraging MI, GetSafe provides tailored insurance recommendations to customers while simplifying the information-gathering process. GetSafe also offers a comprehensive app that allows users to manage all their insurance policies in one centralized location, enhancing convenience and accessibility for policyholders. Trov, headquartered in San Francisco, CA, United States, has secured $87 million in funding for innovative on-demand property insurance services. Trov streamlines the claims process by integrating an AI chatbot, enabling customers to initiate insurance coverage immediately via a user-friendly app interface.

Trov offers flexibility by allowing users to adjust insurance coverage for their valuables dynamically, reflecting the adaptability and responsiveness enabled by AI-driven solutions. Lemonade emerges as a trailblazer in insurance operations, leveraging AI-powered claim analysis to expedite claims processing. By employing eighteen anti-fraud algorithms on customer-submitted image and video claims, Lemonade ensures swift and accurate assessment, with responses delivered within minutes. Furthermore, Lemonade's unique business model, where small insurance groups contribute to a shared claim pool, demonstrates how AI can foster innovative approaches to risk management and resource allocation within the insurance industry (Deloitte Digital, 2017).

In parallel to MI, RPA is a transformative force within the insurance industry, revolutionizing operations by automating mundane and repetitive tasks, enhancing operational efficiency and elevating customer service standards. Through the deployment of software bots, RPA streamlines a wide array of rule-based tasks, encompassing activities like policy creation, deposit collection, background verification, and more (Deloitte, 2017). By embracing a hyper-automation strategy, insurers can extend this efficiency to processes requiring decision-making capabilities, enhancing overall operational agility. Adopting RPA equips insurance organizations with a competitive edge, enabling them to refine their operations and amplify customer satisfaction metrics. The impact of RPA extends across various functions within the insurance sector, ranging from underwriting and regulatory compliance to sales and distribution, finance and accounts, policy administration, business analytics, fraud detection, policy cancellation, and query resolution. By integrating RPA into these diverse areas, insurers can streamline workflows, mitigate risks, and drive innovation, positioning themselves as industry leaders in a dynamic and competitive landscape. RPA's versatility and effectiveness make it an indispensable tool for insurance companies seeking to navigate the complexities of the modern marketplace while delivering exceptional value to their customers.

One notable example is HDFC Life, which unveiled the inaugural life insurance chatbot in collaboration with Haptik, India's largest platform. This innovative chatbot serves as a financial advisor, assisting users in selecting the most appropriate life insurance plans and solutions. With a focus on providing comprehensive insurance advice covering various aspects, from health to tax planning and retirement, the chatbot utilizes a straightforward 60-second quiz to assess users' needs and preferences. Through this interactive process, the chatbot computes personalized recommendations tailored to each individual's requirements, simplifying decision-making and enhancing accessibility to essential insurance services. This initiative underscores HDFC Life's commitment to leveraging technology to offer seamless and customer-centric solutions, reaffirming its position as a leader in the Indian insurance industry (The Economic Times, 2017).

Zurich Insurance Group exemplifies a forward-thinking approach by embracing RPA technology in 2016 to elevate services across the policy life cycle within its international programs business. This strategic move stemmed from Zurich's unwavering commitment to prioritizing the needs of its customers and brokers. With a core objective of optimizing the efficiency of policy handlers, adopting RPA aimed to liberate their time and enhance data accuracy. The outcome has been transformative, as the implementation of RPA has not only elevated service quality but also minimized re-work and eliminated tedious, repetitive tasks, thereby significantly enhancing the overall customer experience. Developed in collaboration with Capgemini, the RPA solution employed by Zurich Insurance Group is tailored to meet the organization's specific requirements, leveraging advanced BluePrism software to automate many policy issuance tasks. From harmonizing terms in master policies to generating invoices and drafting policy documents, these intelligent robots streamline processes seamlessly, alleviating the workload of policy handlers considerably. Importantly, RPA is not positioned to replace human effort but to complement it, fostering a harmonious coexistence between humans and technology. This symbiotic relationship facilitates the delivery of rapid, precise outcomes, enabling Zurich to allocate human resources more effectively, resulting in superior service delivery and an enriched customer experience (Zurich, 2021).

Integrating Robotic Process Automation bots with Natural Language Processing capabilities has ushered in a new era for the insurance industry, fundamentally transforming how insurers approach customer service. This convergence of advanced technologies has enabled insurers to respond to customer queries swiftly and accurately, thereby significantly enhancing overall customer satisfaction. RPA, with its ability to automate repetitive tasks and NLP's capacity to understand and interpret human language, has streamlined communication channels and empowered insurers to deliver personalized and efficient service. In a highly competitive market landscape where customer expectations constantly evolve, adopting RPA with NLP has become a strategic imperative for insurers seeking to differentiate themselves and gain a competitive edge.

Beyond its impact on customer service, deploying RPA with NLP capabilities has profound implications for internal processes and operational risk management within insurance organizations. By automating repetitive tasks and streamlining workflows, RPA bots equipped with NLP can significantly improve operational efficiency and resource utilization. The integration of NLP further enhances the capabilities of RPA bots by enabling them to understand and interpret customer inquiries more accurately, thereby reducing the likelihood of errors and misunderstandings. As a result, insurers can achieve greater agility and responsiveness in addressing customer needs while minimizing the potential for costly errors or compliance breaches.

Looking ahead, the transformative potential of RPA with NLP extends beyond immediate operational improvements to drive broader strategic objectives within the insurance industry. As insurers continue to invest in digital transformation initiatives, RPA with NLP emerges as a foundational technology that enables organizations to adapt and thrive in an increasingly digital world. By harnessing the power of automation and natural language understanding, insurers can unlock new opportunities for innovation, differentiation, and growth. Whether streamlining claims processing, optimizing underwriting workflows, or enhancing customer engagement, RPA with NLP is poised to play a central role in shaping the future of insurance services and driving value for insurers and policyholders.

In the rapidly evolving landscape of industries today, the comprehensive adoption and seamless integration of cutting-edge technologies like automation, deep learning, external data ecosystems, and Robotic Process Automation are critical for organizations to stay competitive and relevant. These technologies reshape business operations, optimize processes, and drive innovation across various sectors. However, to fully leverage the potential of these technologies, organizations must prioritize gaining expertise in AI-related technologies and trends.

To navigate this transformative landscape effectively, organizations must invest in continuous learning initiatives to ensure that their teams are equipped with the knowledge and skills required to harness the potential of AI and RPA. This involves training programs, workshops, and resources to upskill employees and enable them to adapt to new technologies and methodologies. Organizations can empower their workforce to embrace change and drive digital transformation initiatives by fostering a continuous learning and innovation culture.

Furthermore, developing and implementing a coherent strategic plan is essential for successful AI and RPA adoption. This entails aligning AI initiatives, including RPA implementation, with broader business objectives and goals. Organizations must identify key use cases where AI and RPA can add the most value, whether streamlining operations, improving efficiency, enhancing customer experiences, or driving revenue growth. Organizations can ensure that their technology investments translate into tangible business outcomes by prioritising these initiatives and setting clear objectives.

Moreover, organizations must develop a robust data strategy to capitalize on the insights derived from data assets. This involves prioritizing data collection, management, and analysis to extract actionable insights and drive informed decision-making. By leveraging advanced analytics techniques and ensuring data privacy and security, organizations can build trust and mitigate risks associated with data-driven initiatives.

Creating the right talent and technology infrastructure is crucial for successful AI and RPA adoption and integration. This includes attracting and retaining top talent with expertise in AI and investing in scalable technology infrastructure to support AI-driven applications and workflows. By prioritizing these initiatives and embracing a holistic approach to AI and RPA adoption, organizations can position themselves for success in today's data-driven economy. They can drive innovation, improve operational efficiency, enhance customer experiences, and gain a competitive edge in their respective industries. Ultimately, AI and RPA offer tremendous opportunities for organizations to transform their business operations and achieve sustainable growth in the digital age (Balasubramanian et al., 2021).

3.3.4 Cloud Computing

The insurance industry is increasingly prioritizing cloud solutions to enhance their operational efficiency and customer service. These solutions facilitate the streamlining of operations and the management of project and product portfolios, while also delivering customer-centric services (Yang & Zhou, 2021). Modern users demand personalized services, smooth navigation, and seamless experiences, which are not typically provided by traditional insurance methods. Cloud-based insurance solutions are software systems hosted on cloud servers rather than on-premises servers. These systems enable insurance companies to manage operations, projects, and customer services from anywhere at any time. Additionally, they offer scalability to meet changing requirements (Accenture, 2023). The numerous features and functions of cloud-based systems help insurance companies improve both operational efficiency and customer satisfaction.

The insurance industry is gradually moving towards its digital transformation. Cloud technology has become one of the key elements of this process. Increasingly, insurance companies are defining "cloud strategies" not just as part of the IT ecosystem but as an essential aspect of their digital transformation plan, as it has a significant impact on transforming business operations across the insurance sector. This is not surprising, as cloud computing brings with it several benefits. Insurance companies can use it to, among other things, increase their innovation, improve cost-efficiency, enhance risk management, and boost a positive customer experience—and this is certainly not a close-ended list.

Data integrity, system availability, elasticity, and performance will be key to success, as will high degrees of automation and extensive use of cloud-native technologies. Leading insurers are cultivating a more flexible cost base by adopting software-as-a-service (SaaS), platform-as-a-service (PaaS), and other cloud-based computing models. These benefits help explain why so many insurers have big plans to expand their public cloud adoption. Indeed, most insurers aim to move at least 80% of their business to the cloud in the coming years, building on the workloads they have already migrated (Betz & Payne, 2021).

In the insurance industry, many cloud computing methodologies cater to diverse platform architectures and operational requisites. These methodologies offer various options, from public cloud infrastructure provided by leading service providers like Amazon Web Services (AWS), Microsoft Azure, or Google Cloud Platform (GCP) to private cloud infrastructures managed by insurance platforms. Public cloud services, renowned for their scalability, flexibility, and an array of managed services, are favoured for their ability to support decentralized insurance applications effectively. They offer a broad spectrum of resources and services that can be tailored to meet the varied needs of insurance platforms, enabling seamless adaptation to evolving demands. On the other hand, insurance platforms may opt for private cloud deployments to retain greater control over security, compliance, and data privacy. These deployments can be on-premises or hosted in third-party data centres, offering dedicated resources to enhance performance and customization options. Hybrid cloud environments merge elements of both public and private clouds, allowing insurance platforms to enjoy the scalability and cost-efficiency of public cloud services while safeguarding sensitive data and workloads within a private cloud setting. This hybrid approach facilitates seamless integration between on-premises infrastructure and cloud resources, offering unparalleled flexibility.

Moreover, insurance platforms may embrace multi-cloud strategies to distribute workloads across multiple cloud providers, mitigating the risk of vendor lock-in and optimizing performance and cost-effectiveness. By leveraging the strengths of various cloud providers, insurance platforms can enhance resilience and capitalize on geographic redundancy and diverse service offerings. Edge computing technologies play a pivotal role in processing and analysing data closer to the source, thereby reducing latency and improving responsiveness for decentralized insurance applications. Whether deployed at the network edge, in regional data centres, or on IoT devices, edge computing resources support real-time data processing and decision-making, enhancing the efficiency of insurance transactions. Furthermore, serverless computing platforms, such as AWS Lambda or Azure Functions, empower decentralized insurance platforms to execute code in response to events without the need to manage server infrastructure. These serverless architectures minimize operational overhead, enhance scalability, and optimize costs by only charging for the computing resources consumed during execution, offering a cost-effective solution for insurance platforms. The choice of cloud computing method in decentralized insurance depends on scalability requirements, data sensitivity, compliance considerations, budget constraints, and the desired level of control and customization. By leveraging cloud computing technologies effectively, insurance platforms can build scalable, resilient, and cost-effective solutions that offer innovative insurance products and services to a global audience.

One example of an insurance platform that uses cloud technology is Boost Insurance, a subsidiary of Axiata Group Berhad, which has revolutionized the insurance landscape in Malaysia through its innovative use of public cloud infrastructure, specifically AWS. Boost has emerged as a leading figure in Malaysia's e-wallet and payment landscape, offering a comprehensive suite of financial services encompassing micropayments, remittances, insurance, lending, and savings. Recognizing the potential of data-driven insights to enhance customer experiences and refine marketing strategies, Boost encountered the challenge of efficiently managing and analysing substantial customer data as its user base expanded rapidly.

Boost Insurance turned to AWS's cloud infrastructure to address this challenge and implement a robust data lake solution. This solution effectively consolidated disparate data sources into a centralized repository, empowering Boost to conduct various analytics, including real-time processing, machine learning, and predictive modelling. The seamless integration of AWS services such as Amazon S3, Amazon Redshift, and AWS Glue facilitated the deployment of advanced analytics tools, enabling Boost Insurance to gain invaluable visibility into the entire customer lifecycle. The enhanced data analytics capabilities enabled Boost to achieve significant improvements across key performance metrics, including a 17% increase in customer spending, a 50% surge in active users, and a 15% reduction in churn rate. Moreover, AWS's agility and scalability empowered Boost Insurance to expedite decision-making processes, enabling strategic decisions based on real-time insights rather than waiting for perfect information. This accelerated pace of data analysis, from weeks to days, enabled Boost to respond promptly to evolving market dynamics and customer needs, driving sustained business growth and bolstering competitiveness. AWS's robust analytics dashboards and automated reporting capabilities enhanced departmental heads' visibility and control over operational data, facilitating more informed decision-making and resource allocation across internal departments (AWS, 2020).

Slice Labs Inc. is renowned for its cloud-based, on-demand, pay-per-use insurance platform, which enables the rapid deployment of innovative insurance products. By leveraging design, data, and technology, Slice redefines insurance and enhances customer engagement. Introducing the Insurance Cloud Services (ICS), Slice Labs Inc. offers a groundbreaking platform that empowers insurers to transition into digital-first entities efficiently and affordably. ICS is a fully digital, end-to-end solution hosted in the cloud, designed to facilitate experimentation and deployment for insurers seeking to embrace digital transformation. With ICS, insurers can swiftly launch fully digital insurance products with minimal risk and cost, catering to customers' evolving needs in the digital age. The key features of the Slice Insurance Cloud Services platform include rapid time to market, cost-effective deployment of new products, flexible monthly subscription models, and significant reductions in operating expenses. This platform supports insurers in introducing, evaluating, and adopting new products, technologies, and business models, enabling them to stay ahead in a fast-paced and competitive market landscape. ICS offers insurers the flexibility and scalability needed to innovate and excel through its comprehensive suite of services, including pricing, rating, licensing, real-time and automated underwriting, servicing, and capacity. The platform is fully embeddable via API, facilitating seamless integration for insurers looking to enhance their product offerings and customer experiences.

The vision behind ICS is to create a digital insurer-as-a-service platform that optimizes speed and cost efficiencies for deployment and ongoing operations. By prioritizing customer experience, Slice has developed a platform that accelerates insurers' time to market, scales infinitely, and synchronizes product offerings with customer behaviours. Moreover, ICS is designed for versatility, configurability, and usability, ensuring it meets the diverse needs of insurers across various product lines and business functions. Currently operational in the US marketplace and fully localized for the United Kingdom with multi-currency and multilingual capabilities, ICS is poised to revolutionize the insurance landscape globally. With standard and surplus lines licenses across all 50 states, Slice is committed to driving innovation and empowering insurers to thrive in the digital era (Mertz, 2018).

Numerous traditional insurers have also harnessed the power of cloud computing to enhance internal operations and expand service offerings, enabling customers to navigate the complexities of a rapidly evolving environment effectively. AXA Switzerland is a pioneer, boldly embracing cloud computing to redefine operations and enhance customer experiences. With Google Cloud as its strategic partner, AXA Switzerland embarked on a transformative journey aimed at future-proofing its business model and maintaining its position as the leading insurance provider in Switzerland. As traditional insurers grapple with the rapid pace of change driven by shifting customer behaviours and technological advancements, AXA Switzerland recognized the urgent need for innovation. Leveraging its rich heritage of 143 years, AXA Switzerland decided to transition from conventional analogue practices to a digitally driven approach. Google Cloud emerged as the catalyst for this transformation, offering unparalleled technological expertise and resources. AXA Switzerland gained invaluable insights into customer preferences and market trends by leveraging Google Cloud analytics solutions, including BigQuery, Dataflow, and Cloud Functions. This empowered AXA Switzerland to develop tailored services and precisely anticipate evolving customer needs. To unlock the full potential of cloud computing, AXA Switzerland embarked on a comprehensive modernization of its IT infrastructure. By embracing the flexible multi-cloud approach offered by Google Cloud, AXA Switzerland gained agility and scalability, enabling rapid innovation without compromising security. This modernization effort laid the foundation for a seamless integration of applications and processes, driving operational efficiency and cost savings (Google Cloud, 2024).

Cloud-based solutions have revolutionized the insurance industry, offering various applications that enhance efficiency, improve customer experiences, and mitigate risks. These innovative technologies empower insurers to streamline operations, optimize processes, and drive digital transformation across various facets of their businesses. Policy administration and management systems powered by the cloud enable insurers to handle policy creation, management, and administration tasks efficiently. These systems reduce manual effort and enhance productivity by automating policy issuance and renewals. Cloud-based solutions also provide insurers with real-time access to policy information, enabling seamless task management and improved service delivery to policyholders. Claims processing is another area where cloud-based solutions play a critical role. Insurers can automate and streamline the claims process by leveraging cloud-based claims management software from submission to settlement. These solutions facilitate efficient communication with policyholders, expedite claims processing, and minimize errors, enhancing customer satisfaction and operational efficiency. Customer self-service portals powered by the cloud empower policyholders to manage their policies online, reducing reliance on intermediaries and enabling convenient self-service functionalities.

With cloud-based portals, policyholders can submit claims, make payments, and update their information independently, improving customer satisfaction and reducing the workload on customer support teams. Cloud-based analytics tools provide insurers with valuable insights derived from data analysis, enabling informed decision-making and strategic planning. These tools enable insurers to identify trends, assess risks, and optimize pricing strategies, enhancing their competitiveness in the market. By leveraging advanced analytics capabilities, insurers can gain deeper insights into customer behaviour, market trends, and emerging risks, driving business growth and innovation. Integration with telematics devices and IoT sensors enables insurers to offer usage-based insurance products personalized to individual policyholders' needs.

Cloud-based fraud detection solutions leverage advanced AI and ML algorithms to detect and prevent fraudulent activities in insurance claims. These solutions analyse vast amounts of data to identify suspicious patterns and anomalies, enabling insurers to mitigate financial losses and safeguard operations. By leveraging cloud-based fraud detection systems, insurers can enhance fraud detection capabilities and preserve the integrity of their business. Digital marketing tools powered by the cloud enable insurers to optimize marketing campaigns, target specific customer segments, and track sales performance. These solutions provide insights into customer preferences, behaviours, and interactions, enabling targeted marketing campaigns and improved customer engagement. Cloud-based marketing tools empower insurers to build stronger brand relationships, drive customer acquisition, and achieve business growth objectives. Cloud-based compliance and regulatory reporting systems streamline compliance management processes and ensure adherence to industry regulations and standards. These solutions automate data collection, analysis, and reporting, reducing the administrative burden on insurers and enhancing transparency and compliance. By leveraging cloud-based compliance solutions, insurers can mitigate regulatory risks, improve operational efficiency, and ensure compliance with evolving regulatory requirements. Document management systems powered by the cloud provide insurers with secure and centralized storage for critical documents and records. These solutions streamline document organization, retrieval, and version control, enhancing collaboration and workflow efficiency. Cloud-based document management systems enable insurers to improve data governance, mitigate risks, and ensure compliance with data protection regulations. Cloud-based collaboration tools facilitate remote work and enable seamless communication and collaboration among team members. These solutions support virtual meetings, document sharing, and project collaboration, fostering productivity and teamwork. By leveraging cloud-based collaboration tools, insurers can adapt to remote work environments, ensure business continuity, and maintain high operational efficiency. Cloud-based underwriting and risk assessment solutions leverage AI and ML technologies to automate risk assessment processes and optimize underwriting decisions. These solutions analyse vast amounts of data to evaluate risks, determine appropriate premium rates, and improve underwriting accuracy.

Insurers can enhance risk management capabilities by leveraging cloud-based underwriting solutions, streamlining processes, and driving profitability. Cloud-based CRM systems centralize customer data and enable insurers to deliver personalized services and experiences. These solutions provide insights into customer preferences, behaviours, and interactions, enabling targeted marketing campaigns and improved customer engagement. Cloud-based CRM systems empower insurers to build stronger customer relationships, drive retention, and increase lifetime value. Cloud-based disaster recovery capabilities enable insurers to quickly recover critical data and restore operations during a disaster or system failure. These solutions offer automated backups, failover, and recovery mechanisms, ensuring business continuity and data integrity. Insurers can mitigate risks, enhance resilience, and safeguard their operations and assets by leveraging cloud-based disaster recovery solutions.

Despite recognizing the importance of cloud technology, many insurers still have a long road ahead regarding full adoption. They must address critical risks and internal challenges to leverage cloud investments effectively and achieve increased agility and digital transformation goals. These include establishing a culture conducive to change, mitigating data security risks, and executing a comprehensive public cloud roadmap aligned with digital transformation initiatives. Insurance firms should take a holistic approach to maximize returns on cloud investments, focusing on key actions to drive success. Firstly, infusing cloud knowledge into board and business leadership ensures alignment with organizational objectives. Conducting readiness and maturity assessments helps gauge the organization's preparedness for cloud adoption and transformation. Building holistic cloud strategies centred around creating business value and defining clear success criteria further guides the implementation process. Establishing a dedicated cloud competence centre involving legal, risk management, compliance teams, and regulators ensure compliance with industry standards and regulations. Embracing robust change management practices facilitates smooth transitions and adoption of cloud technologies across the organization. Prioritizing data security and risk management safeguards sensitive information and minimizes potential threats. Designing a target operating model tailored to the cloud environment optimizes operational efficiency and resource allocation. Formalizing a cost management framework enables efficient resource utilization and cost optimization strategies. By embracing these actions and taking a comprehensive approach to cloud adoption, insurance companies can unlock the full potential of cloud technology and drive meaningful digital transformation within their organizations.

3.3.5 Data Analytics and Predictive Analytics

Data analytics involves collecting, processing, and analysing large data sets to uncover meaningful insights and trends. It encompasses various techniques and methodologies to extract valuable information from structured and unstructured data sources. Predictive analytics, a branch of data analytics, focuses on interpreting and analysing data to generate forecasts regarding future events, risks, and probabilities.

In the context of the insurance industry, predictive analytics is crucial in underwriting, claims management, risk assessment, and customer relationship management. Insurance companies leverage predictive analytics tools to collect data from many sources, including telematics, customer interactions, agent interactions, smart homes, and social media. By analysing this diverse dataset, insurers can better understand customer behaviour, preferences, and risks.

Predictive modelling in insurance is a key application of predictive analytics, wherein techniques such as data mining, statistics, artificial intelligence, machine learning, and deep learning are employed to analyse and comprehend large datasets. These models enable insurers to make informed predictions about future events, such as the likelihood of a customer filing a claim, the probability of a particular risk occurring, or the potential impact of external factors like natural disasters or economic fluctuations.

One of the significant advantages of predictive analytics in insurance is its ability to improve decision-making processes and operational efficiency. By leveraging predictive models, insurers can optimize underwriting processes, identify high-risk policies or customers, and allocate resources more effectively. For example, predictive modelling can help insurers accurately assess the level of risk associated with a particular policyholder, allowing them to adjust premiums accordingly or take preventive measures to mitigate potential losses. Predictive analytics enables insurers to anticipate and prepare for future changes or disruptions in the market. For instance, the COVID-19 crisis highlighted the importance of predictive modelling in helping insurers anticipate shifts in customer behaviour, market dynamics, and risk profiles. By utilizing "what-if" modelling techniques, insurers can simulate different scenarios and evaluate the potential impact of changes in their business strategies or market conditions.

The strategic incorporation of data analytics has emerged as a pivotal strategy for leading insurance providers, transforming their operational frameworks and redefining industry standards in risk assessment, customer satisfaction, and operational efficiency across the underwriting continuum. This shift in approach encompasses risk evaluation and proactive measures for loss prevention, marking a significant departure from traditional methodologies. These industry leaders are able to harness extensive repositories of third-party data from various domains, including environmental conditions, industry-specific metrics, geographical indicators, governmental records, and more. With agile infrastructures in place, they demonstrate agility in acquiring, validating, managing, and iteratively leveraging this data within their analytical frameworks, enabling swift and informed responses to the ever-evolving dynamics of the market landscape (Javanmardian et al., 2021).

For example, Allstate Insurance, established in 1931 as the insurance arm of Sears Roebucks, has proactively embraced data integration into its business operations. In contrast to Sears' failure to adapt to the digital age, Allstate has demonstrated resilience and innovation, positioning itself as the second-largest provider of property and casualty insurance in the United States. The company's ambitious "D3" organization embodies its commitment to a data-driven analytics journey, focusing on the three core pillars: Data, Discovery, and Decision Science. This organization, comprising 300 individuals, is structured around horizontal activities such as Data Strategy, Technology, and Analytics Center of Excellence, supporting vertical business functions like product development, claims processing, and marketing. The Analytics Center of Excellence within Allstate leads transformative analytical initiatives, leveraging partnerships with universities to educate the company's workforce on the potential of analytics and Artificial Intelligence. Collaborations with institutions like Northwestern University have led to groundbreaking initiatives, including applying AI techniques to analyse policyholder interactions and predict policy renewals, enhancing the overall customer experience. Data and analytics permeate every facet of Allstate's operations, enabling the company to derive actionable insights from vast amounts of free-form text and voice data, informing strategic decisions and enhancing customer satisfaction.

One notable innovation by Allstate is the QuickFoto Claim initiative, which enables customers to submit collision photographs through the Allstate Mobile App, streamlines the claims process, and enhances customer convenience. This represents a significant shift towards digital transformation and automation within the insurance industry. Moreover, Allstate leverages advanced analytics to drive product development and pricing decisions, operating its Analytics Center of Excellence as a shared service to accelerate the adoption of analytics across business units. By deploying "analytics sandboxes," Allstate explores new data sources and expands its data collection capabilities, driving innovation and agility.

Allstate's D3 organization relies on a robust data ecosystem to quantify business benefits and prioritize data activities that deliver the greatest value to the firm. In the face of competitive threats from tech giants like Amazon and FinTech solutions like Lemonade, Allstate remains committed to building rich data and analytics capabilities within an elegant, highly agile environment. Allstate demonstrates that an 87-year-old insurance company can adapt and compete in the digital age by embracing innovation and leveraging data as a strategic asset. As the company motto suggests, "The Good Hands Are Doing More Than Ever Before," highlighting Allstate's dedication to innovation, customer service, and data-driven excellence in the insurance industry (Bean, 2018).

Some decentralized insurance platforms, such as Ethos Life, Qover, Kin, and Boost, also used data analytics and predictive modelling in their operations. Ethos Life uses predictive analytics technology to underwrite the policy based on self-reported data verified with the person's medical and pharmaceutical records. The insurance commissioner has validated all the data used to underwrite the policy for underwriting purposes. That allows Ethos to issue life insurance on the spot. Ethos also eliminated the commission model, enabling it to put customers in products that match their needs regardless of how much it will make. Fintech partners with large insurance carriers, including Assurity Life Insurance Company and Banner Life Insurance Company, a Legal & General America subsidiary, to issue the policies (Fuscaldo, 2019).

3.3.6 Internet of Things

Integrating IoT into insurance marks a transformative shift in how the industry approaches risk management. This strategic amalgamation of real-time data sourced from IoT devices with decentralized insurance structures empowers the sector with advanced capabilities for precise risk assessment, dynamic pricing strategies, and streamlined claims processing. Key IoT devices in this integration include sensors, wearables, and telematics devices, which actively collect and transmit real-time data from insured assets like homes and vehicles. This paradigm shift is evident across various insurance sectors, each adopting IoT integration to revolutionize their offerings.

In auto insurance, telematics devices have become pivotal tools for monitoring driving behaviour. This innovation translates into tangible benefits for policyholders, with incentives such as discounts for safe driving practices. Leading insurance companies, including Progressive Snapshot and Allstate's Drivewise, leverage IoT data from telematics devices to tailor auto insurance rates based on individual driving habits. This personalized approach aligns insurance costs more closely with actual risk and fosters a culture of responsible driving. Property insurance has embraced the potential of IoT by integrating smart home devices, resulting in reduced premiums and enhanced risk prevention. Collaborations such as that between Liberty Mutual and Nest exemplify this trend. By partnering with Nest, a prominent provider of smart home devices, Liberty Mutual extends discounts to policyholders who adopt these devices. Smart thermostats, smoke detectors, and security cameras create safer home environments and a more accurate risk assessment. This data-driven approach allows for personalized premium discounts, reflecting policyholders' proactive investment in smart home technology.

In health insurance, wearables have become integral to monitoring health metrics, promoting preventive measures, and encouraging a healthy lifestyle. Oscar Health, a technology-driven health insurance company, illustrates this integration by providing members with free Misfit fitness trackers. Members are incentivized to sync their health data with the Oscar app, earning rewards for achieving daily step goals. This initiative encourages physical activity and contributes to a comprehensive understanding of individuals' health. The collected data enables insurers to implement personalized and preventive health measures, transforming the traditional health insurance model. Commercial insurance has reaped substantial benefits from Industrial IoT, particularly in reducing downtime and operational risks. Zurich Insurance Group stands out as an example, leveraging IoT to offer enhanced risk management solutions to manufacturing, construction, and logistics businesses. Integrating IoT sensors into industrial processes allows Zurich to tailor policies addressing specific operational challenges. This proactive approach reduces the likelihood of disruptions and enhances overall resilience in commercial operations.

Agriculture insurance has witnessed a transformation by integrating IoT devices like soil sensors and drones. These technologies provide data-driven coverage and compensation for weather-related losses. Agriculture insurers can offer farmers more accurate and timely coverage by actively monitoring soil conditions and weather patterns through IoT devices, mitigating risks associated with unpredictable weather events. Life insurance has incorporated wearable safety devices to improve risk assessment and facilitate timely assistance. The data collected from these wearables contributes to more accurately evaluating an individual's risk profile, allowing life insurers to tailor coverage plans accordingly. Wearable safety devices also facilitate timely assistance in emergencies, enhancing the overall value proposition of life insurance. Travel insurance has embraced IoT devices for better risk assessment during travel, offering tailored coverage for specific conditions. This integration allows travel insurers to assess risks more accurately, considering location, weather conditions, and specific activities planned during the trip. By leveraging IoT data, travel insurance providers can offer travellers more personalized and relevant coverage options, enhancing the overall customer experience. Commercial property insurance rewards businesses with smart building technologies, enhancing risk management and reducing insurance costs. Companies that invest in smart building technologies can receive incentives and reduced premiums from insurers. These technologies, including IoT-enabled sensors and automation systems, contribute to better risk prevention and management. Insurers, in turn, benefit from a reduced likelihood of claims and losses, fostering a mutually beneficial relationship with business clients.

These examples illustrate how IoT integration contributes to personalized, data-driven, risk-aware insurance offerings across various sectors. The benefits extend to insurers and policyholders, fostering a collaborative and preventive approach to risk management. Real-time data from IoT devices enables dynamic risk assessment, allowing insurers to adapt coverage and premiums based on current risk factors. Additionally, behavioural analytics derived from IoT data offer insights into policyholders' habits, facilitating more informed risk assessments and personalized premium structures. The advantages of IoT integration in decentralized insurance are substantial. It provides precision in risk assessment, contributes to risk prevention through early warnings, enables the customization of policies based on monitored behaviours, and accelerates claims processing through smart contract automation.

Moreover, blockchain technology enhanced the security and integrity of the vast amounts of data IoT devices generate. It provides a tamper-resistant and transparent record for insurance-related data. Moreover, smart contracts are programmed to automate predefined actions based on the data received from IoT devices, facilitating processes like policy adjustments, premium discounts, or claims processing. However, challenges and considerations arise in integrating IOT, including concerns about data privacy due to extensive data collection. Ensuring compliance with regulations becomes crucial. The standardization and interoperability of IoT devices also become essential for seamless integration across different ecosystems.

Additionally, the susceptibility of IoT devices to cybersecurity threats necessitates robust security measures. Hence, IoT integration in decentralized insurance fosters a data-driven, responsive, preventive insurance model. It enhances risk management, improves customer experiences, and drives innovation. As the IoT ecosystem evolves, its integration into decentralized insurance promises to create a more resilient and adaptive insurance landscape.

3.3.6.1 On-Demand Insurance: Leveraging IoT for Real-Time, Personalized Coverage

On-demand insurance, coupled with the transformative capabilities of the IoT, brings many benefits that redefine the insurance landscape, creating a win–win scenario for insurers and policyholders. On-demand insurance allows individuals to tailor coverage precisely to their immediate needs. The flexibility to activate and deactivate insurance as necessary aligns with the dynamic nature of modern lifestyles, offering a level of customization that traditional insurance models often lack. This is particularly advantageous for individuals engaged in activities with varying levels of risk, such as travel, recreation, or short-term projects. The flexibility of On-Demand Insurance caters to a broader market by accommodating diverse coverage needs. By leveraging IoT technology for real-time data, insurers can seamlessly adapt to the changing requirements of policyholders, fostering a responsive and customer-centric approach. In the on-demand insurance market, various players leverage digital technology, big data, computing power, and data analytics to provide coverage for specific periods or episodes (Kulia, 2023). The spectrum of risks covered by on-demand insurance spans travel and recreation, mobility, valuable belongings, equipment, electronics, small businesses, gig workers, and healthcare (KPMG, 2017).

Take, for instance, InsureandGo, a UK-based insurance carrier specializing in travel insurance that covers various sports and activities during holidays. Travellers can conveniently purchase policies online, specifying the type of coverage needed (annual multi-trip or single trip) and selecting the duration. Another notable example is Cuvva, a UK-based car insurer specializing in providing car insurance for durations ranging from one hour to 28 days. The pricing for their one-hour car insurance, starting at £8.70, is influenced by factors such as the buyer's age, driving duration, claims history, current location, and the time of day when coverage is required. Thimble offers on-demand coverage for small businesses and specific professions, including general liability, professional liability, business equipment, commercial property, and data protection. San Francisco-based insurer Trov has introduced a user-friendly app allowing consumers to buy short-term insurance on-demand, protecting against loss or damage to sports equipment and computers. Users can effortlessly activate or deactivate coverage based on specific activities like riding an expensive bike or bringing a laptop on vacation.

The on-demand insurance model not only brings significant convenience and affordability to consumers but also aligns seamlessly with the evolving landscape of IoT. Data from wearables and telematics devices, integral components of IoT, enable risks to be quantified with heightened accuracy and dynamism throughout a contract. This technological integration has spurred discussions on discrimination, as "bad" risks may face higher premiums, while "good" risks enjoy discounts or lower premiums. This intersection of on-demand insurance and IoT technology signifies a paradigm shift in the insurance industry, offering consumers personalized, real-time coverage precisely when needed, redefining the traditional insurance model.

3.3.6.2 Categories of On-Demand Insurance: Usage-Based and Episodic Insurance

On-demand Insurance is a relatively new phenomenon categorized as usage-based and episodic Insurance. However, these terms are often used interchangeably. Yet, there are notable differences between these emerging concepts.

Usage-Based Insurance: Usage-Based Insurance, commonly known as UBI, represents a dynamic form of coverage tailored to an individual's needs and behaviours. Unlike traditional insurance models, UBI incorporates a personalized approach, with premiums determined based on an individual's usage patterns. Telematics-based auto insurance is a prime example of UBI, where insurers equip policyholders with telematics devices installed in their vehicles or a smartphone app that tracks driving behaviour. This integration of IoT allows for real-time monitoring and collection of data on safer driving habits, such as maintaining safe speeds and avoiding sudden braking. Safer drivers are then rewarded with lower insurance premiums, fostering a more personalized and fair approach to coverage.

In usage-based insurance, the contractual relationship between the insured and the insurance company persists continuously, even when the insured item is inactive. This component is often integrated into traditional insurance coverage. For instance, basic liability and theft insurance may always remain in force in usage-based car insurance. Additional liability and collision coverage premiums are calculated based on usage factors, such as the number of kilometres driven and driving habits. Metromile is an exemplary company offering this type of coverage, where customers pay a base rate covering the vehicle when parked and not in use and an additional per-mile rate reflecting the actual distance driven. This IoT-enabled approach enables drivers who infrequently use their vehicles to save significantly on insurance costs.

Integrating IoT technology in usage-based insurance transforms the pricing model and enhances risk assessment through real-time data collection, providing a more accurate representation of an individual's driving habits. This innovative approach to insurance empowers policyholders with the flexibility to pay for insurance precisely in proportion to their actual usage, making UBI an appealing option for occasional drivers or those seeking cost-effective coverage.

Episodic Insurance: Episodic Insurance allows individuals to purchase coverage for specific events or periods when needed. Unlike traditional insurance policies, usually annual contracts, episodic insurance policies can be activated for a few hours, days, or weeks, depending on the specific need. In episodic insurance, the contract ends when the insurance is turned off. Customers can choose to turn on insurance from different providers at different times. The mode of activation can range from manual to automatic: coverage can be activated manually, recommended by a smart device and activated manually by the user, or activated automatically based on criteria like location, activity, or context. While this automatic mode of activation might be the future for car or embedded Insurance, it does not necessarily extend to all areas of on-demand Insurance.

One practical example of episodic Insurance is rental car coverage. When renting a car for a short period, individuals can purchase episodic Insurance to cover the rental duration. This approach offers a cost-effective and convenient solution, as it avoids purchasing an annual auto insurance policy for a temporary vehicle.

Another example of episodic Insurance is event-based coverage. Imagine someone planning a vacation and engaging in activities like snorkelling or zip-lining. They can obtain episodic insurance coverage for the days they will participate in these activities. This way, they are insured only during high-risk events and do not need continuous coverage when not engaged in such activities. Episodic Insurance is particularly popular in the sharing economy. For instance, individuals renting out their properties on short-term rental platforms like Airbnb can purchase episodic Insurance to cover the rental period.

Usage-Based Insurance and Episodic Insurance are two innovative forms of on-demand Insurance that cater to policyholders' evolving needs and preferences. UBI utilizes telematics technology to reward safe driving behaviour with personalized premiums. At the same time, episodic Insurance offers flexibility and cost-effectiveness for individuals who only need insurance coverage for specific events or periods. These on-demand insurance models demonstrate how the insurance industry is adapting to technological advancements and providing tailored solutions that meet the diverse requirements of today's consumers. The integration of IoT technology amplifies the transformative potential of on-demand insurance. This integration makes real-time monitoring, data collection, and dynamic risk assessment possible. This evolution aligns with the broader trend of insurance adapting to technological advancements, providing tailored solutions that meet today's consumers' evolving needs and preferences.

3.3.6.3 Benefits and Ethical Challenges in On-Demand Insurance

On-demand insurance, situated at the nexus of innovation and adaptability, represents a paradigm shift in the insurance landscape. Its integration with the IoT introduces a transformative dynamic that unfolds a myriad of benefits and ethical considerations, reshaping the contours of the industry.

One of the key benefits is the concept of instant coverage, which allows policyholders to access and activate insurance within minutes. This real-time responsiveness enhances customer experience and empowers individuals with unparalleled convenience and peace of mind. Moreover, on-demand Insurance upends the traditional one-size-fits-all approach, offering unparalleled flexibility and customization for policyholders. Instead of committing to long-term policies, individuals can tailor insurance coverage to specific events or periods, paying only for the necessary protection. This flexible pricing model ensures that individuals pay only for the duration and extent of coverage they require, making on-demand Insurance more cost-effective, especially for those who do not need constant or extended coverage.

Beyond convenience and cost-efficiency, on-demand Insurance can serve as an effective mechanism to encourage responsible risk management behaviours. With coverage activated when specific events occur, policyholders are incentivized to safeguard against potential risks proactively. This aligns with the broader insurance industry's goal of promoting risk mitigation and prevention, benefiting insurers and policyholders.

However, amidst its promising prospects, on-demand Insurance also presents complex ethical challenges that warrant careful consideration. As on-demand Insurance facilitated by IOT allows for dynamic and real-time pricing, ethical dilemmas arise in ensuring transparent and justified pricing decisions. Policyholders must comprehend the factors influencing pricing and be informed about how their actions can affect premiums. Insurers must diligently avoid discriminatory practices based on age, gender, ethnicity, or socioeconomic status. Fair and transparent underwriting guidelines are essential to mitigate these ethical challenges, ensuring that policyholders are treated fairly and equitably.

Like other innovative insurance models, such as peer-to-peer and parametric Insurance, on-demand Insurance relies on vast amounts of personal data for risk assessment and pricing. Using such data raises significant ethical concerns concerning individual privacy and data security. Insurers must prioritize robust data security measures and transparent data handling practices to protect policyholders' sensitive information from misuse or unauthorized access.

Additionally, the real-time nature of on-demand Insurance can raise questions about the accuracy and reliability of risk evaluations. Ethical dilemmas arise when policyholders lack complete information about the factors influencing the assessment of their risk and the potential outcomes. Clear and transparent communication about the underwriting and pricing process becomes imperative to avoid misunderstandings and disputes during the claims process.

To address these ethical challenges, on-demand insurers must prioritize fairness, transparency, and inclusivity. Implementing clear policies and guidelines for risk assessment, ensuring data privacy, and actively engaging with the community are critical steps to build trust and mitigate ethical challenges. Regular reviews of underwriting and pricing practices can help identify and rectify potential biases, contributing to a more sustainable and ethical on-demand insurance landscape.

3.4 Conclusion

Decentralized insurance platforms driven by cutting-edge technologies like blockchain, machine intelligence, and digital platforms stand as formidable game-changers, challenging the traditional norms of insurance operations. Decentralized platforms foster heightened transparency and efficiency, eliminating the need for intermediaries and traditional centralized authorities. Blockchain technology, in particular, is pivotal in ensuring trust and security within the decentralized ecosystem. Moreover, the integration of machine intelligence and digital platforms amplifies the transformative potential of decentralized insurance. Machine learning algorithms enable sophisticated data analysis, empowering platforms to assess risks accurately, price policies competitively, and process claims efficiently. Digital platforms and mobile apps offer seamless user experiences, facilitating direct engagement between insurers and policyholders. These technological advancements streamline insurance operations and enhance user satisfaction and trust. Categorizing decentralized insurance platforms based on their approaches to managing on-chain and off-chain risks provides valuable insights into the diverse strategies adopted in modernizing insurance practices. Platforms specializing in on-chain risks offer coverage tailored to blockchain activities, addressing vulnerabilities such as smart contract bugs and hacking incidents. On the other hand, platforms focusing on off-chain risks extend coverage to real-world events like natural disasters, health issues, and liability claims. By catering to both on-chain and off-chain risks, decentralized platforms demonstrate versatility in addressing the evolving needs of insurance consumers.

Furthermore, the strategic alliances between traditional insurers and technology firms underscore the convergence of traditional and decentralized insurance models. Established insurers recognize the disruptive potential of decentralized platforms and seek to harness it through strategic collaborations. By leveraging blockchain and smart contracts, traditional insurers enhance operational efficiency, streamline claims processing, and explore innovative insurance products. These partnerships bridge the gap between tradition and innovation, fostering synergies that drive industry-wide transformation. Looking ahead, the future of decentralized insurance platforms appears promising, marked by continued innovation and widespread adoption. Through technological innovation, strategic partnerships, and regulatory collaboration, decentralized platforms are reshaping insurance operations enhancing transparency, efficiency, and user engagement. As the journey towards decentralized insurance continues, stakeholders must remain agile and collaborative to navigate the evolving landscape successfully.

References

Accenture. (2023). *Reimagining insurance: The new cloud imperative*. Accessed on 6 March 2024 from https://www.accenture.com/content/dam/accenture/final/industry/insurance/document/Accenture-Reimagining-insurance-the-new-cloud-imperative.pdf#zoom=40

Anchen, J. (2022). *Machine intelligence in insurance*. Accessed on 4 February 2024 from https://www.swissre.com/risk-knowledge/advancing-societal-benefits-digitalisation/machine-intelligence-in-insurance.html

AWS. (2020). *Boost unlocks the value of customer data with AWS*. Accessed on 4 May 2024 from https://aws.amazon.com/solutions/case-studies/boost/

Balasubramanian, R., Libarikian, A., & McElhaney, D. (2021). *Insurance 2030—The impact of AI on the future of insurance*. Accessed on 8 January 2024 from https://www.mckinsey.com/industries/financial-services/our-insights/insurance-2030-the-impact-of-ai-on-the-future-of-insurance

Bean, R. (2018). Allstate's data-driven business transformation initiative. *Forbes*. Accessed on 6 May 2024 from https://www.forbes.com/sites/ciocentral/2018/11/11/allstates-data-driven-business-transformation-initiative/?sh=57ba3f764d9e

Betz, S., & Payne, C. (2021). How insurers can transform by adopting public cloud. *Ernst and Young*. Accessed on 16 March 2024 from https://www.ey.com/en_gl/insights/financial-services/emeia/how-insurers-can-transform-by-adopting-public-cloud

Biener, C., Eling, M. & Wirfs, J. H. (2014). Insurability of Cyber Risk: An Empirical Analysis. *The Geneva Papers*, 1– 28.

Chekriy, S., & Mukhin Y. (2018). Blockchain platform for insurance-related products. *Glass Cube*, 1–33. https://www.ico196.com/uploads/ico_whitepaper/153552952982i-chain.net.wpaper_rev_005.pdf

Crawford, S., Meadows, I., & Piesse, D. (2016). Blockchain technology as a platform for digitization: Implications for the insurance industry. *Viitattu*, 2. http://www.ey.com/Publication/vwLUAssets/EY-blockchain-technology-as-a-platform-fordigitization/$FILE/EY-blockchain-technology-as-a-platform-for-digitization.pdf

Daley, S. A. M. (2020). *Nine companies using blockchain to revolutionize insurance*. Accessed on 16 March 2024 from https://builtin.com/blockchain/blockchain-insurance-companies

Deloitte Digital. (2017). *From mystery to mastery: Unlocking the business value of artificial intelligence in the insurance industry*. Accessed on 6 May 2024 from https://www2.deloitte.com/content/dam/Deloitte/xe/Documents/financial-services/Artificial-Intelligence-in-Insurance.pdf

Deloitte. (2016). *Blockchain in insurance Turning a buzzword into a breakthrough for health and life insurers*. Accessed on 4 May 2024 from https://www2.deloitte.com/us/en/pages/life-sciences-and-health-care/articles/blockchain-in-insurance.html

Deloitte. (2016). *How robotics and cognitive automation will transform the insurance industry*. Accessed on 4 May 2024 from https://www2.deloitte.com/us/en/pages/operations/articles/robotic-process-automation-insurance.html

Fuscaldo, D. (2019). *Life insurance startup Ethos valued at more than $400 million after series C raise*. Accessed on 6 May 2024 from https://www.forbes.com/sites/donnafuscaldo/2019/08/27/life-insurance-startup-ethos-valued-at-more-than-400-million-after-series-c-raise/?sh=13facfd53e61

Gatteschi, V., Lamberti, F., Demartini, C., Pranteda, C., & Santamaría, V. (2018). Blockchain and smart contracts for insurance: Is the technology mature enough? *Future Internet, 10*(2), 20.

Google Cloud. (2024). *AXA Switzerland: Future-proofing the insurance business to help clients in a changing world*. Accessed on 6 May 2024 from https://cloud.google.com/customers/axa-switzerland

Grima, S., Spiteri, J., & Romānova, I. (2020). A STEEP framework analysis of the key factors impacting the use of blockchain technology in the insurance industry. *The Geneva Papers on Risk and Insurance-Issues and Practice, 45*, 398–425.

IAIS. (2023). *Regulation and supervision of AI/ML in insurance: A thematic review*. Accessed on 6 May 2024 from https://www.iaisweb.org/uploads/2023/12/Regulation-and-supervision-of-AI-ML-a-thematic-review.pdf

Javanmardian, K., Ramezani, S., Srivastava, A., & Talischi, C. (2021). *How data and analytics are redefining excellence in P&C underwriting*. Accessed on 6 May 2024 from https://www.mckinsey.com/industries/financial-services/our-insights/how-data-and-analytics-are-redefining-excellence-in-p-and-c-underwriting

Kar, A. K., & Navin, L. (2021). Diffusion of blockchain in insurance industry: An analysis through the review of academic and trade literature. *Telematics and Informatics, 58*, 101532.

KPMG. (2017). *Will on-demand insurance become mainstream?* Accessed on 19 August 2023. https://assets.kpmg.com/content/dam/kpmg/uk/pdf/2017/09/will-on-demand-insurance-become-mainstream.pdf

Kulia, S. (2023). On-demand insurance: The rise of customizable, usage-based coverage. *The Times of India*. Accessed 19 August 2023. https://timesofindia.indiatimes.com/blogs/voices/on-demand-insurance-the-rise-of-customizable-usage-based-coverage/

Kumar, P., Taneja, S., Özen, E., & Singh, S. (2023). Artificial Intelligence and machine learning in insurance: A bibliometric analysis. In P. Tyagi, S. Grima, K. Sood, B. Balamurugan, E. Özen, & T. Eleftherios (Eds.), *Smart analytics, Artificial Intelligence and sustainable performance management in a global digitalised economy* (*Contemporary studies in economic and financial analysis*, Vol. 110A, pp. 191–202). Emerald Publishing Limited. https://doi.org/10.1108/S1569-37592023000110A010

Ladva, P., & Grasso, A. (2023). *Benefits and use cases of AI in insurance*. Accessed on 6 May 2024 from https://www.swissre.com/risk-knowledge/advancing-societal-benefits-digitalisation/opportunities-ai-insurance.html

Mertz, E. (2018). *Slice launches its on-demand digital insurer-as-a-service*. Accessed on 6 May 2024 from https://blog.slice.is/icsondemand

NAIC. (2024). *Artificial Intelligence*. Accessed on 6 March 2024 from https://content.naic.org/cipr-topics/artificial-intelligence

Neale, F. R., Drake, P. P., & Konstantopoulos, T. (2020). InsurTech and the disruption of the insurance industry. *Journal of Insurance Issues, 43*(2), 64–96.

Shetty, A., Shetty, A. D., Pai, R. Y., Rao, R. R., Bhandary, R., Shetty, J., Nayak, S., Keerthi Dinesh, T., & Dsouza, K. J. (2022). Block chain application in insurance services: A systematic review of the evidence. *SAGE Open*. https://doi.org/10.1177/2158244022107987

The Economic Times. (2017). *HDFC Life brings country's first life insurance Chatbot with Haptik*. Accessed on 6 October 2023 from https://economictimes.indiatimes.com//hdfc-life-brings-countrys-first-life-insurance-chatbot-with-haptik/articleshow/57518145.cms?utm_source=contentofinterest&utm_medium=text&utm_campaign=cppst

Wang, Y., & Kogan, A. (2018). Designing confidentiality-preserving Blockchain-based transaction processing systems. *International Journal of Accounting Information Systems, 30*, 1–18.

Yang, W., & Zhou, J. (2021). Service innovation of insurance data based on Cloud Computing in the era of Big Data. *Complexity*. https://doi.org/10.1155/2021/2303129

Yong, W. (2023). Is artificial intelligence relevant to insurance? *IBM*. Accessed on 6 May 2024 from https://www.ibm.com/blog/is-artificial-intelligence-relevant-to-insurance/

Zhao, L. (2020). The analysis of application, key issues and the future development trend of blockchain technology in the insurance industry. *American Journal of Industrial and Business Management, 10*(02), 305–314. https://doi.org/10.4236/ajibm.2020.102019

Zurich. (2021). *Robotics take the tedium from policy administration—and give back efficiency*. Accessed on 16 October 2024 from https://www.zurich.com/en/commercial-insurance/sustainability-and-insights/commercial-insurance-risk-insights/robotics-take-the-tedium-from-policy-administration-and-give-back-efficiency

CHAPTER 4

Regulatory, Economic, and Political Challenges for Decentralized Insurance: A Global Perspective

4.1 Regulatory Frameworks and Legal Structures for Insurance

The insurance industry operates under a stringent regulatory framework worldwide. Regulations cover capital requirements, investment practices, reinsurance agreements, and loss reserve adequacy to ensure insurers can meet future claims. Additionally, the design, pricing, and sales of insurance products are regulated to protect consumers. According to public interest theory, this regulation aims to serve the public good by enhancing safety, improving social welfare, and preventing market failures. Skipper (1997) asserts that government intervention is necessary when actual or potential market failures threaten public welfare, provided that such intervention can mitigate these failures. Market failures can stem from factors such as market power concentration, information asymmetries, externalities, or free rider issues. However, in the highly competitive insurance markets, concerns about market power are minimal.

Information asymmetry is a well-documented issue in traditional insurance. Insured parties often possess more information about their risks than insurers, leading to adverse selection and moral hazard problems. Adverse selection occurs when individuals know about risks and seek insurance coverage when anticipating higher potential losses. In this case, insurers may struggle to accurately assess risk, resulting in suboptimal

N. Singhal et al., *Potential, Risks, and Ethical Implications of Decentralized Insurance*, Technology, Work and Globalization,
https://doi.org/10.1007/978-981-97-5894-4_4

pricing and potentially unsustainable business models. For example, an individual with a pre-existing health condition might actively pursue health insurance, knowing that the insurer might not be fully aware of their higher-risk profile. This selective participation undermines the principle of risk sharing, leading to a concentration of higher-risk individuals within the insured pool. Moral hazard, another consequence of information asymmetry, arises when the insured party alters their behaviour because they know they are protected by insurance (Sun et al., 2020). This behaviour change can involve taking risks that they otherwise wouldn't if they did not have insurance coverage. For instance, a person with comprehensive auto insurance might drive more recklessly, knowing that the insurer would bear the financial consequences of an accident. The implications of information asymmetry extend to the insurers, who may grapple with substantial challenges in accurately assessing risks. The lack of complete and transparent information hampers the ability of insurers to make informed decisions, leading to suboptimal pricing. This suboptimal pricing affects insurers' profitability and has broader implications for the sustainability of business models within the industry. In this context, the role of a proper regulator becomes paramount. A regulator serves as a crucial entity to mitigate the adverse effects of information asymmetry by implementing and enforcing regulations that promote transparency, fairness, and ethical conduct within the insurance market. Regulatory frameworks can stipulate disclosure requirements, ensuring that insured parties provide accurate and comprehensive information about their risks. By doing so, regulators contribute to a more level playing field, reducing the potential for adverse selection and moral hazard.

Within the insurance framework, externalities present profound challenges to traditional models that are predominantly structured to evaluate and address risks at an individual or organizational level. These externalities embody the unintended and often widespread consequences of insured events, transcending the immediate parties involved to impact society or the environment on a larger scale. A concrete illustration of this challenge could be a major industrial accident causing environmental harm or a natural disaster with extensive implications, where the repercussions extend well beyond the directly affected entities. The inherent complexity of externalities lies in their diffuse and frequently unpredictable nature, creating a substantial obstacle for insurers in accurately quantifying and incorporating these broader social impacts into their risk assessment processes. Traditional insurance models, finely tuned to evaluate discrete risks, encounter significant hurdles when confronted with the intricacies of external effects. Unlike direct losses experienced by the insured party, externalities are inherently challenging to quantify, and they often involve unprecedented events that defy conventional modelling approaches. The reliance on historical data and actuarial models, which traditionally guide premium calculations, may prove inadequate when externalities come into play. The unpredictability and far-reaching consequences of these events make it challenging for insurers to establish fair and accurate premiums that genuinely reflect the true societal cost of an insured event. This inadequacy in pricing not only contributes to market inefficiencies but also poses a substantial threat to the financial viability of insurance companies. The ramifications of improperly pricing externalities extend beyond market inefficiencies to potential insolvency risks for insurers. If insurance companies consistently underestimate the broader social or environmental impacts of events, they may face financial losses that strain their financial resilience. This underscores the critical importance of a robust risk assessment framework that can effectively account for externalities and align premiums with the true societal costs of insured events. Regulations can stipulate incorporating external impact assessments into risk evaluation processes, ensuring that insurers account for the broader societal and environmental consequences of insured events. Through its oversight and enforcement mechanisms, a regulator becomes instrumental in creating a more resilient and sustainable insurance industry that can effectively navigate the complexities posed by externalities.

The free rider problem poses another persistent challenge in traditional insurance models, disrupting the fundamental principle of risk-sharing upon which these systems are built. This issue arises when individuals selectively seek insurance coverage precisely when they anticipate a need or imminent risk. In doing so, they exploit the protective benefits of insurance without contributing their fair share to the risk pool during periods of lower risk or when they don't anticipate needing coverage. The consequence is a distortion of the risk-sharing mechanism, as a subset of participants bears a disproportionate burden of the overall risk. This behaviour directly undermines the core principle of insurance, which relies on collectively sharing risks among all participants. When individuals strategically join the insurance pool only when they foresee a potential loss or claim, the risk pool becomes imbalanced. Those who consistently participate and contribute premiums throughout their lower-risk periods find themselves subsidizing the increased claims from opportunistic latecomers. This imbalance leads to adverse selection, as the risk pool becomes skewed towards higher-risk individuals, necessitating an adjustment in premiums to cover the heightened overall risk. The implications of the free rider problem extend beyond the immediate impact on risk-sharing dynamics. The increased claims and subsequent adjustment of premiums create a cycle that further exacerbates the problem. As premiums rise due to the adverse selection induced by free riders, active participants may find the insurance cost less attractive, potentially leading to a decline in overall participation. A regulator can play a pivotal role in mitigating the free rider problem by establishing and enforcing rules and regulations that promote fair and equitable participation. For instance, regulators can implement policies discouraging opportunistic behaviour, such as waiting until a need arises before seeking coverage. These policies may include penalties for latecomers or incentives for consistent and continuous participation. Furthermore, a regulator can advocate for transparency in insurance practices, ensuring that policies and premium calculations are communicated to all participants. This transparency fosters a sense of trust among participants, potentially reducing the incentive for free riding.

Asymmetric information, free rider issues, and externalities highlight the critical need for proactive regulation to ensure the financial stability of insurance companies. Prudential regulators are responsible for establishing and enforcing standards that maintain the proper functioning of the insurance market. The financial crisis of 2008 demonstrated that market discipline alone is insufficient to prevent market failure without regulatory oversight. This crisis revealed the necessity of financial transparency for effective market discipline and underscored the need for robust post-crisis regulations if proactive measures fail to prevent financial distress. Regulation must include corrective actions to avert insurer failures and the development of effective distress resolution plans. This might involve formalized solvency insurance. A well-implemented post-crisis regulatory framework reduces the likelihood of market failure by increasing participants' confidence in entering financial contracts, even in the presence of asymmetric information.

The regulatory framework for the global insurance industry is characterized by multifaceted requirements that collectively aim to ensure the stability, reliability, and financial robustness of insurance companies. These regulations issued various regulations, guidelines, and circulars that offer insights into diverse approaches and structures of insurance regulation across jurisdictions. Each regulation by the regulatory and supervisory authorities serves a distinct purpose and contributes to the overarching goals of safeguarding policyholders, maintaining market integrity, and fostering a resilient insurance sector. These requirements span licencing, capitalization, solvency, technical supervision, investment practices, and financial reporting.

Licencing requirements are the initial gateway, establishing stringent criteria and conditions for entities aspiring to be insurance providers. The attainment of a licence is contingent upon factors such as financial stability, professional competence, and adherence to regulatory guidelines. This meticulous licencing process functions as a protective mechanism, ensuring that only qualified and financially stable organizations gain entry into the market. The outcome is enhanced consumer protection, as policyholders are likelier to engage with reputable and secure insurance entities. Capitalization requirements constitute a fundamental pillar, mandating that insurance companies uphold a minimum level of capital to cover potential liabilities and unforeseen losses. These requirements, often formulated through risk-based approaches, play a pivotal role in fortifying insurers against financial vulnerabilities. The stipulated capitalization standards ensure the fulfilment of obligations to policyholders and act as a preventive measure against insolvency, contributing to the overall resilience of the insurance sector. Solvency requirements complement capitalization measures by ensuring insurers possess adequate financial resources to meet their obligations and operate robustly. Regulatory authorities employ sophisticated stress testing and risk assessment methodologies to evaluate insurers' solvency positions. Established solvency ratios serve as critical benchmarks, assuring financial stability and the ability to weather adverse scenarios. Technical supervision emerges as a cornerstone of effective regulation, involving continuous monitoring of insurers' operations, risk management practices, and compliance with regulatory standards. Regulatory authorities conduct regular examinations and audits to scrutinize underwriting practices, investment strategies, and overall risk management frameworks. This meticulous oversight is instrumental in maintaining the insurance market's integrity and upholding prudence standards. Regulations governing insurers' investment practices strike a delicate balance between risk-taking and prudent investment. Regulatory bodies set guidelines that specify permissible types of assets for investment, ensuring insurers maintain a diversified and risk-conscious investment portfolio. This regulatory intervention aims to mitigate investment activity risks and safeguard policyholder funds. Regulatory authorities meticulously review submitted financial statements, fostering market confidence and reinforcing adherence to regulatory standards.

4.1.1 *Licencing and Authorization*

Pursuing a licence is a prerequisite for insurance companies operating worldwide. This imperative licensure is typically granted by competent supervisory authorities, which may vary in form, ranging from ministries to independent administrative bodies, depending on the jurisdiction. Notably, establishing insurance companies universally hinges on obtaining a licence sanctioned by the insurance supervisory authority. While this process is common across nations, the specifics of licencing requirements exhibit regional disparities. Insurance companies must comply with several requirements to obtain a licence, such as predefined insurance contracts and terms and conditions. Across diverse nations, insurers are universally mandated to assume a recognized legal persona, commonly adopting the form of a legal entity. This legal form, however, varies extensively from country to country (Castelluccio, 2022). For instance, in the United States, a diverse array of "town mutuals" or "county mutuals" specializes in covering agricultural property risks. Contrastingly, within the European Union, mutual or cooperative insurance entities find common ground, particularly in sectors such as livestock, small vessels, and burial benefits. The spectrum of permissible legal forms extends to Asian countries, with unique models such as Singapore's "societies," Chinese Taipei's cooperatives, and Vietnam's authorization of mutual associations. This intricate regulatory tapestry governing legal forms underscores a nuanced interplay between global standards, regional preferences, and the ever-evolving nature of insurance markets (Gatteschi et al., 2018).

Moving towards the procedural aspects of licencing, most countries, especially those in three major regions, necessitate submitting a comprehensive business plan. The business plan of operations outlines the risks intended to be covered, proposed reinsurance, information on initial-year expenses, and the financial resources available. Specific requirements related to business plans vary in Asia, where countries like Hong Kong,

Laos, Macao, Malaysia, the Philippines, and Sri Lanka mandate a business plan for the first three years. Chinese Taipei, Thailand, and Vietnam require plans for the first five years.

Within the managerial domain, a critical facet of insurance regulations is the "fit and proper" requirement employed by several nations to ensure the credibility and proficiency of insurance company management. In some countries, for example, Hong Kong, Macao, Malaysia, Singapore, Chinese Taipei, and Vietnam, stringent legal prerequisites dictate that company managers must meet specific standards of reputability and competence. The "fit and proper" criterion becomes a cornerstone, safeguarding the interests of policyholders and fostering a robust insurance sector.

The licencing regulation also extends to the specific supervision of share ownership, aiming to prevent any reduction in the capital base of insurance companies. In the European Union, insurance companies, with few exemptions for foreign entities, must notify the competent authority of the identity of direct and indirect shareholders holding qualified participations. Belgium, the Czech Republic, Germany, Italy, Japan, Korea, Luxembourg, Mexico, the Netherlands, Poland, Portugal, Sweden, the United Kingdom, and the United States require approval of the list of shareholders. In Asia, Macao emphasizes shareholders being "of good repute," some countries, such as Bulgaria, Croatia, Latvia, Slovenia, and Ukraine, require a list of principal shareholders and particulars of their stake in the company.

Another important licencing regulation is reinsurance arrangement, which influences global insurance companies' resilience and risk management strategies. Some nations, including Australia, Germany, Italy, Japan, Luxembourg, Mexico, Poland, Sweden, the United Kingdom, and the United States, mandate regulatory approval for reinsurance plans, necessitating insurers to craft and navigate these plans through a stringent process meticulously. In contrast, countries like Belgium, the Czech Republic, Finland, France, Hungary, Iceland, Norway, Portugal, Spain, Switzerland, and Turkey adopt an informative submission approach, acknowledging supervisory interest in understanding risk mitigation strategies without a formal approval mandate. In the Asian landscape, jurisdictions like Macao and Hong Kong exemplify meticulous adequacy checks by supervisory authorities on reinsurance programs, emphasizing regulatory oversight to ensure the financial stability of insurance operations.

4.1.2 Capital Adequacy and Solvency

The minimum capital required for licencing must be available the whole time the company carries on business. Minimum solvency requirements are the mandated levels of capital and financial reserves that insurance companies must maintain to guarantee their ability to fulfil policyholder claims and remain solvent. These requirements are established by regulatory authorities across various countries, with variations influenced by factors such as the type of insurance business, associated risks, and specific regulatory frameworks (Castelluccio, 2022). Each country adopts a unique approach to ensure insurers maintain sufficient financial reserves to meet policyholder claims and guarantee solvency.

In the United States, solvency requirements are decentralized and regulated at the state level, with each state adopting the National Association of Insurance Commissioners (NAIC) Risk-Based Capital (RBC) model. The United Kingdom adheres to the European Union's Solvency II Directive, emphasizing a comprehensive risk-based approach. Germany follows suit with Solvency II, emphasizing risk-sensitive calculations for solvency requirements. Japan employs a solvency margin overseen by the Financial Services Agency (FSA), reflecting a balance between fostering competition and ensuring financial security. China adopts a risk-based approach, considering market, credit, and underwriting risks in determining solvency requirements. India sets solvency norms under the Insurance Regulatory and Development Authority of India (IRDAI), aligning with the country's unique market dynamics. Canada's provinces each have their regulatory framework, utilizing a risk-sensitive approach to set solvency requirements. Australia employs a risk-based capital framework, which emphasizes assessing various risks in determining solvency. France complies with the Solvency II Directive, ensuring a risk-sensitive evaluation of solvency needs. In South America, Brazil follows solvency regulations outlined by the Superintendence of Private Insurance (SUSEP), aligning with the country's market conditions. South Africa utilizes a risk-sensitive approach to set solvency requirements, considering factors like market and underwriting risks. European countries like the Netherlands, Sweden, and Switzerland adhere to the Solvency II Directive, employing risk-based approaches to regulate solvency requirements. Turkey utilizes a risk-based model, aligning with the country's regulatory priorities. Russia adopts a risk-sensitive approach, reflecting the country's unique economic conditions. Asian countries such as Singapore,

Italy, and Mexico adopt risk-based approaches tailored to specific market conditions. Switzerland implements risk-sensitive solvency requirements, aligning with the country's financial and regulatory landscape. Sweden adheres to the Solvency II Directive, employing a risk-based approach. In the Middle East, Saudi Arabia utilizes a risk-sensitive approach, considering factors like market and credit risks to set solvency requirements for insurers. Poland adheres to the Solvency II Directive, ensuring a comprehensive and risk-sensitive assessment of solvency needs. Greece employs a risk-based approach, considering specific risks associated with the Greek insurance market in determining solvency standards. These examples highlight the diverse methodologies employed globally to assess minimum solvency requirements, showcasing the adaptability of regulatory frameworks to each country's unique economic, market, and risk conditions.

4.1.3 Underwriting and Pricing Standards

Underwriting and pricing standards regulations encompass various guidelines and requirements to ensure fairness, transparency, and financial stability within the insurance industry. These standards typically cover several key areas. Insurance companies are expected to establish robust risk assessment methodologies and underwriting criteria to evaluate the potential risks associated with insuring individuals, businesses, or assets. This includes assessing age, health status, occupation, location, and past claims history to determine appropriate coverage and premiums. Insurers must adopt transparent pricing practices, providing clear explanations of premium calculations and factors influencing pricing decisions. Pricing should be based on actuarial principles and risk assessment, ensuring fairness and consistency across policyholders. Discriminatory pricing based on factors such as gender, race, or ethnicity is often prohibited from promoting equity and non-discrimination. The supervisory authority's role is further emphasized in submitting specifications regarding calculating premium rates. Various countries, including the Czech Republic, Hungary, Japan, Korea, Mexico, Poland, Switzerland, and the United States, mandate domestic and foreign direct insurance companies to submit general policy conditions. In the EU Member countries, systematic submission or approval of general policy conditions may not be required, with exceptions for compulsory and supplementary health insurance. The evolving regulatory landscape within the EU, marked by harmonization under the third generation of Insurance Directives, has led to a significant reduction in prior approval of premiums and tariffs, except for specific cases. The oversight of premium rates and policy conditions varies globally, with certain jurisdictions conducting exhaustive checks, particularly for very high-risk classes. Underwriting and pricing standards regulations aim to promote market efficiency, consumer confidence, and financial stability within the insurance industry. These standards evolve in response to emerging risks, market developments, and regulatory priorities, reflecting a commitment to maintaining a fair, transparent, and sustainable insurance marketplace.

4.1.4 Technical Provisions and Supervisions

Technical provisions are critical in ensuring insurance companies meet their commitments to policyholders, but the regulatory frameworks and supervisory approaches guiding these provisions vary significantly across countries. In nations such as Belgium, Denmark, Finland, France, Iceland, Mexico, Netherlands, Norway, Sweden, Switzerland, and Turkey, a prevailing a posteriori supervisory model is adopted. This entails regulatory assessments occurring after the establishment of technical provisions. The European Union (EU) mirrors this approach, assigning responsibility to the home country of an insurer for rule establishment and compliance oversight. The EU's focus, particularly in life insurance, centres on mathematical reserves, while non-life insurance encompasses provisions for unearned premiums, outstanding claims, and incurred but not reported claims. Additionally, countries like Finland, France, and Iceland introduce equalization reserves as valuation adjustments in non-life insurance, employing calculation methods that can be statistical or case-specific.

Across Asia, technical provision frameworks have been widely embraced, albeit with distinct nuances. For life insurance, regulations predominantly refer to "mathematical reserves." In contrast, non-life insurance typically involves calculations for "unearned premium reserves" (e.g., Indonesia, the Philippines, Sri Lanka) and "claims reserves" (e.g., Macao, Malaysia, Singapore). Vietnam introduces the concept of an equalization provision. Despite legislation, many countries encounter challenges due to imprecise rules and inadequate supervision, posing potential risks to insurers' solvency and policyholder security. Precision takes centre stage in the technical provision landscape of the United Kingdom, Canada, Australia, South Africa, and Brazil. These nations prioritize accuracy in determining mathematical reserves for life insurance, relying on actuarial methods that consider factors such as mortality rates, interest rates, and policy terms. Their approach in the non-life insurance sector involves assessing risk profiles to ensure meticulous calculations of unearned premium reserves. Countries like India, UAE, Russia, Saudi Arabia, and Singapore adopt a risk-sensitive approach to supervising technical provisions. In life insurance, actuarial assessments guide the calculation of mathematical reserves, considering the nuanced risks associated with policyholders. For non-life insurance, calculations of unearned premium reserves are intricately tied to evaluating policy risks and market conditions, demonstrating a keen awareness of risk factors. Several countries, including Mexico, Japan, South Korea, Thailand, and Malaysia, champion comprehensive risk-based frameworks for technical provisions. These countries utilize advanced actuarial models in life insurance to calculate mathematical reserves, considering intricate risk assessments. The non-life insurance sector witnesses detailed calculations for provisions related to outstanding claims. It Incurred But Not Reported claims showcase a commitment to a resilient insurance sector through thorough risk evaluations.

4.1.5 Investments Management Regulations

Most national legislations encompass explicit provisions governing the investments of insurance companies, delineating rules for portfolio composition and diversification. Specifically, in life insurance, meticulous regulations dictate the selection of assets representing technical provisions. Noteworthy is the inclusion of rules in certain countries like Iceland, Japan, Norway, Turkey, and the United States, which extend to assets covering various liabilities beyond life insurance. The management of investments in insurance companies follows two distinct paradigms: quantitative restrictions on investment choices and the "prudent person" approach. The latter, emphasizing managerial skills and expertise, find favour in jurisdictions such as the United Kingdom and the United States. Within the European Union, a hybrid approach prevails, blending prudent person rules that offer general guidelines with quantitative restrictions, manifesting as fixed ceilings on specific asset types. Across Asia, ceilings on certain assets are a common feature, complemented by introducing floors representing minimum percentages. Sri Lanka, for instance, mandates a minimum of 50% investment in government securities for life insurance.

Similarly, in the Philippines, insurers must invest at least 25% of the minimum paid-up capital in bonds, while India stipulates a 25% investment in government securities. Unique requirements exist in Croatia, where a minimum of 30% of mathematical reserves must be invested in state bonds. In Russia, limitations restrict foreign investments to 20% of provisions. Furthermore, the methods employed to value investments as counterparts to technical provisions exhibit considerable divergence across countries. Insurance companies value investments in some jurisdictions based on their current market prices. This practice is observed in countries such as Australia, Denmark, Luxembourg, Mexico, Portugal, Spain, Turkey, the United Kingdom, Indonesia, the Philippines, Thailand, Belarus, Croatia, Lithuania, and Slovenia.

Other countries mandate the application of the principle of the lower historical cost or market value as directed by supervisory authorities. Notable examples include Belgium, Denmark, Finland, Germany, Iceland, Italy, the Netherlands, Poland, Sweden, Malaysia, Singapore, Croatia, Latvia, and Slovenia. There are also some countries necessitate investments to be valued at historical cost, exemplified by the Czech Republic, France, Germany, Hungary, Italy, Japan, Korea, Poland, Macao, Estonia, and Slovakia. Interestingly, Asia, Brunei, Hong Kong, Sri Lanka, and Vietnam lack specific legislation on investment valuation, contributing to a spectrum of global approaches in this critical aspect of insurance regulation.

4.1.6 Consumer Protection and Fraud Detection Regulations

Consumer protection and fraud detection regulations for insurance companies are designed to safeguard the interests of policyholders, ensure fair treatment, transparency, and integrity in insurance transactions, and mitigate the risks associated with fraudulent activities. Insurance companies must provide consumers with clear and comprehensive information about insurance products, coverage terms, premiums, deductibles, limitations, and exclusions. This includes disclosing policy features, terms and conditions, renewal provisions, and claims procedures in a language easily understandable to policyholders. For instance, the California Department of Insurance enforces disclosure requirements that mandate insurers to provide consumers with clear and comprehensive information about insurance products, coverage terms, and claims procedures. Additionally, the Fair Credit Reporting Act (FCRA) and the Health Insurance Portability and Accountability Act (HIPAA) protect consumer privacy rights and regulate insurers' use of personal information.

Insurers must treat customers fairly and ethically throughout the insurance lifecycle, from product marketing and sales to claims handling and dispute resolution. This includes ensuring customers are not subjected to unfair or discriminatory practices based on gender, race, ethnicity, age, or health status. The Prudential Regulation Authority (PRA) and the Financial Conduct Authority (FCA) oversee consumer protection regulations in the United Kingdom. The FCA ensures fair treatment of customers throughout the insurance lifecycle, while the PRA focuses on maintaining solvency and financial stability within the industry. For example, insurers like Aviva and Prudential must adhere to transparency requirements, disclosing policy features, terms, and conditions in a language accessible to policyholders.

Consumers have certain rights and remedies under consumer protection laws, including the right to cancel policies within a specified cooling-off period, receive timely and accurate information about policy changes or updates, and file complaints or seek redress for grievances through regulatory channels. Insurers must also implement robust fraud detection, prevention, and investigation mechanisms to combat insurance fraud effectively. This includes employing advanced analytics, data mining techniques, and predictive modelling to identify suspicious claims patterns, anomalies, and fraudulent activities. Across Asia, countries like Singapore enforce consumer protection and fraud detection regulations through the Monetary Authority of Singapore (MAS). Insurers such as NTUC Income and AIA must adhere to strict guidelines on fair treatment of customers, transparency in pricing, and claims handling procedures. MAS encourages collaboration between insurers and law enforcement agencies to combat insurance fraud and protect policyholders' interests effectively. Consumer protection and fraud detection regulations for insurance companies aim to promote market integrity, consumer confidence, and financial stability within the insurance industry. These regulations help mitigate risks, protect policyholders' interests, and maintain trust and credibility in insurance transactions. Compliance with regulatory requirements is essential for insurers to uphold ethical standards, maintain public trust, and mitigate the adverse impact of fraudulent activities on insurance markets and stakeholders.

4.1.7 *Financial reporting, On-Site Inspection, and Main Accounting Principles*

The insurance industry's landscape is marked by its commitment to financial transparency and regulatory compliance. This commitment is reflected in insurance companies' comprehensive financial reporting practices worldwide. These financial reports, including balance sheets, income, and cash flow statements, are crucial communication tools to convey insurers' financial standing to various stakeholders. Furthermore, insurers delve into intricate details about their underwriting practices, investment portfolios, and risk management strategies. They introduce specialized reporting elements such as loss reserves and incurred but not reported (IBNR) claims.

The demand for financial reports exhibits significant variation across countries, each imposing unique reporting requirements and frequencies. In Australia, reports encompassing the balance sheet and profit and loss account are presented annually and quarterly. Austria mandates financial annual accounts and an annual report, coupled with a quarterly submission of a list of assets covering mathematical reserves. Belgium requires an annual submission of the balance sheet, profit and loss account, and the annual statement of solvency margin. The Czech Republic incorporates an enclosure to the balance sheet, profit and loss account, and a list of technical provisions in its annual reporting. Denmark's annual reports consist of the balance sheet, profit and loss account, notes to the annual report, and a 5-year review. Finland adheres to annual reporting standards, covering balance sheets, profit and loss accounts, solvency margin items, and a detailed analysis of technical provisions based on the EU-15 Directive on accounting. France stands out with its dual commitment to both annual and quarterly reporting. Companies in France submit balance sheets, profit and loss accounts, and an annual report within 5 months, while quarterly reports focus on business activities and investments. Hungary mandates annual reports featuring an auditor's clause, reports on reinsurance contracts, and solvency reports submitted exclusively to the supervisor. Japan adopts a varied frequency, with balance sheets, profit and loss accounts, audit records, business reports, and financial statements submitted annually, quarterly, and monthly. Korea's reporting demands encompass a mix of annual, quarterly, and monthly reports, covering balance sheets, profit and loss accounts, business reports, property lists, income statements, and monthly asset statements. The Netherlands requires annual reporting of balance sheets, profit and loss accounts, and annual returns, providing comprehensive information on investments, technical results, technical provisions, solvency, and actuarial reports. Poland sets forth a comprehensive set of documents, including balance sheets, profit and loss accounts, technical insurance accounts, cash flow reports, and solvency declarations, to be submitted annually, quarterly, and monthly. In the EU 15, financial reporting includes balance sheets, profit and loss accounts, and annual accounts submitted annually and periodically, emphasizing the industry's dedication to transparency and accountability on a global scale.

While financial reporting is a cornerstone, regulatory bodies and supervisory authorities are pivotal in ensuring adherence to insurance regulations and financial reporting standards through on-site inspections. These inspections are designed to meticulously examine an insurance company's financial records, risk management practices, and the adequacy of reserves. The primary objective is to verify the company's financial soundness, capacity to meet obligations to policyholders, and adherence to regulatory requirements, thereby contributing to the overall stability of the insurance sector and safeguarding the interests of policyholders. Portugal conducts on-site inspections based on the EU-15 Directive on accounting, with variable periodicity for insurance companies' headquarters and branches. Spain follows a similar approach, conducting on-site inspections for headquarters and branches of insurance companies with variable periodicity. Sweden opts for a once-every-three-year on-site inspection for domestic insurance companies' headquarters and their domestic branches. Switzerland conducts on-site inspections every four years for insurance companies' headquarters and branches. In Turkey, on-site inspections are performed for the headquarters and branches of insurance companies with variable periodicity. The United Kingdom also conducts on-site inspections with variable periodicity for both headquarters and branches of insurance companies. In the United States, on-site inspections occur once every 1–5 years for the headquarters and branches of insurance companies. Korea conducts biennial on-site inspections for the headquarters of domestic insurance companies and their branches. Luxembourg, adhering to the EU-15 Directive on accounting, conducts on-site inspections every five years, on average, for the headquarters of domestic insurance companies and their domestic branches.

In Mexico, on-site inspections are carried out annually for the headquarters of domestic insurance companies. These inspections are conducted periodically, with specific frequency variations based on factors such as the size and risk profile of the insurance company. This systematic and globally widespread approach to on-site inspections contributes to a robust regulatory framework, ensuring the stability and integrity of the insurance sector.

4.2 Regulatory Challenges in Decentralized Insurance

The emergence of decentralized insurance, fuelled by advanced technologies promises to reshape the traditional landscape of the insurance industry. Unlike conventional insurance models, decentralized insurance operates on decentralized manner, fostering transparency, reducing operational costs, and promoting accessibility. However, this revolutionary shift towards decentralized insurance introduces various regulatory challenges that require careful examination (Saeed & Arshed, 2022). As governments and regulatory bodies grapple with the implications of decentralized technologies, a comprehensive understanding of the unique regulatory hurdles becomes imperative (International Insurance Society, 2021). There is an intricate web of regulatory challenges confronting decentralized insurance due to difficulty recognizing them in legal frameworks related to licencing requirements, solvency standards and capital requirements, investments, financial reporting and inspection, and integrating innovative technologies within established regulatory frameworks (Alvin et al., 2022).

4.2.1 Identifying a Legal Form for Decentralized Insurance Entities

In the regulatory landscape governing insurance companies, adherence to licencing requirements has long been a cornerstone. These requirements, meticulously detailed in regulatory Sect. 4.1.1, serve as a means to establish the legal identity of insurance companies, maintain financial stability, ensure consumer protection, and guarantee the overall integrity of insurance providers. Traditional regulatory frameworks are built on overseeing transactions conducted in fiat currencies and maintaining a structured environment to uphold industry standards (Popovic et al., 2020). However, the rise of decentralized insurance entities operating on blockchain technology introduces a paradigm shift, necessitating a reevaluation of these well-established regulatory norms. Blockchain-based insurance platforms, such as Etherisc and Nexus Mutual, operate on decentralized networks where transactions, including premium payments and claims settlements, are executed through cryptocurrencies. This departure from traditional fiat currency transactions challenges the conventional licencing requirements for centralized financial systems. The inherent characteristics of blockchain, characterized by the utilization of smart contracts and DAOs, complicate the regulatory task of identifying appropriate legal forms within the established regulatory structures. For example, DAOs operate on smart contracts, enabling the automatic execution of claims and premium transactions based on predefined rules. This automation challenges traditional distinctions between various entities within the insurance ecosystem, such as insurers, intermediaries, and policyholders. Regulators find themselves in the intricate position of categorizing DAOs and determining the most suitable legal forms for their functioning, as these innovative structures blur the lines of conventional regulatory frameworks. An instance is Tezos, a blockchain platform that employs on-chain governance mechanisms. In decentralized insurance, a governance structure where participants make policy decisions collectively could create challenges in identifying the responsible party for regulatory compliance.

Similarly, the global nature of blockchain technology poses challenges for regulators in determining applicable laws and regulations. This is particularly evident when participants and transactions span multiple countries, each with its regulatory framework. Take the example of a decentralized insurance platform with users and smart contracts distributed across multiple countries (Malhotra et al., 2022). Determining the applicable laws and regulations becomes intricate, leading to potential conflicts between legal jurisdictions (Amponsah et al., 2021). For instance, a user in one jurisdiction might face a different regulatory environment than another, raising questions about harmonizing global standards. The decentralized nature of these platforms also complicates identifying responsible entities and the location of data storage, exemplified by cases where regulators from different countries assert jurisdiction over aspects of a blockchain-enabled insurance platform (Shetty et al., 2022). The lack of uniformity in international regulations further exacerbates challenges. This is illustrated by variations in data protection laws, financial regulations, and consumer rights across jurisdictions. The

General Data Protection Regulation (GDPR) in the European Union imposes stringent data protection requirements. Decentralized insurance platforms must navigate varying data protection laws, financial regulations, and consumer rights across different jurisdictions. The absence of a cohesive global regulatory framework can result in a fragmented legal landscape, increasing decentralized insurance entities' complexity and compliance burden.

4.2.2 Solvency Assurance in Decentralized Insurance Models

In the decentralized context, ensuring solvency becomes particularly intricate due to the unique features of decentralized insurance models. One primary challenge lies in establishing standardized metrics for determining minimum solvency. Unlike centralized insurers that may follow well-established regulatory frameworks, decentralized platforms often do not have any such regulation and decentralized governance structures (Popovic et al., 2020). Governing bodies face the challenge of devising metrics that adequately assess the solvency of these entities, considering the decentralized and often algorithmic nature of their financial operations. Striking a balance between ensuring robust financial health and accommodating the unique decentralized features poses a significant hurdle for regulators in formulating effective minimum solvency requirements.

Furthermore, the dynamic and volatile nature of cryptocurrency markets, often utilized in several decentralized insurance platforms, introduces additional complexity to minimum solvency regulations. The valuation and liquidity of digital assets can fluctuate rapidly, impacting the financial standing of decentralized insurers. Regulators must devise adaptive frameworks that account for the volatility inherent in decentralized finance and cryptocurrency markets, ensuring that minimum solvency requirements remain resilient in the face of market fluctuations. In decentralized insurance, it will be very difficult for regulators to avoid cross sectorial activity since the insurance contract in a decentralized world is designed mutually by the people themselves, and they are highly customized, which may lead to several problems such as lack of funds for settling claims, etc. Whether insurance companies may hold shares in non-insurance entities sparks varied opinions across the globe. Countries like the Czech Republic, Hungary, Japan, Korea, Switzerland, and the United States impose limits on such shareholding. At the same time, within the European Union, a more lenient stance prevails, accepting shareholding without construing it as engaging in primary business activities. Regulatory nuances extend to insurance companies' creation of banking subsidiaries, with prohibitions in some countries and permissive approaches in others.

Moreover, the traditional regulatory landscape in the insurance industry typically includes specific supervision of share ownership, with the overarching goal of preventing any reduction in the capital base of insurance companies. This scrutiny ensures companies maintain a stable financial foundation to meet their obligations and cover potential risks. However, in the context of decentralized insurance entities, adhering to such regulatory oversight becomes challenging due to the lack of a defined ownership structure or identifiable shareholders. In the traditional insurance landscape, well-established guidelines govern reinsurance arrangements, providing a structured framework for insurance companies to manage and mitigate risks. These guidelines are typically designed to ensure the financial stability of insurance providers, maintain a balanced risk portfolio, and uphold industry standards. However, adhering to such guidelines becomes challenging in decentralized insurance.

Another major challenge is related to capital adequacy in a decentralized insurance system. Balancing capital allocation priorities and optimizing risk-adjusted returns while maintaining solvency ratios may also be challenging in decentralized environments due to regulatory uncertainty and dynamic market conditions. This necessitates the establishment of frameworks for capital allocation, risk management, and solvency assessment. However, defining and assessing the appropriate level of capital that decentralized insurance entities should maintain is very challenging. Moreover, digital asset valuations can experience significant fluctuations, introducing uncertainties in the financial standing of decentralized insurers. Regulators need to address these market dynamics by developing frameworks that account for the unique risks associated with digital assets. Establishing guidelines that mitigate the impact of market volatility on capital adequacy becomes crucial to maintaining the stability and solvency of decentralized insurance platforms.

4.2.3 Customized Pricing and Policies of Decentralized Insurance

In the traditional insurance landscape, regulatory bodies oversee and set general policy conditions and premium rates. This centralized approach ensures standardized policies and pricing across the industry. However, in decentralized insurance, achieving a high level of customization presents significant challenges. However, decentralized insurance embraces various innovative approaches that redefine how policies are determined. For instance, in a peer-to-peer model of decentralized insurance, the determination of policy conditions and premium rates shifts from regulatory authorities to the involved peers themselves. This introduces a dynamic where the terms of the insurance agreement are collectively decided by the participants, allowing for a more personalized and context-specific approach. In parametric decentralized insurance, the customization process takes on a different form. Here, policy conditions are automatically triggered based on predefined parameters. Instead of manual negotiations or regulatory interventions, the insurance contract terms are automatically activated in response to specific, quantifiable events or conditions. This automation streamlines the customization process and aligns it with smart contracts' decentralized and automated nature.

On the other hand, on-demand insurance in a decentralized context is tailored to the usage patterns of the insured. The actual usage of the insured asset or service drives the customization in this model. For instance, the insurance coverage and associated premiums may vary based on the frequency or duration of usage, providing a more flexible and usage-driven approach compared to traditional, fixed-term policies. The difficulty regulating decentralized insurance entities arises from these models' diverse and evolving nature. While offering flexibility and innovation, it challenges the traditional regulatory frameworks accustomed to standardization. Regulators are faced with the task of adapting to these novel approaches, ensuring a balance between customization and the need for regulatory oversight to protect the interests of participants and maintain the integrity of the insurance industry.

4.2.4 Managing Risks in Decentralized Insurance

Effective risk management in insurance involves a comprehensive approach that integrates risk identification, assessment, mitigation, and monitoring across various aspects of insurance operations. Insurers must proactively identify and manage risks to safeguard financial stability, protect policyholder interests, and maintain regulatory compliance in an increasingly dynamic and challenging insurance landscape. Several kinds of risk are involved in insurance operations, such as underwriting, market, and operational risks (Popovic et al., 2020). Underwriting risk refers to the risk of adverse selection and inadequate pricing of insurance policies. Insurers must assess the likelihood of policyholders filing claims and accurately price policies to cover potential losses while generating profits. Underwriting risk management involves evaluating policyholder characteristics, estimating loss probabilities, and setting appropriate premium rates to maintain underwriting profitability. Claims risk encompasses the potential for unexpected and large claim payments that may exceed policy reserves and strain insurer solvency. Insurers must manage claims risk by accurately assessing claim liabilities, reserving adequate funds to cover anticipated losses, and implementing effective claims management practices to mitigate claims leakage and fraud. Market risk refers to the impact of fluctuations in financial markets, including interest rates, equity prices, and currency exchange rates, on insurer investments and liabilities. Insurers must manage market risk by diversifying investment portfolios, hedging against adverse market movements, and maintaining liquidity buffers to withstand market volatility and economic downturns. Credit risk arises from counterparties' potential default or non-payment, including policyholders, reinsurers, and investment issuers. Insurers must manage credit risk by assessing counterparties' creditworthiness, establishing credit limits, and monitoring credit exposures to mitigate the risk of financial losses due to counterparty defaults. Operational risk encompasses the risk of disruptions, errors, and inefficiencies in insurance operations, including underwriting, claims processing, and policy administration. Insurers must manage operational risk by implementing robust internal controls, leveraging technology solutions to automate processes, and establishing business continuity plans to mitigate the impact of operational disruptions and ensure operational resilience.

In traditional insurance frameworks, regulators have regulations for managing each risk. But, regulators face several challenges in a decentralized insurance framework due to technological complexity, regulatory ambiguity, and jurisdictional complexity. Assessing underwriting risk in decentralized insurance platforms is challenging due to the lack of centralized data and standardized underwriting practices. Since, in decentralized platforms, assessing policyholder risk profiles and pricing insurance policies may rely on decentralized data sources and algorithmic models. Regulators may struggle to verify the accuracy and fairness of underwriting practices without centralized oversight and transparency mechanisms. Managing claims risk in decentralized insurance platforms requires an accurate assessment of claim liabilities, adequate reserves, and effective claims management practices. Without standardized claims management practices, regulators may struggle to verify the accuracy and integrity of claims data and processes. Decentralized platforms may invest premiums and reserves in volatile assets, exposing insurers to market fluctuations and liquidity risks. Regulators may struggle to assess the adequacy of risk management practices and the resilience of investment portfolios in decentralized environments. Assessing credit risk in decentralized insurance platforms requires evaluating the creditworthiness of counterparties, including policyholders, reinsurers, and investment issuers. Decentralized platforms may interact with counterparties across different jurisdictions, making it challenging for regulators to assess credit risk and enforce creditworthiness standards. Without centralized credit assessment mechanisms, regulators may struggle to effectively monitor and mitigate credit risk. Managing operational risk in decentralized insurance platforms requires implementing robust internal controls, leveraging technology solutions, and establishing business continuity plans to mitigate the impact of operational disruptions. Decentralized platforms may face operational challenges related to system outages, cyberattacks, and process inefficiencies, posing risks to insurer operations and policyholder service. Regulators may struggle to monitor and enforce operational risk management standards in decentralized environments.

4.2.5 Fund Optimization Challenges

Regulating optimization in decentralized insurance platforms is inherently difficult due to the distinctive features of decentralized insurance models. Decentralized insurance platforms often involve investments in digital assets, cryptocurrencies, and smart contracts, presenting novel challenges for regulatory bodies. Traditional regulatory frameworks may not fully encompass the complexities and risks associated with digital assets. Regulators must develop guidelines that address the volatile nature of cryptocurrency markets, ensuring that investors are protected against market fluctuations and potential losses. Balancing the need for investor protection with the desire to encourage the growth of decentralized insurance platforms requires a nuanced and adaptive approach to regulation. The lack of a centralized authority or intermediaries in decentralized insurance complicates investment regulatory oversight. Unlike traditional investments, where centralized entities may facilitate compliance checks and due diligence, decentralized platforms often operate without intermediaries. Regulators face challenges in monitoring and enforcing compliance with investment regulations, requiring innovative solutions such as blockchain analytics, decentralized audits, and collaboration with decentralized governance mechanisms to ensure transparency and adherence to regulatory standards (Shetty et al., 2022).

Regulating smart contract risk in decentralized insurance platforms involves addressing security vulnerabilities, coding errors, and potential exploits that can compromise fund security and disrupt insurance operations (Zhao, 2020). Mitigating smart contract risk requires technical expertise, regulatory guidance, and industry collaboration to develop best practices and standards for smart contract development, auditing, and monitoring. Regulators must develop frameworks for auditing and monitoring smart contracts, addressing potential vulnerabilities, and establishing standards for secure and transparent coding practices within decentralized insurance platforms. Regulating liquidity management in decentralized insurance platforms is difficult due to the dynamic nature of decentralized environments. Fluctuations in demand for insurance products, variations in premium payments, and unforeseen claim events can make it challenging to ensure adequate liquidity. Hence, regulators must coordinate with other regulatory bodies overseeing various aspects of decentralized insurance. Harmonizing regulatory approaches across different sectors becomes essential to create a cohesive and effective framework for investment-related activities within decentralized insurance.

4.2.6 Consumer Protection and Compliances Complexity

As decentralized insurance platforms aim to redefine traditional models, ensuring robust consumer protection becomes a crucial aspect that regulators worldwide are grappling with. Let's take the instance of the United States, where the decentralized insurance space is gaining momentum. The Securities and Exchange Commission (SEC) and the Commodity Futures Trading Commission (CFTC) are actively exploring ways to enhance consumer safeguards because decentralized insurance consumer protection is difficult due to a lack of central authority, limited consumer redress mechanism, and diverse regulatory frameworks.

The DAO incident in 2016 is the best example of consumer protection and compliance complexity. The Decentralized Autonomous Organization launched on the Ethereum blockchain. It aimed to operate without traditional management structures, relying instead on smart contracts to automate investment decisions and distribute profits to token holders (Cousaert et al., 2022). However, a critical flaw in the DAO's smart contract code allowed an attacker to exploit a vulnerability, siphoning off millions of dollars worth of ether cryptocurrency. This incident revealed the inherent risks of decentralized platforms and highlighted the lack of a central authority to address security breaches and resolve disputes. Consumer protection mechanisms were virtually non-existent, leaving investors with limited avenues for recourse. The Ethereum community was divided over potential solutions, leading to a contentious hard fork to reverse the unauthorized transactions and restore funds to affected investors. The DAO incident underscored the need for robust security measures, code audits, and governance structures in decentralized platforms to safeguard consumer interests and mitigate systemic risks.

There is also regulatory complexity due to the difficulty of compliance across jurisdictions. Decentralized insurance platforms that operate globally must navigate a complex regulatory landscape characterized by varying regulatory frameworks and compliance requirements across different jurisdictions. For example, consider a decentralized insurance platform offering coverage to users in the European Union, the United States, and Asia. Each jurisdiction may have distinct regulatory standards governing insurance products, consumer protection laws, and data privacy requirements. Compliance with these regulations necessitates meticulous legal analysis, regulatory engagement, and ongoing monitoring to ensure adherence to evolving regulatory requirements.

However, EU regulators, including the European Insurance and Occupational Pensions Authority (EIOPA), are tasked with developing frameworks that transcend national boundaries, addressing the unique challenges of decentralized insurance models. The goal is to create a cohesive regulatory approach that protects consumers while fostering innovation within the EU's decentralized insurance sector. Singapore stands as a pioneer in addressing consumer protection challenges in decentralized insurance. The MAS recognizes the need for adaptable regulatory frameworks through a regulatory sandbox. MAS actively engages with industry stakeholders to develop guidelines that enhance consumer protection without stifling innovation (MAS, 2017). Striking this delicate balance serves as a testament to Singapore's commitment to fostering a conducive environment for decentralized insurance platforms to thrive while safeguarding the interests of policyholders.

4.2.7 Fraud Detection and Prevention

Fraud detection and prevention is a very complex task in a decentralized insurance platform due to several reasons, such as anonymity, pseudonymity, and smart contract vulnerabilities. For example, Consider a decentralized platform that offers peer-to-peer health insurance coverage. A user has joined the platform, contributed premiums, and expected healthcare benefits based on the terms of their chosen policies. Smart contracts automate policy management and claims processing, ensuring transparency and efficiency in the insurance process. However, when the user experiences a medical emergency and submits a claim to reimburse his medical expenses, he encounters unexpected challenges. Despite providing all the necessary documentation and meeting the criteria outlined in his policy, his claim is repeatedly denied by the decentralized insurance platform. Upon further investigation, the user discovers that a group of fraudulent users has been manipulating the claims processing system by submitting falsified claims and exploiting loopholes in the smart contracts governing the insurance policies. These fraudulent actors have devised sophisticated schemes to inflate claims, misrepresent medical conditions, and circumvent the platform's fraud detection mechanisms. As a result, the decentralized insurance platform struggles to distinguish legitimate claims from fraudulent ones, leading to delays, disputes, and mistrust among policyholders.

Hence, regulators must ensure that these platforms have mechanisms to detect and prevent fraudulent activities without compromising user privacy. Compliance with AML and KYC regulations is essential to prevent fraud and illegal activities. Decentralized insurance platforms must find ways to integrate robust identity verification processes while still maintaining the principles of decentralization and privacy. However, regulators will find several problems in implementing regulations to detect and prevent fraud in decentralized insurance entities for several reasons: First, users on decentralized platforms often interact pseudonymously or anonymously, using cryptographic keys instead of personal identifiers. This anonymity complicates regulatory efforts to identify and trace individuals engaged in fraudulent activities, hindering law enforcement and regulatory enforcement measures. Second, using smart contracts, users can create and trade insurance policies directly on the platform. Since the platform operates on a decentralized blockchain network, there's no central entity responsible for regulatory compliance or oversight. Regulators may struggle to define the legal framework and jurisdiction for regulating such platforms, especially if they operate across multiple jurisdictions with varying regulatory requirements.

However, regulatory bodies worldwide have intensified their efforts to address fraudulent activities. Australia is a proactive example, where entities like the Australian Securities and Investments Commission (ASIC) actively collaborate with industry players to integrate technological solutions. Adopting cutting-edge tools such as advanced data analytics, artificial intelligence, and blockchain-based identity verification systems is gaining traction, reflecting a concerted effort to stay ahead of fraudsters (OECD, 2017). Similarly, Japan's Financial Services Agency recognizes the inherent risks associated with emerging technologies in insurance. Consequently, regulatory frameworks are being refined to ensure decentralized insurance platforms deploy robust fraud detection and prevention measures, underscoring the imperative of staying abreast of technological advancements to uphold the sector's integrity. Meanwhile, regulators like the Financial Conduct Authority are grappling with the challenge of enhancing anti-fraud measures within the insurance landscape in the United Kingdom (OECD, 2017). As the industry witnesses a proliferation of innovative models leveraging blockchain and smart contracts, regulatory bodies are intensifying their focus on ensuring the agility and effectiveness of fraud detection mechanisms. This endeavour necessitates a delicate balance between fostering innovation and mitigating fraudulent activities, highlighting the complexities inherent in regulatory adaptation to evolving technologies and emphasizing the importance of global collaboration in shaping effective regulatory frameworks.

4.2.8 Financial Reporting and Inspection Challenges

Financial reporting in decentralized insurance introduces complexities related to the transparency and accuracy of reported data. Traditional reporting mechanisms may not seamlessly integrate with the decentralized and distributed ledger technologies underpinning these platforms. Regulators face the challenge of developing standardized reporting requirements that capture the decentralized nature of transactions, ensuring that financial information remains reliable and accessible (Popovic et al., 2020). Striking a balance between fostering transparency and avoiding excessive reporting burdens poses a significant regulatory challenge in the dynamic context of decentralized insurance.

On-site inspection, a common regulatory practice in traditional insurance, faces challenges in the decentralized realm. The absence of centralized physical entities or offices makes traditional on-site inspections difficult. Regulators must explore alternative means, such as utilizing blockchain analytics, engaging third-party auditors, or collaborating with decentralized governance structures to conduct effective inspections. Ensuring the integrity and security of on-site inspections becomes crucial, given the reliance on decentralized technologies. (Fig. 4.1).

The application of main accounting principles in decentralized insurance encounters challenges due to the unique characteristics of blockchain-based financial systems. Smart contracts, which automate and execute insurance policies, introduce complexities in aligning with traditional accounting standards. Regulators must address the accounting treatment of smart contract transactions, the valuation of digital assets, and the recognition of revenue and liabilities within a decentralized framework. Establishing accounting principles that effectively capture the economic substance of decentralized insurance transactions is essential for maintaining consistency and comparability in financial reporting.

Additionally, these platforms' decentralized and cross-border nature poses challenges for harmonizing accounting principles globally. Regulators must collaborate across jurisdictions to develop internationally accepted accounting standards that can accommodate the unique features of decentralized insurance. This involves navigating differences in regulatory approaches and fostering a cooperative environment to ensure a consistent and comprehensive accounting framework for decentralized insurance entities operating across borders.

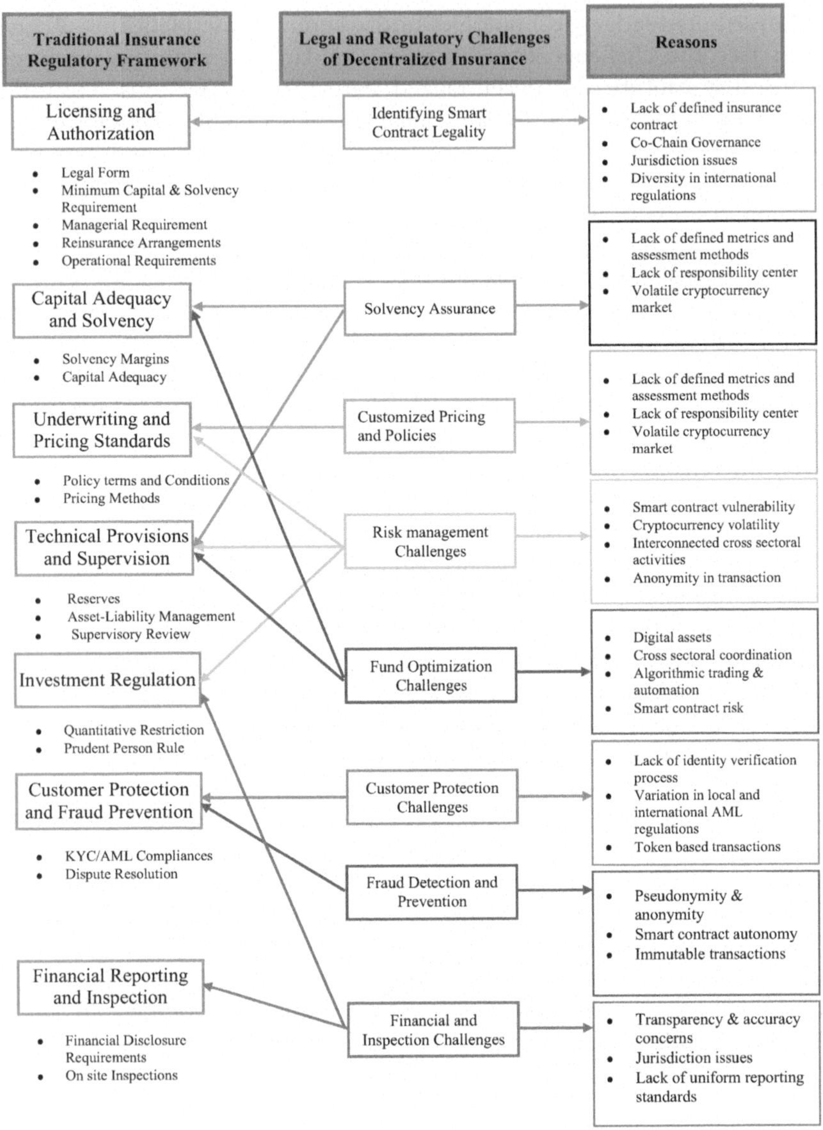

Fig. 4.1 Regulatory and legal challenges of decentralized insurance (*Source* Developed by authors)

4.3 Economic Challenges of Decentralized Insurance

4.3.1 *Scalability and Efficiency*

Scalability and efficiency are pivotal economic challenges confronting the landscape of decentralized insurance. The challenge lies in seamlessly expanding decentralized platforms to accommodate a burgeoning user base while upholding operational efficiency (International Insurance Society, 2021). This raises the need for robust technological infrastructures to handle increased activity without compromising speed and resource consumption (Popovic et al., 2020). Transaction costs constitute another economic facet demanding careful consideration. During decentralized insurance endeavours to reduce reliance on traditional intermediaries, the transactional overhead on distributed networks introduces economic complexities. Striking an equilibrium between fostering affordability for policyholders and ensuring the economic viability of insurers in the face of transactional expenses becomes a focal point.

Moreover, the resource-intensiveness inherent in implementing and sustaining decentralized insurance platforms introduces economic challenges. Significant investments in computing power, energy consumption, and infrastructure become imperative, impacting overall operational efficiency and economic feasibility. Effectively addressing these scalability and efficiency dilemmas is paramount for the sustainable evolution of decentralized insurance as a dynamic force in the modern insurance landscape (McKinsey & Company, 2016). The recent failures of the B3i Consortium (See Box 4.1) show that the short-term hurdles and risks must not be underestimated (The Geneva Association, 2023). In 2022, B3i, the re/insurance industry's blockchain initiative, became insolvent due to failure to raise new capital (Howard, 2022). This highlights the challenges associated with achieving expected efficiency gains and profitability in mass adoption in the short term.

These developments have led insurers and investors to doubt:

- Whether decentralized applications in insurance will achieve the expected scale and efficiency gains in the foreseeable future;
- Whether technology is mature and safe enough for mass insurance applications;
- The extent to which technology benefits or challenges the traditional insurance industry.

Box 4.1: The B3i Saga—Lessons from a Consortium's Demise

The B3i consortium, once a beacon of hope for revolutionizing the re/insurance industry through blockchain, succumbed to insolvency in 2022 amidst its quest for new capital. B3i was formed to enhance efficiency and scale with investments from international re/insurers. This failure underscores the formidable highlights in achieving swift mass adoption and immediate profitability in insurance (The Geneva Association, 2023).

B3i, born as 'The Blockchain Insurance Industry Initiative' in 2016, was a collaboration of major re/insurers such as Aegon, Allianz, Munich Re, Swiss Re, and Zurich. It sought to leverage blockchain for end-to-end solutions in reinsurance transactions, aiming for speedier access with reduced operational risks. The consortium's journey took a fateful turn in 2022 when insolvency was announced due to an inability to secure USD 20 million in new capital. Despite raising USD 22.7 million, B3i's aspirations crumbled, leaving a void in the once-promising landscape.

Among the notable projects attempted by B3i, 'B3i Re' focused on creating reinsurance smart contracts, streamlining information flow and mitigating fraud risks. Another initiative, 'B3i Fluidity', introduced an insurance platform for application distribution, featuring components like 'Ritablock' for technical accounting and 'Claimshare' for confidential claims data processing.

The reasons behind B3i's downfall are multi-faceted. The consortium's technology-centric approach overshadowed the importance of clear problem-solving goals, leading to a misalignment of emphasis. The complexity of consortium governance hindered collective decision-making and external funding efforts. Timing also played a crucial role, as the demand for blockchain reinsurance was not robust, and the supply remained experimental. Legacy system integration and the lack of a comprehensive blockchain ecosystem in the insurance industry compounded B3i's challenges.

Implications for Decentralized Insurance

B3i's collapse resonates beyond its immediate stakeholders, echoing the fragility of DeFi ecosystems. This fragility casts a shadow over decentralised insurance's short- and medium-term prospects. Cryptocurrency markets, including Bitcoin and Ethereum, bore the brunt of these concerns, with significant value drops in response to B3i's failures in May and November 2022. The aftermath of B3i serves as a cautionary tale, prompting reflections on the intricacies and vulnerabilities inherent in decentralized insurance and blockchain-based initiatives within the broader financial landscape.

4.3.2 *Interoperability Issues and Immature Technology*

Interoperability and immature technology emerge as a formidable economic hurdle, casting shadows on the seamless integration and widespread adoption of decentralized insurance solutions (Walsh et al., 2021). The bedrock of cohesive collaboration interoperability falters as diverse networks struggle to communicate effectively, thwarting promised gains in efficiency, accessibility, and functionality (Sakho et al., 2019). This lack of standardized communication not only introduces additional costs and complexities but also jeopardizes the economic viability of decentralized insurance, challenging its transformative potential. Simultaneously, the spectre of immature technology, plagued by design errors, amplifies economic concerns within decentralized insurance ecosystems. Smart contracts and the underlying blockchain infrastructure, marred by these design flaws, become breeding grounds for vulnerabilities, security breaches, and operational malfunctions. Beyond compromising the reliability of decentralized insurance processes, these issues precipitate economic repercussions. The financial toll incurred in rectifying design errors, fortifying security measures, and compensating affected stakeholders adds a layer of uncertainty, undermining the economic viability of decentralized insurance initiatives.

The recent incidents of the Terra crash underscore the pressing need to address design failures and the overall immaturity of technology. The TerraUSD instability is a stark reminder that the short-term hurdles and risks of immature blockchain systems should not be underestimated within the decentralized insurance landscape (The Geneva Association, 2023). The Terra crash serves as a wake-up call, prompting a reassessment of the risk landscape associated with decentralized insurance. Insurers and investors are now questioning the effectiveness of risk management protocols within these systems and are wary of potential vulnerabilities that could compromise financial stability. The need for greater transparency, accountability, and comprehensive risk mitigation strategies has become more apparent as stakeholders seek assurances that decentralized insurance can navigate challenges and uphold the security of their investments.

Box 4.2: TerraUSD Breakdown and Its Implication on Decentralized Insurance

TerraUSD's Collapse: Unraveling the Story

Originally launched in 2018, TerraUSD (UST) boasted the title of the largest non-collateralized stablecoin. From the conventional approach of fiat-backed or crypto-collateralized stablecoins, TerraUSD maintained its dollar parity through a straightforward arbitrage algorithm—UST 1 ⊃ USD 1 worth of LUNA. Acting as Terra's companion coin, LUNA was designed to balance and uphold Terra's values. However, the cryptocurrency's catastrophic collapse resulted from a significant dip in LUNA's value and recurring volatility in the crypto market. This drop made it impossible for TerraUSD to sustain its dollar value, setting off a series of events highlighting a critical design flaw—its lack of collateralization through physical or digital assets.

Following its de-pegging from USD 1, the Luna Foundation Guard, responsible for overseeing Terra's ecosystem, took drastic measures. Deploying USD 3.5 billion from reserves to repeg UST to the U.S. dollar was a swift but ultimately unsustainable intervention. The reserve buffer quickly depleted, and by May 25, 2022, investors introduced a new LUNA, termed Terra 2.0, marking the decoupling of UST and LUNA.

Factors Behind TerraUSD's Downfall

The downfall of TerraUSD can be dissected by examining an intricate interplay of contributing factors. At its core was the fundamental flaw of operating without collateralization—a stark contrast to traditional stablecoins backed by tangible assets or fiat currency. Relying solely on an arbitrage algorithm tied to LUNA exposed TerraUSD to market fluctuations, especially when LUNA's value experienced a substantial decline. The cryptocurrency's vulnerability was compounded by its heavy reliance on LUNA's value, intricately linked to TerraUSD's stability. The failure to adapt to changing market conditions and insufficient collateralization underscored critical weaknesses in its design.

The inherent volatility of the cryptocurrency market played a pivotal role in TerraUSD's failure. The abrupt and substantial drop in LUNA's value reflected broader market fluctuations, spotlighting the challenges and risks of navigating the unpredictable crypto landscape. The inadequacy of TerraUSD's collateralization mechanism, lacking robust support through physical or digital assets, left it without a secure buffer to absorb the impact of market shocks, ultimately failing to adapt to changing conditions.

Efforts to stabilize TerraUSD post-depegging led to the exhaustion of its reserve buffer. The Luna Foundation Guard's deployment of USD 3.5 billion to repeg UST to the U.S. dollar highlighted the inherent challenges of relying on reserves. It marked a critical turning point in TerraUSD's collapse. Finally, TerraUSD's model as a non-collateralized stablecoin introduced inherent risks associated with algorithmic mechanisms. Unlike collateralized stablecoins, which use assets as a guarantee, non-collateralized stablecoins rely on algorithmic processes. The failure of these mechanisms, as witnessed in TerraUSD, underscores the inherent challenges and uncertainties associated with non-collateralized stablecoin models.

Decoding the Impact on Decentralized Insurance

The collapse of TerraUSD reverberates with significant implications for the decentralized insurance landscape. The first lesson emerges in the risk associated with overreliance on algorithmic models within decentralized insurance, mirroring the challenges faced in the stablecoin. Platforms utilizing intricate algorithms for risk assessment and smart contract execution must ensure the robustness and adaptability of these models to navigate unforeseen market dynamics effectively.

The incident underscores the critical need for adequate collateralization in decentralized finance applications, particularly insurance. Decentralized insurance platforms must prioritize securing assets or reserves to absorb potential shocks, fortifying stability and resilience against market volatility. Furthermore, the TerraUSD failure sheds light on the market sensitivity and susceptibility of decentralized insurance, to broader market conditions and external influences. This underscores the importance of implementing robust risk management strategies within decentralized insurance platforms, safeguarding insurers and policyholders.

The incident may also impact the reputation and trust associated with decentralized systems. Stakeholders, including insurers, investors, and users, may exercise increased caution when engaging with these platforms. Transparent governance, robust risk management practices, and industry-wide collaboration become essential to maintain and restore confidence in decentralized insurance. This calls for a heightened focus on user education and awareness within the decentralized insurance landscape. Ensuring that users, insurers, and investors are well-informed about these systems' complexities and potential pitfalls is crucial for fostering informed decision-making and reducing uncertainties associated with insurance initiatives. Regulatory scrutiny will likely intensify after the TerraUSD failure, prompting authorities to assess the risks and implications for decentralized financial instruments. This may pave the way for the development of clearer regulatory frameworks, ensuring that decentralized insurance platforms adhere to standards prioritising stability, security, and the protection of stakeholders.

4.3.3 Governance and Accountability

Decentralized insurance faces intricate challenges related to governance and accountability that are central to its operational dynamics. The complexity of governance structures in decentralized insurance poses a significant hurdle, as decision-making involves a diverse array of stakeholders, including insurers, reinsurers, and blockchain developers. Achieving consensus and effective coordination becomes a delicate balance, potentially resulting in delays, disputes, or suboptimal outcomes due to the absence of a centralized authority. The decentralized decision-making landscape demands innovative solutions to streamline governance and ensure alignment among diverse interests. Internal control failures present a critical risk within decentralized insurance ecosystems. The lack of traditional hierarchical structures, a characteristic of decentralized models, can lead to lapses in internal control mechanisms (Godefroid et al., 2022). This exposes decentralized insurance systems to risks such as fraud, operational inefficiencies, and security breaches. Establishing robust internal control frameworks is imperative to uphold the integrity and reliability of decentralized insurance operations. Furthermore, fiduciary responsibilities owed to clients must be clearly defined and enforced in the decentralized landscape (Popovic et al., 2020). Ensuring transparency, fairness, and client protection becomes challenging, necessitating innovative solutions to navigate the unique challenges posed by decentralized insurance models.

The FTX scandal further underscores that traditional pain points, such as agency problems, incompetence, and fraud, are also present in self-proclaimed decentralized systems. This revelation heightens the importance of addressing governance and accountability challenges in decentralized insurance to mitigate risks and instil stakeholder confidence (The Geneva Association, 2023). Risks associated with concentrated decision-making and token holdings underscore the importance of equitable governance to prevent conflicts of interest and maintain the principles of decentralization. Addressing these governance and accountability challenges is crucial to fostering trust, promoting widespread adoption, and unlocking decentralized insurance's transformative potential in the broader insurance landscape.

Box 4.3: Collapse of FTX and the Implications for Decentralized Insurance

The collapse of FTX: Established in 2017, FTX, a centralized exchange for buying and selling cryptocurrencies, faced a catastrophic failure triggered by a critical revelation. On 2 November 2022, an article exposed that Alameda Research, a trading firm affiliated with FTX and owned by FTX Chief Executive Sam Bankman-Fried, held a significant amount of FTX's exchange token, FTT. This token was employed as collateral for Alameda's liabilities. Binance, a leading cryptocurrency exchange, divested all FTT holdings in response. The fallout was swift; on 11 November 2022, FTX filed for bankruptcy protection. The collapse was attributed to failures in internal controls, a lapse in fiduciary responsibilities for clients, and concentrated holdings of FTT cryptos by the exchange.

Reasons for Failure: The failure of FTX can be traced back to several interconnected factors. One of the primary catalysts was the revelation that Alameda Research, closely linked to FTX, held a substantial amount of FTT, using it as collateral. The ensuing loss of confidence, exemplified by Binance's decision to sell off its FTT holdings, precipitated a severe liquidity crisis for FTX. The failure of internal controls within the exchange and neglect of client fiduciary responsibilities exacerbated the situation. The concentrated holding of its own FTT cryptos significantly heightened risks, leaving FTX vulnerable to market shocks and triggering a cascading effect that led to its eventual collapse.

Implications for Decentralized Insurance: The collapse of FTX sends reverberations throughout the decentralized insurance landscape, serving as a stark reminder of the challenges inherent in financial systems (The Geneva Association. 2023). The failure underscores the critical importance of robust internal controls and fiduciary responsibilities in decentralized insurance ecosystems. Like centralized exchanges, decentralized insurance platforms must prioritize effective governance, transparent risk management, and client protection. The concentrated holding of assets, as witnessed in FTX, highlights the need for decentralized platforms to diversify and minimize risks associated with holding their tokens. This event emphasizes the imperative for decentralized insurance to learn from centralized failures, fortify risk management practices, and instil confidence in stakeholders to ensure the long-term sustainability of the decentralized financial ecosystem.

4.3.4 Financial Stability and Systematic Risks

Operating within the volatile landscape of cryptocurrencies, decentralized insurance platforms are exposed to the inherent price swings of digital assets. Cryptocurrency market volatility can directly impact the financial health of these platforms, affecting the valuation of assets, reserves, and overall liquidity. Sudden and significant fluctuations pose a constant risk to the stability of decentralized insurance, requiring robust risk management strategies to navigate this challenging environment. At the core of decentralized insurance operations are smart contracts intricate lines of code designed to execute and enforce insurance agreements. However, the reliance on these smart contracts introduces a technological risk. Vulnerabilities or flaws in the code can lead to exploits, hacks, or operational disruptions, jeopardizing the financial integrity of the decentralized insurance platform. The financial stability of these platforms is intricately linked to the resilience and security of their smart contract infrastructure, making it imperative to invest in rigorous code audits and continuous improvements to mitigate potential risks. Decentralized insurance commonly employs collateralization mechanisms to secure funds for potential claim payouts. However, the effectiveness of these mechanisms is contingent on various factors, including market dynamics and regulatory frameworks. Inadequate collateralization, whether due to market fluctuations or regulatory uncertainties, poses a substantial risk to financial stability.

Moreover, the lack of clear regulatory frameworks introduces additional risks, as regulatory interventions or legal challenges can impact the financial stability of decentralized insurance platforms by introducing compliance costs, legal disputes, and potential regulatory scrutiny. The governance structures of decentralized insurance platforms play a crucial role in decision-making and overall stability. The concentration of decision-making power and token holdings within a small group can lead to conflicts of interest and compromise the equitable management of the platform. Additionally, decentralized insurance involves interactions among multiple parties, introducing counterparty risks. Failures or defaults among insurers, reinsurers, or users can disrupt the smooth functioning of operations, creating financial instability. Balancing governance structures and mitigating counterparty risks are essential to bolstering financial stability in decentralized insurance ecosystems.

4.3.5 *Risk Modelling and Pricing*

Decentralized insurance grapples with intricate risk modelling and pricing challenges, both foundational elements in the traditional insurance paradigm. The distinctive nature of decentralized systems introduces complexities that demand innovative solutions to ensure accurate risk assessment and fair pricing, which is crucial for the sustained growth of this evolving sector. One of the primary hurdles in decentralized insurance is the paucity of historical data and actuarial models. Unlike traditional insurers who leverage extensive historical data to inform their risk models, decentralized platforms often operate in emerging markets or with novel financial instruments where such data is scarce or absent. This scarcity poses a significant challenge in developing robust risk models that accurately reflect the unique dynamics of decentralized insurance, requiring the industry to explore alternative methodologies to assess risk effectively.

Decentralized insurance heavily relies on smart contracts for automated and transparent policy execution. However, the vulnerabilities intrinsic to smart contracts present a substantial risk. Coding errors, security breaches, or unforeseen operational malfunctions can compromise the reliability of risk models. The challenge lies in adequately accounting for and mitigating these technological risks to ensure the integrity of risk assessments and pricing strategies, necessitating continuous advancements in blockchain technology and smart contract development. Cryptocurrencies, commonly used as assets within decentralized insurance, are prone to high volatility. The dynamic nature of cryptocurrency markets introduces uncertainties that challenge traditional risk modelling and pricing approaches. Developing models that accurately capture and predict the value fluctuations of these digital assets becomes a critical hurdle in ensuring fair and sustainable pricing structures for decentralized insurance products. Innovations in data analytics and predictive modelling are essential to navigate the intricate landscape of cryptocurrency markets and develop resilient risk management strategies.

To surmount these challenges, the decentralized insurance sector must embrace innovation and collaboration. Leveraging advancements in data analytics, machine learning, and blockchain technology can enhance risk model development, even without extensive historical data. Collaborative efforts between decentralized insurance platforms, technology experts, and regulatory bodies are crucial to establishing industry-wide standards and best practices that foster transparency and reliability in risk assessments. As the decentralized insurance sector matures, addressing these challenges becomes instrumental in building a resilient and sustainable ecosystem that can effectively serve the needs of users and investors.

4.3.6 Dependency Challenges and Investor Confidence

The dependency issue is a prominent challenge exemplified by the case of FidentiaX. The failure of FidentiaX, a blockchain-based insurtech startup, underscores the risks associated with overreliance on incumbent insurance companies for the success of a decentralized insurance marketplace. FidentiaX's strategic approach heavily relied on onboarding traditional insurance players to populate its marketplace, leading to a dependency on these incumbents. Rather than fostering a self-contained ecosystem, this approach exposed the startup to the challenges of convincing established insurers to embrace new technological paradigms. The reluctance of these incumbents to adapt their technology became a crucial bottleneck, ultimately contributing to the downfall of the FidentiaX project. Dependency challenges in decentralized insurance highlight the need for innovative strategies that reduce reliance on traditional players and promote self-sustainability within the insurance ecosystem.

Another critical dimension of challenges in decentralized insurance, as illustrated by the FidentiaX case, revolves around investor confidence. The project's failure was not solely attributed to technological hurdles but was exacerbated by a lack of confidence from investors. The decentralized insurance landscape, being relatively nascent and innovative, requires substantial investor trust to thrive. FidentiaX's inability to instil confidence stemmed from the difficulties in convincing traditional insurers and investors to embrace the decentralized model. This case emphasizes investor education, transparent communication, and robust value propositions in fostering confidence within the decentralized insurance sector. Addressing investor concerns and building trust becomes paramount for the sustainable growth and development of decentralized insurance initiatives.

Hence, dependency challenges associated with traditional insurers and the critical aspect of investor confidence emerge as significant hurdles in the decentralized insurance landscape. Overcoming these challenges requires a strategic shift towards self-sustainability, innovative solutions to bridge technological gaps, and proactive efforts to build trust among traditional players and investors. Decentralized insurance must navigate these complexities to realize its transformative potential and establish itself as a reliable and robust alternative in the broader insurance industry.

4.4 Political Challenges of Decentralized Insurance

Political challenges within the realm of decentralized insurance unfold as intricate hurdles and issues stemming from the interplay between innovative insurance models and the dynamic political environment. This intricate relationship poses challenges requiring careful consideration of government policies and an understanding of the geopolitical landscape, both of which can wield substantial influence over the operational landscape of decentralized insurance platforms. The global presence of decentralized insurance platforms demands an acute awareness of geopolitical factors that can influence cross-border coordination, regulatory standards, and the overall acceptance of decentralized insurance solutions (Anguiano & Parte, 2024). Global political events, such as diplomatic tensions or international policy shifts, may reverberate within the decentralized insurance sphere, necessitating strategic planning and adaptability to ensure sustained operations. Moreover, public perception and political backlash become critical dimensions influencing decentralized insurance. Political decisions and narratives can significantly shape how decentralized insurance is perceived by the public, influencing adoption rates and, consequently, the success of these innovative financial models.

4.4.1 Cross Border Collaboration

Cross-border collaboration emerges as a pivotal political challenge confronting decentralized insurance initiatives, necessitating seamless cooperation between jurisdictions. This collaborative imperative faces many hurdles rooted in diverse regulatory frameworks, geopolitical considerations, and national interests (Amponsah et al., 2021; Malhotra et al., 2022). One example highlighting the complexity of cross-border collaboration is seen in the European Union. The EU consists of member states with varying insurance regulations and legal frameworks. Decentralized insurance platforms seeking to operate across EU countries encounter the challenge of adhering to different rules, making navigating a complex regulatory landscape imperative. In the United States, each state has its insurance regulations, creating a decentralized regulatory environment within the country itself. Decentralized insurance projects aiming to provide coverage nationally must navigate the intricacies of state-specific requirements, demonstrating the need for tailored approaches to comply with diverse regulatory frameworks.

Geopolitical considerations further compound the challenges of cross-border collaboration. Diplomatic tensions, varying economic interests, and divergent policy priorities can influence the willingness of nations to engage in cooperative efforts concerning decentralized insurance. Regional geopolitical unrest may result in increased regulatory scrutiny, with governments emphasizing stringent controls on financial activities, potentially hindering the free-flowing nature of decentralized insurance platforms. Moreover, the absence of an international regulatory body for decentralized insurance creates a void that decentralized platforms must navigate independently. The lack of a centralized authority overseeing cross-border insurance activities leads to a fragmented landscape, wherein decentralized insurance providers are compelled to establish bilateral agreements with individual countries. This decentralized approach increases the complexity of operations and heightens the susceptibility to regulatory uncertainties and political interventions. Engaging in diplomatic dialogues, advocating for standardized international regulations, and fostering mutual understanding between jurisdictions become imperative. Establishing transparent communication channels with regulatory bodies and policymakers across borders is essential to navigating the intricate web of political considerations and creating an environment conducive to the global expansion of decentralized insurance. As the decentralized insurance landscape continues evolving, effective cross-border collaboration remains a cornerstone for sustainable growth and global acceptance.

4.4.2 Public Perception and Political Backlash

Public perception and potential political backlash present formidable challenges for decentralized insurance initiatives. The success and acceptance of decentralized insurance models hinge on technological advancements and how the public and the political establishment perceive these innovations. Negative perceptions and political resistance can impede the growth and adoption of decentralized insurance. An illustrative example of public perception impacting decentralized insurance is found in China. The country has been at the forefront of exploring blockchain applications, including DeFi and insurance. However, decentralized insurance platforms faced scepticism and criticism due to concerns about the reliability of smart contracts, data privacy, and the overall security of blockchain-based systems. This public scepticism has the potential to translate into political resistance and increased regulatory scrutiny, creating hurdles for the decentralized insurance ecosystem. The political backlash against decentralized insurance can also manifest in regulatory interventions. In the European context, as decentralized insurance gains prominence, there are instances where political authorities have expressed reservations about the potential risks associated with these models. Concerns about consumer protection, financial stability, and adherence to existing regulatory frameworks have been raised. This has led to political discussions on introducing measures that could curtail the expansion of decentralized insurance platforms.

To address the political challenge of public perception and potential backlash, decentralized insurance initiatives must prioritize transparent communication and education. Engaging in public awareness campaigns, clearly articulating the benefits of decentralized insurance, and addressing concerns through open dialogue contribute to building positive public perception. Moreover, collaboration with regulatory authorities to establish guidelines and standards that align with public expectations can help mitigate political resistance. Decentralized insurance platforms must proactively demonstrate their commitment to ethical practices, data security, and consumer protection to foster trust among users and gain political support. Building a positive narrative around the societal benefits of decentralized insurance, such as increased financial inclusion and efficiency, is essential in shaping public and political opinions in favour of these innovative models.

4.4.3 Lobbying and Industry Influence

Lobbying and industry influence represent a nuanced political challenge for decentralized insurance initiatives. As these innovative models gain traction, various stakeholders may lobby to shape regulatory frameworks, policies, and public perception in their favour. While lobbying is common in traditional industries, its impact on the decentralized insurance sector raises unique considerations. As decentralized finance and insurance gain prominence, different entities within the blockchain and cryptocurrency space may lobby policymakers to create a regulatory environment that aligns with their business models. Industry players, from decentralized insurance platforms to blockchain developers, may seek to influence legislation to favour decentralized technologies.

The challenge arises in finding the right balance between allowing industry players to contribute to the regulatory discourse and preventing undue influence that could compromise the integrity of decentralized insurance systems. Excessive lobbying efforts can lead to regulations favouring specific interests over broader societal benefits. Striking a balance that accommodates innovation while safeguarding consumer protection and systemic stability is crucial. To address the political challenge of lobbying and industry influence, decentralized insurance initiatives should prioritize transparency in their interactions with policymakers. Engaging in open and inclusive dialogues involving diverse stakeholders, including consumer advocacy groups, can help ensure that regulatory decisions consider the broader public interest. Regulators must remain vigilant to avoid regulatory capture, where industry interests excessively influence the regulatory process. Implementing disclosure requirements for lobbying activities and maintaining a transparent regulatory framework can help mitigate the risks associated with undue industry influence.

4.5 Conclusion

Examining existing regulatory structures reveals the challenges inherent in implementing decentralized insurance, while collaborative dialogues between regulators and industry leaders offer glimpses of potential solutions. Real-world examples from pioneering nations like Germany, Japan, and Australia enrich the narrative, providing insights into the evolving global landscape. Licencing and authorization, capital adequacy and solvency, underwriting and pricing standards, technical provisions and supervision, and investment management regulations are scrutinized to highlight the complexities of operating within the insurance sector's stringent regulatory framework. Regulatory challenges encompass difficulty recognizing decentralized insurance within existing legal frameworks. Economic challenges like scalability, interoperability, governance, financial stability, risk modelling, pricing, dependency, and investor confidence pose hurdles to widespread adoption. Political challenges, including cross-border collaboration, public perception, political backlash, lobbying, and industry influence, further complicate the operational landscape of decentralized insurance platforms. Despite these challenges, decentralized insurance holds immense potential to revolutionize the insurance industry, offering increased transparency, reduced operational costs, and enhanced accessibility. Collaborative efforts between regulators, industry stakeholders, and policymakers are essential to navigate the complexities and realize the full transformative potential of decentralized insurance. Stakeholders can pave the way for decentralized insurance to thrive in an ever-evolving global landscape by addressing regulatory uncertainties, fostering technological innovation, and promoting regulatory clarity.

References

Alvin, K., Erik, L., Gwen, W., & Rex, Z. (2022). *Decentralized insurance alternatives: Market landscape, opportunities and challenges*. The Society of Actuaries Research Institute. Accessed on 18 August 2023 from https://www.soa.org/resources/research-reports/2022/decentralized-ins-alt/

Amponsah, A. A., Weyori, B. A., & Adekoya, A. F. (2021). Blockchain in insurance: Exploratory analysis of prospects and threats. *International Journal of Advanced Computer Science and Applications, 12*(1). https://doi.org/10.14569/IJACSA.2021.0120153

Anguiano, D. T. T., & Parte, L. (2024). The state of art, opportunities and challenges of blockchain in the insurance industry: A systematic literature review. *Management Review Quarterly, 74*(2), 1097–1118. https://doi.org/10.1007/s11301-023-00328-6

Castelluccio, J. A. (2022). Decentralized insurance—A new frontier. https://www.mayerbrown.com/en/insights/publications/2022/03/decentralized-insurance-a-new-frontier

Cousaert, S., Vadgama, N., & Xu, J. (2022). Token-based insurance solutions on blockchain. In *Blockchains and the token economy: Theory and practice* (pp. 237–260). Springer International Publishing.

Gatteschi, V., Lamberti, F., Demartini, C., Pranteda, C., & Santamaría, V. (2018). Blockchain and smart contracts for insurance: is the technology mature enough? *Future Internet, 10*(2), 20. https://doi.org/10.3390/fi10020020

Godefroid, M., Plattfaut, R., & Niehaves, B. (2022). How to measure the status quo bias? A review of current literature. *Management Review Quarterly*, 1–45. https://doi.org/10.1007/s11301-022-00283-8

Howard, L. S. (2022, July 29). Industry's Blockchain Project, B3i, ceases to trade after filing for insolvency. *Insurance Journal*. https://www.insurancejournal.com/news/international/2022/07/29/677926.htm

International Insurance Society. (2021). Decentralized Finance (DeFi)—Risks and opportunities for the insurance industry. https://www.internationalinsurance.org/sites/default/files/2021-09/Decentralized%20Finance%209.2021_2.pdf

Malhotra, A., O'Neill, H., & Stowell, P. (2022). Thinking strategically about blockchain adoption and risk mitigation. *Business Horizons, 65*(2), 159–171. https://doi.org/10.1016/j.bushor.2021.02.033

MAS. (2017). MAS issues "Regulatory Sandbox" guidelines for FinTech experiments. Accessed on 18 August 2023 from https://www.mas.gov.sg/news/media-releases/2016/mas-issues-regulatory-sandbox-guidelines-for-fintech-experiments#:~:text=Singapore%2C%2016%20November%202016.,deliver%20financial%20products%20or%20services

McKinsey & Company. (2016). Blockchain in insurance—Opportunity or threat? https://www.mckinsey.com/~/media/mckinsey/industries/financial%20services/our%20insights/blockchain%20in%20insurance%20opportunity%20or%20threat/blockchain-in-insurance-opportunity-or-threat.ashx

OECD. (2017). Technology and innovation in the insurance sector. Accessed on 18 August 2023 from https://www.oecd.org/pensions/Technology-and-innovation-in-the-insurance-sector.pdf

Popovic, D., Avis, C., Byrne, M., Cheung, C., Donovan, M., Flynn, Y., Fothergill, C., Hosseinzadeh, Z., Lim, Z., & Shah, J. (2020). Understanding blockchain for insurance use cases. *British Actuarial Journal, 25*(e12), 1–23. https://doi.org/10.1017/S1357321720000148

Saeed, M., & Arshed, N. (2022). Revolutionizing insurance sector in India: A case of blockchain adoption challenges. *International Journal of Contemporary Economics and Administrative Sciences, 12*(1), 300–324.

Sakho, S., Jianbiao, Z., Essaf, F., & Mbyamm Kiki, M. J. (2019). Blockchain: Perspectives and issues. *Journal of Intelligent & Fuzzy Systems, 37*(6), 8029–8052. https://doi.org/10.3233/JIFS-190449

Shetty, A., Shetty, A. D., Pai, R. Y., Rao, R. R., Bhandary, R., Shetty, J., Nayak, S., Dinesh, K. T., & Dsouza, K. J. (2022). Block chain application in insurance services: A systematic review of the evidence. *SAGE Open, 12*(1), 21582440221079876.

Skipper, H. D. (1997). *Foreign insurers in emerging markets: Issues and concerns*. International Insurance Foundation, Occasional Paper no.1.

Sun, R. T., Garimella, A., Han, W., Chang, H. L., & Shaw, M. J. (2020). Transformation of the transaction cost and the agency cost in an organization and the applicability of blockchain—A case study of peer-to-peer insurance. *Front Blockchain, 3*, 1–24. https://doi.org/10.3389/fbloc.2020.00024

The Geneva Association. (2023). *Assessing the potential of decentralised finance and blockchain technology in insurance*. https://www.genevaassociation.org/sites/default/files/2023-08/DeFi%20insurance_WEB.pdf

Walsh, C., O'Reilly, P., Gleasure, R., McAvoy, J., O'Leary, K. (2021). Understanding manager resistance to blockchain systems. *European Management Journal, 39*(3), 353–365. https://doi.org/10.1016/j.emj.2020.10.001

Zhao, L. (2020). The analysis of application, key issues and the future development trend of blockchain technology in the insurance industry. *American Journal of Industrial and Business Management, 10*(02), 305–314. https://doi.org/10.4236/ajibm.2020.102019

CHAPTER 5

Emerging Trends in Regulatory and Legal Frameworks for Decentralized Insurance

5.1 Emerging Trends in Regulatory and Legal Frameworks for Decentralized Insurance

The dynamic landscape of decentralized insurance is witnessing a profound evolution in regulatory and legal frameworks, encapsulating a spectrum of innovative trends and strategic initiatives. In this multifaceted exploration, emerging trends reveal a concerted effort to integrate DeFi principles, foster innovation through sandbox regulatory frameworks, establish RegTech and SupTech, prioritize enhanced consumer protection mechanisms, and embrace sustainability through carbon credits and climate risk mitigation measures. These initiatives underscore a global convergence towards establishing uniform standards within the decentralized insurance sector, particularly in regulatory reporting. This comprehensive endeavour aims to cultivate a secure, transparent, and sustainable environment while promoting global regulatory clarity and efficiency in decentralized insurance operations. Through collaborative efforts and strategic partnerships, regulatory authorities across diverse jurisdictions are shaping the future of decentralized insurance, fostering an ecosystem that prioritizes consumer protection, innovation, and environmental sustainability on a global scale (Table 5.1).

N. Singhal et al., *Potential, Risks, and Ethical Implications of Decentralized Insurance*, Technology, Work and Globalization, https://doi.org/10.1007/978-981-97-5894-4_5

Table 5.1 Regulatory trends in decentralized insurance

	Purpose	*Benefits*	*Insights for regulatory bodies*
Regulation and Guidelines on AI implementation	– To draft regulations and guidelines on AI Implementation in the Insurance Sector	– Enhanced operational efficiency in insurance processes – Improved accuracy in risk assessment and pricing decisions – Greater transparency and accountability in AI-driven practices	– The need for clear guidelines to govern AI implementation in insurance – Addressing challenges related to data privacy, algorithmic bias, and regulatory compliance – Harmonizing regulations across jurisdictions while considering cultural and legal contexts
Integration of DeFi Protocols in Regulatory Frameworks	– To adapt to the evolving landscape of decentralized insurance while maintaining compliance with established standards	– Increased transparency and accountability in decentralized insurance operations – Mitigate DeFi protocols' risks, such as smart contract vulnerabilities and financial fraud – Promotion of innovation and financial inclusion within a regulated environment – Facilitate international collaboration and standardization in DeFi regulation	– Understanding decentralized insurance's unique characteristics and challenges within the broader DeFi ecosystem – Learning from existing regulatory frameworks for DeFi platforms to inform the development of decentralized insurance regulations – Collaborating with international bodies and stakeholders to establish global standards for decentralized insurance regulation
Sandbox Regulatory Frameworks	– To create controlled environments where innovative financial services and technologies can be tested under regulatory supervision	– Encourages experimentation and innovation within the financial sector – Provides a safe space for fintech startups to test new products and services without full regulatory compliance – Facilitates collaboration between regulators and industry stakeholders to address emerging challenges and opportunities – Enables regulators to gather insights and data on new technologies and business models before implementing broader regulatory changes	– Learning from successful sandbox initiatives to develop effective regulatory frameworks for emerging technologies – Collaborating with industry participants to design sandbox programs that meet the needs of both innovators and regulators – Continuously monitor and evaluate sandbox projects to identify risks and best practices for future regulation

	Purpose	*Benefits*	*Insights for regulatory bodies*
Supervisory Technology (SupTech)	– To improve regulatory activities' efficiency, effectiveness, and transparency while addressing emerging risks and challenges	– Increased efficiency in data collection, analysis, and interpretation for regulatory purposes – Enhanced risk identification and monitoring capabilities, leading to more proactive supervision – Improved regulatory compliance through automated processes and real-time monitoring – Greater transparency and accountability in regulatory decision-making processes – Reduction of operational costs and resource requirements for regulatory agencies	– Understanding the potential of SupTech to transform regulatory functions and processes – Recognizing the importance of investing in technology infrastructure and talent to support SupTech initiatives – Embracing collaboration with industry stakeholders and technology providers to develop and implement SupTech solutions – Adapt regulatory frameworks and guidelines to accommodate advanced technologies under supervision
Regulatory Technology (RegTech)	– To address regulatory and compliance requirements more effectively and efficiently	– Enhanced compliance with complex regulations by applying innovative technologies such as machine learning, artificial intelligence, biometrics, and data analytics – Streamlined regulatory reporting processes, risk modelling for stress testing, and monitoring of capital requirement compliance – Improved anti-money laundering (AML) and know-your-customer (KYC) programs, fraud prevention, and detection of in-house violations – Increased transparency and accountability in regulatory processes and reporting	– Acknowledgement of the pivotal role of RegTech in modernizing regulatory approaches and ensuring effective compliance – Emphasis on collaboration with industry stakeholders and startups to drive innovation and adoption of RegTech solutions – Consideration of regulatory sandboxes and pilot programs to test and evaluate RegTech applications in real-world scenarios – Focus on talent development and infrastructure investment to support the integration and deployment of RegTech solutions
Data Privacy and Security Regulations	– To establish frameworks and standards that protect individuals' privacy rights and sensitive information	– Protection of individuals' privacy rights and sensitive information against data breaches and unauthorized access – Compliance with regulatory requirements enhances consumer trust and confidence in decentralized insurance platforms – Safeguarding against cybersecurity threats and data breaches mitigates legal and financial risks for insurance companies – Encouragement of responsible data handling practices and accountability among insurance providers	– Collaboration with international counterparts to harmonize data privacy standards and ensure cross-border data transfer mechanisms – Implement robust notification requirements for data breaches to facilitate timely response and mitigate potential damages – Enforcement of fines and penalties for non-compliance with data privacy regulations to incentivize adherence to regulatory standards – Promotion of transparency and accountability in data processing practices through data protection impact assessments and consent mechanisms

(continued)

Table 5.1 (continued)

	Purpose	*Benefits*	*Insights for regulatory bodies*
Sustainable Integration	– To incorporate carbon credits and climate risk mitigation measures into decentralized insurance frameworks	– Encourages insurance companies to adopt sustainable practices and contribute to environmental conservation efforts – Mitigates climate-related risks and enhances resilience against natural disasters and extreme weather events – Aligns insurance practices with international sustainability goals and commitments to combat climate change – Fosters innovation in decentralized insurance solutions by incorporating carbon credits and climate risk mitigation measures	– Collaboration with environmental agencies and stakeholders to develop regulatory frameworks that promote sustainable integration within decentralized insurance – Integrating climate risk assessments and sustainability criteria into insurance licencing and approval processes – Development of guidelines and standards for transparent reporting and disclosure of climate-related risks and sustainability initiatives by insurance companies – Implementation of incentives and support mechanisms to encourage adopting eco-friendly insurance practices and investment in sustainable projects

	Implementation and scope	*Regulatory initiatives*	*Technological integration*
Regulation and Guidelines on AI implementation	– Developing robust frameworks to ensure responsible AI deployment – Establishing standards for transparency, accountability, and data governance – Adapting regulatory approaches to emerging challenges and technological developments	– International efforts such as the European Union's AI Act – National regulations focusing on AI ethics and human centricity – Sector-specific guidelines for AI implementation in insurance	– Incorporating AI technologies into risk assessment, underwriting, and claims processing – Developing methodologies for evaluating the fairness and transparency of AI systems – Collaboration between regulatory bodies and industry stakeholders to address emerging risks and promote responsible AI adoption in insurance

	Implementation and scope	*Regulatory initiatives*	*Technological integration*
Integration of DeFi Protocols in Regulatory Frameworks	– Incorporating DeFi principles into existing legal structures for insurance regulation – Addressing regulatory gaps and challenges specific to decentralized insurance – Balancing innovation and compliance to foster a dynamic and inclusive regulatory environment	– Developing guidelines and standards for issuing, trading, and custody of digital assets within decentralized insurance platforms – Establishing clear regulatory frameworks to protect investors and maintain market stability in decentralized insurance – Collaborating with international organizations to harmonize decentralized insurance regulations across jurisdictions	– Leveraging blockchain technology and distributed ledger technology to enhance transparency and auditability in decentralized insurance – Encouraging innovation in decentralized insurance while ensuring adherence to regulatory requirements – Providing support and guidance to insurance entities and fintech startups to navigate the regulatory landscape and promote responsible innovation
Sandbox Regulatory Frameworks	– Designing sandbox programs that are flexible, transparent, and accessible to a wide range of stakeholders – Setting clear objectives and criteria for participation in sandbox projects – Providing regulatory guidance and support to participants throughout the testing process – Evaluating the outcomes of sandbox experiments to inform broader regulatory decisions and policy changes	– Establishing formal frameworks and guidelines for sandbox programs within regulatory agencies – Engaging with industry stakeholders to solicit feedback and input on sandbox design and implementation – Collaborating with other regulatory bodies and international organizations to share best practices and lessons learned from sandbox initiatives – Monitoring the impact of sandbox projects on consumer protection, market integrity, and financial stability	– Leveraging digital platforms and tools to streamline the application and review process for sandbox participants – Incorporating emerging technologies such as blockchain, artificial intelligence, and machine learning into sandbox experiments – Ensuring that sandbox programs are equipped to handle the unique regulatory challenges posed by new technologies and business models – Promoting cross-sector collaboration and knowledge-sharing to enhance the effectiveness of sandbox initiatives in fostering innovation

(continued)

Table 5.1 (continued)

	Implementation and scope	*Regulatory initiatives*	*Technological integration*
Supervisory Technology (SupTech)	– Developing customized SupTech solutions tailored to regulatory agencies' needs and priorities – Integrating data analytics, machine learning, natural language processing, and visualization techniques into supervisory processes – Establishing data standards and protocols to ensure interoperability and compatibility across different systems and platforms – Providing training and capacity-building programs for regulatory staff to enhance their technical skills and expertise in SupTech	– Launching pilot programs and proof-of-concept initiatives to test and evaluate SupTech solutions in real-world environments – Collaborating with international regulatory bodies and standard-setting organizations to share best practices and develop common SupTech standards – Engaging with industry participants and technology firms to foster innovation and adoption of SupTech tools and methodologies – Monitoring regulatory developments and trends in SupTech to stay abreast of new opportunities and challenges	– Integrating SupTech solutions with existing regulatory frameworks and systems to enhance effectiveness and efficiency – Leveraging big data analytics and predictive modelling to identify and assess potential risks and vulnerabilities in the financial system – Implementing real-time monitoring and surveillance capabilities to detect and mitigate compliance breaches and misconduct – Exploring emerging technologies such as distributed ledger technology and cloud computing to improve data security and scalability in SupTech applications

	Implementation and scope	*Regulatory initiatives*	*Technological integration*
Regulatory Technology (RegTech)	– Integration of RegTech platforms with existing regulatory frameworks and systems to enhance oversight and enforcement capabilities – Establishment of interoperability standards and protocols to facilitate seamless data exchange and integration across jurisdictions – Promoting cross-border collaboration and knowledge-sharing to foster innovation and standardization in the RegTech ecosystem – Conducting regular assessments and evaluations of RegTech implementations to ensure alignment with regulatory objectives	– Collaboration with industry associations and standard-setting bodies to develop common RegTech standards and best practices – Launching public–private partnerships and innovation hubs to incubate and accelerate the development of RegTech solutions – Implementing regulatory sandboxes and innovation labs to foster experimentation and regulatory compliance – Enhancing regulatory guidance and oversight to address emerging challenges and risks associated with RegTech adoption	– Leveraging advanced technologies such as machine learning, AI, blockchain, and cloud computing to power RegTech solutions – Utilizing data analytics and predictive modelling techniques to identify compliance risks and enhance decision-making processes – Addressing challenges related to algorithmic bias, transparency, and accountability in using algorithms for regulatory compliance – Monitoring and assessing the impact of RegTech solutions on regulatory outcomes and market dynamics

(continued)

Table 5.1 (continued)

	Implementation and scope	*Regulatory initiatives*	*Technological integration*
Data Privacy and Security Regulations	– Adoption of data protection laws and regulations, such as the General Data Protection Regulation, to govern the processing of personal data – Integration of privacy-by-design principles into decentralized insurance platforms to embed data protection measures from the outset – Implement robust data governance frameworks to ensure compliance with data privacy regulations and mitigate risks associated with data processing – Enhancement of cybersecurity measures and incident response protocols to address emerging threats and vulnerabilities in decentralized insurance ecosystems	– Development of regulatory frameworks to address emerging technologies such as artificial intelligence and machine learning in insurance pricing and underwriting – Monitoring developments in international jurisdictions to inform regulatory approaches and ensure alignment with global best practices – Collaboration with industry stakeholders and technology experts to address ethical and regulatory challenges associated with using big data and analytics in insurance – Promotion of transparency and accountability in algorithmic decision-making processes to prevent biases and ensure fairness in insurance practices	– Integration of privacy-enhancing technologies (PETs) such as encryption and anonymization to protect sensitive data and preserve privacy rights – Adopting secure data storage and transmission protocols to prevent unauthorized access and data breaches – Implement robust identity and access management solutions to control and monitor user access to sensitive information – Utilization of advanced analytics and machine learning techniques to detect and mitigate cybersecurity threats and identify potential vulnerabilities in decentralized insurance platforms

	Implementation and scope	*Regulatory initiatives*	*Technological integration*
Sustainable Integration	– Establishment of regulatory guidelines for insurance companies to incorporate carbon credits and climate risk mitigation strategies into their underwriting and investment practices – Integration of sustainability criteria into insurance product design, pricing models, and claims management processes – Promotion of research and development initiatives to explore innovative technologies and solutions for climate risk assessment and mitigation within decentralized insurance – Facilitation of international collaborations and partnerships to exchange best practices and promote global standards for sustainable integration in insurance regulations	– Tailored regulations by FINMA, CVM, and APRA promote sustainable practices in decentralized insurance – NAIC leads state-level efforts in the US, notably in California, to integrate sustainability into insurance regulations – Regulatory bodies worldwide like FSA, DNB, and FSCA explore sustainability and climate risk mitigation – Global authorities such as BaFin, MAS, and ACPR actively engage in discussions and regulatory measures to advance sustainability in decentralized insurance	– Tech Integration for Carbon Credits & Climate Risk: Blockchain and data analytics aid in transparently integrating carbon credits and climate risk measures into decentralized insurance – Climate Risk Assessment with Satellite Imagery: Satellite imagery and geospatial analytics enable climate risk assessment, aiding informed decisions by insurers – Digital Platforms for Sustainable Insurance: Digital platforms and mobile apps enhance consumer awareness and engagement in sustainable insurance practices and climate risk mitigation

Source Prepared by authors

5.1.1 *Regulation and Guidelines on AI Implementation in the Insurance Sector*

AI represents a paradigm shift in how insurers assess risks, underwrite policies, and process claims. AI technologies offer unprecedented opportunities to enhance operational efficiency, improve risk management practices, and deliver personalized services to policyholders. However, alongside these opportunities, it brings significant challenges related to data privacy, algorithmic bias, and regulatory compliance. Against this backdrop, regulatory bodies and policymakers worldwide are grappling with the complex task of developing robust frameworks to govern the responsible implementation of AI within the insurance sector. These frameworks aim to establish clear guidelines, standards, and safeguards to ensure that AI systems are deployed ethically, transparently, and in accordance with legal requirements (The Geneva Association, 2023).

The regulatory landscape surrounding AI implementation in insurance is multifaceted and dynamic, reflecting different jurisdictions' diverse approaches and priorities. At the international level, initiatives such as the European Union's AI Act seek to harmonize regulations across member states while addressing the unique challenges posed by AI-driven insurance practices (Chatzara, 2020). The AI Act introduces risk-based categorizations for AI applications, including those deemed "high risk", such as those used in risk assessment and pricing decisions. It mandates specific requirements for transparency, accountability, and data governance. Similarly, regulatory bodies in other regions, including the United States, Asia–Pacific, and beyond, are developing guidelines and standards tailored to their respective legal and cultural contexts. From Japan's emphasis on human-centric AI principles to Singapore's focus on fairness, ethics, accountability, and transparency, each jurisdiction seeks to balance promoting innovation and safeguarding consumer interests. Moreover, the regulatory landscape is evolving in response to emerging challenges and technological developments. Recent discussions surrounding the use of AI in insurance have centred on issues such as algorithmic discrimination, data protection, and the need for greater transparency and explainability in AI-driven decision-making processes.

In this context, understanding the intricacies of regulatory frameworks and guidelines on AI implementation is paramount for insurers, regulators, policymakers, and other stakeholders. By fostering dialogue, collaboration, and knowledge-sharing, stakeholders can collectively navigate the complexities of AI regulation, foster a culture of responsible innovation, and build public trust in AI-enabled insurance practices.

The Chinese government is actively developing regulations focused on AI ethics. This is important in ensuring ethical principles govern AI applications involving human interaction. Furthermore, the legislation implemented in 2023 will cover a wide range of sectors and grant regulators the right to request companies' source codes for explanation and documentation. This proactive approach by the Chinese government demonstrates their commitment to upholding principles such as human centricity, human autonomy, security, controllability, fairness, and justice in AI.

The EU is one of the most ambitious organizations regulating AI, with several guidelines and regulations. The European Commission proposed the EU AI Act in 2021, creating regulations for several businesses. The Act seeks to protect AI systems and ensure they abide by current basic rights and EU principles laws. It aims to improve governance and the efficient implementation of current rules, create legal clarity to encourage investment and innovation in AI and speed up the creation of a single market for legitimate, reliable, and safe AI applications. Because it covers a wide range of sectors and businesses, the EU AI Act is "horizontal". It uses a risk-based methodology to distinguish between AI applications with possible low, restricted, high, or intolerable dangers. Insurance is one of the sectors impacted by the AI Act, especially regarding "high-risk" applications. Although AI applications for risk assessment and pricing choices in life and health insurance were not specifically included in the initial plan, it was added as a high-risk application in an amended version in response to lobbying from several parties. Technical documentation and record keeping (e.g., setting up automated logging capabilities to monitor system operation and risk occurrence and record the duration of use, the reference databases checked by the AI system and the identity of the people involved) as well as requirements pertaining to data governance and management practices, risk management systems, and high-risk AI applications in the insurance industry would be subject to specific regulatory requirements. The extent of AI is largely determined by the definition given in the Act's appendix. AI was first described in the proposal as software created using methods and strategies that provide outputs like suggestions, information, forecasts, or judgements that affect the settings in which they operate. Long-standing analytical techniques employed by insurers may fall under the original concept's wide meaning (Gallo & Nair, 2024). Although the AI Act's geographic reach is restricted to AI applications utilized within the EU, the "Brussels effect" should not be undervalued (Soliman, 2024). Given the distinct features of the insurance sector and its existing regulatory frameworks, industry players, including the EIOPA, have underscored the significance of sector-specific regulation instead of cross-sectoral regulation. Additionally, EIOPA supports the notion of proportionality in regulating AI, emphasizing characteristics unique from conventional mathematical models and their implications for basic rights.

Legislative and regulatory measures that specifically control AI use in insurance and other industries are not in place in Japan. The Civil Code, which regulates contracts and agreements, and the Protection of Personal Information Act, which protects data used for AI applications, are examples of current rules and regulations that apply instead. Although there are no official rules or regulations on AI in Japan, several ministries have released non-binding advice on the subject. With an emphasis on human centricity, privacy protection, security, justice, openness, and responsibility, the "Social Principles of Human-Centric AI" were released in 2019. The Ministry of Economy, Trade, and Industry then released guidelines for their application (Habuka, 2023).

Singapore's strategy does not include certain legislative requirements for using AI in insurance; instead, it concentrates on offering ideas and guidelines. In 2018, the insurance sector and the Monetary Authority of Singapore collaborated to produce the Fairness, Ethics, Accountability, and Transparency (FEAT) principles. These guidelines provide high-level direction for the ethical application of AI in the insurance and finance industries. Over thirty individuals from various industries, including IT, finance, and insurance, make up the Veritas consortium, which MAS established to offer helpful advice on implementing the FEAT principles. The consortium intends to offer an open-source toolbox to assess the fairness and transparency of AI systems and propose workable approaches for financial institutions to apply the FEAT principles. AI inspections have demonstrated how successfully the insurance sector has incorporated the FEAT principles. This illustrates how regulators and insurers may work together to address new risks using principles rather than more regulations. In the future, MAS hopes to further global collaboration on use case-specific guidelines for the insurance sector in other nations. This would assist globally operating insurers in adhering to uniform standards instead of disparate ethical and governance frameworks.

The UK does not now have any regulations on AI. To become a worldwide leader in AI, the U.K. government, like Australia, is creating a national AI policy with a 10-year timeline. The government wants to regulate AI in a way that is "clear, innovation-friendly, and flexible to unleash growth and innovation while safeguarding fundamental values," according to this policy. The government also suggested a set of guidelines for the application of AI. Fairness, explainability, and openness are a few of them. The Financial Conduct Authority and the Bank of England released a discussion paper towards the end of 2022 examining how regulatory goals and AI use in UK financial services interacted. To support financial services organizations in adopting AI safely and responsibly, the paper asked stakeholders several questions: Was a sectoral definition of AI necessary? Additionally, suggestions for a good strategy to handle the unique hazards posed by AI were requested. Industry players have responded to this article by suggesting that current technology-neutral insurance regulatory frameworks could address future AI-related challenges. These frameworks should prioritize openness, explainability, fairness, accessibility, and accountability. The Data Protection Act, the Equality Act, and the new FCA Consumer Duty, which will be phased in starting in the summer of 2023, are a few examples of current regulatory frameworks that apply to AI (Bank of England, 2022, 2023).

In the United States, state-based insurance regulations, federal and state anti-discrimination statutes, and state regulatory efforts that particularly target the use of AI are the key factors influencing AI regulation in the insurance industry. A "blueprint for an AI Bill of Rights" was released by the White House Office of Science and Technology Policy. It outlines five principles—safety, protection against algorithmic discrimination, data privacy, notice and explanation, and human alternatives—for the ethical use of AI. State-based insurance regulation exists in the US, and the NAIC is a forum for state insurance regulators to meet. State regulators have a platform to debate technology advancements in insurance, including artificial intelligence, through the NAIC's Innovation Cybersecurity and Technology Committee, also called the "H Committee". Regulatory guidelines on AI applications in insurance have been created and endorsed by the NAIC, focusing on safety, fairness, accountability, compliance, and transparency. The H Committee concluded that the optimal course of action is not to produce a model rule or law but rather regulatory advice (bulletins). The committee recently addressed whether existing insurance regulatory frameworks reflect the (new) dangers connected with AI in insurance. Based on current rules and regulations, these advisories would set expectations for insurers about overseeing and managing the risks associated with AI in decision-making. AI rules for insurers are also being developed by state lawmakers and regulators, with notable progress made in Colorado. Signed into law in 2021, Colorado Senate Bill 21–169 limits insurers' use of outside data and outlaws unjust discrimination based on an individual's protected status. Additionally, utilizing data that has no direct connection to the risk is forbidden by the new regulation. Federal and state laws have long forbade discrimination against individuals based on their protected status; however, Colorado has expanded this prohibition to include handicaps. This is seen as extensive in the context of insurance as it could limit insurers' services to this particular population. The Colorado Division of Insurance responded to this statute by releasing the draft Algorithm and Predictive Model Governance Regulation in February 2023. This regulation outlines the guidelines for the governance of artificial intelligence (AI) and using external data by life insurance businesses.

The insurance business was impacted by new technology breakthroughs in 2023, which led to the implementation of several programs and increased attempts to safeguard customers. The Model Bulletin on the Use of Algorithms, Predictive Models, and Artificial Intelligence Systems by Insurers (as revised during the meeting) was adopted by the Innovation, Cybersecurity, and Technology (H) Committee during the Fall NAIC Meeting in December 2023. The Model Bulletin is a model message that insurance regulators may use to direct insurers to use AI systems in a way that complies with current laws against unfair and deceptive trade practices, corporate governance, and market behaviour. Its goal is to strike a balance between promoting innovation and safeguarding insurance consumers from any potential negative effects of employing AI systems, such as illegal prejudice or discriminatory activities (The Geneva Association, 2023; Waters & Macro, 2023). The NAIC Big Data and Artificial Intelligence Working Group polled home and life insurers separately in 2023. It published papers on the applications of AI used by these insurers in marketing, fraud detection, claims, underwriting, and loss prevention. These surveys were conducted in addition to a comparable one that private passenger motor insurers finished in 2022. On December 8, 2023, European Union legislators approved the A.I. Act, a law that must still be approved through a few stages. To guard against potential threats such as job automation and the transmission of false information, the A.I. Act "set[s] a new global benchmark for countries seeking to harness the potential benefits of the technology" (Waters & Macro, 2023; NAIC, 2023).

5.1.2 Integration of DeFi Protocols in Regulatory Frameworks

The narrative of decentralized insurance unfolds within the dynamic contours of regulatory evolution. A noteworthy trend is at the forefront of this evolution—the increasing acknowledgement and integration of DeFi principles. Regulators are actively exploring integrating DeFi principles into existing legal structures, acknowledging the potential benefits of decentralized insurance while ensuring compliance with established regulatory standards. Since decentralized insurance is an emerging field within the broader DeFi ecosystem, it has not yet seen the same regulatory attention and framework development as DeFi platforms (Deloitte, 2024). However, the principles and challenges related to regulatory frameworks for DeFi platforms can provide insights into how decentralized insurance might be approached from a regulatory perspective.

The European Blockchain Observatory and Forum, an initiative spearheaded by the European Commission, is dedicated to advancing blockchain technology and nurturing the blockchain ecosystem within the EU. To solidify Europe's standing as a frontrunner in this groundbreaking technology, the Observatory and Forum engage in dynamic and continuous dialogues to shape regulations that align with the evolving landscape of DeFi. Within the European Union, the EU Blockchain Observatory and Forum are pivotal platforms for facilitating robust discussions and collaborations among stakeholders, including policymakers, industry experts, and innovators. By actively participating in these dialogues, regulatory frameworks are crafted to accommodate the dynamic developments unfolding within decentralized finance. This proactive stance reflects a strategic commitment to embracing the inherent transformative potential of blockchain-based financial models. By fostering an environment conducive to innovation and regulatory agility, the EU aims to position itself at the forefront of the global blockchain revolution while ensuring that regulatory measures remain adaptive to the rapidly evolving landscape of decentralized finance.

The proposed Markets in Crypto-Assets (MiCA) framework in the EU represents a significant step towards regulating digital assets, including those operating within DeFi platforms. MiCA aims to address the regulatory challenges posed by the rapidly evolving cryptocurrency and DeFi landscape while ensuring investor protection and market stability. Under the MiCA framework, the EU seeks to establish clear guidelines for issuing, trading, and custody of digital assets within DeFi platforms. The regulations aim to provide legal certainty and transparency to investors while mitigating the risks associated with decentralized financial activities. By creating a regulatory framework tailored to the unique characteristics of DeFi, the EU aims to foster innovation while safeguarding the interests of market participants. One of MiCA's key objectives is to promote responsible innovation in the DeFi sector by establishing a regulatory environment that balances risk management with the need for technological advancement. The EU Blockchain Observatory and Forum are crucial in developing DeFi regulations within the MiCA framework. Through ongoing dialogues and collaboration with industry experts, policymakers, and regulators, the Observatory facilitates the exchange of insights and best practices to inform the drafting of effective regulatory measures.

Moreover, the EU's approach to regulating DeFi reflects its commitment to harnessing the potential of blockchain technology while addressing the associated risks. The MiCA regulation is a landmark framework the European Commission (EC) created to maintain financial stability, protect investors, and foster transformative changes in the crypto asset sector across EU countries. MiCA's significance lies in providing providers of digital wallets and other crypto services to market and sell their offerings across the EU bloc, contingent upon their registration with national authorities and compliance with minimum guarantees to safeguard investors and maintain financial stability (Linden & Shivani, 2023; Ferreira, 2021).

The Central Bank of Russia initiated a comprehensive and forward-looking exploration into integrating blockchain-based financial platforms within the country's intricate regulatory framework. With a keen focus on blockchain technology, particularly Distributed Ledger Technology, the Central Bank of Russia has witnessed significant adoption within the domestic financial services industry. Many DLT-based projects are underway in collaboration with various financial institutions and banks nationwide. Specifically, the Central Bank of Russia has been at the forefront of recognizing and endorsing DLT-based initiatives to modernize financial processes. Notable examples include the implementation of electronic mortgages, digital letters of credit, and digital bank guarantees, all of which leverage the innovative capabilities of blockchain technology. Additionally, the National Settlement Depository, which serves as Russia's central securities depository, has developed a blockchain-based platform for e-proxy shareholder voting, revolutionizing the shareholder voting process with enhanced transparency and security measures. Furthermore, the country has extended its blockchain.

The Monetary Authority of Singapore adopts a proactive stance in regulating the application of blockchain technology within the insurance sector. Through extensive research and consultations, MAS recognizes the transformative potential of new technologies to enhance efficiency, manage risks, create opportunities, and improve people's lives. As blockchain technology is still in its experimental phase, MAS provides a secure and supportive environment for Financial Institutions and FinTech players to explore innovative solutions while mitigating the risks of potential failures. Financial institutions are granted autonomy to introduce new solutions without direct MAS guidance, provided they have conducted thorough due diligence and adhered to legal and regulatory requirements. In June/July 2016, MAS conducted a public consultation and released the finalized FinTech Regulatory Sandbox Guidelines in November 2016. These guidelines delineate essential principles and procedures for navigating the regulatory landscape. MAS's proactive approach to regulation reflects its commitment to fostering innovation while ensuring the stability and integrity of Singapore's financial sector. Through collaborative efforts and forward-thinking initiatives, MAS aims to position Singapore as a leading hub for financial technology innovation and adoption (MAS, 2016).

The Australian Securities and Investments Commission introduced groundbreaking measures in December 2016 to foster innovation in the fintech sector. ASIC's initiative included the release of the world's first licencing exemption for eligible fintech businesses, allowing them to test specific services without obtaining a financial services credit licence (ASIC, 2016). Notably, this exemption covers general insurance for personal property and home contents, with a maximum insured amount of $50,000. This move aimed to encourage fintech innovation while minimizing regulatory barriers and facilitating the developing and testing of new financial products and services. ASIC's regulatory sandbox framework provides flexibility within the regulatory landscape for fintech businesses to test innovative services. The framework comprises various components, including existing regulatory flexibility, tailored licencing exemptions, and the fintech licencing exemption introduced by ASIC. This comprehensive approach offers fintech startups multiple pathways to test the viability of their services while ensuring consumer protection and regulatory compliance. By providing clear guidelines and support, ASIC aims to facilitate innovation in financial services while maintaining regulatory oversight and promoting good consumer outcomes. The fintech licencing exemption introduced by ASIC allows eligible businesses to test specified services for up to 12 months with a maximum of 100 retail clients. This exemption reflects ASIC's commitment to promoting innovation in financial services while ensuring consumer protection (ASIC, 2016).

Additionally, ASIC has enhanced its guidance to licensees regarding organizational competence requirements, providing greater flexibility for small-scale, heavily automated businesses. These updates aim to accommodate the unique circumstances of innovative startups and facilitate compliance with regulatory requirements in alternative ways. Furthermore, ASIC encourages businesses ineligible for the fintech licencing exemption to explore individual exemption options, thereby promoting inclusivity and flexibility within the regulatory framework. The regulatory changes implemented by ASIC underscore Australia's commitment to fostering a conducive environment for fintech innovation. By offering regulatory relief and guidance, ASIC seeks to promote competition, encourage investment, and enhance consumer welfare in the financial services sector. The updates to ASIC's regulatory guides and licencing framework reflect the evolving needs of innovative businesses and align with ASIC's ongoing efforts to support the growth and development of the fintech ecosystem. As fintech continues to reshape the financial landscape, regulatory initiatives like those introduced by ASIC play a crucial role in driving innovation, promoting financial inclusion, and ensuring the stability and integrity of the financial system.

In March 2018, The French Prudential Supervision and Resolution Authority surveyed the challenges of the digital revolution in the French banking and insurance sectors (Banque De France, 2018). In March 2017 in New Zealand, The Financial Markets Authority granted an exemption to enable a broader range of products that robo-advisers can provide users, including mortgages and personal insurance, beginning in 2018

(Financial Markets Authority, 2017). This collective effort of regulators, insurance entities and several stakeholders signifies a noticeable shift towards a more inclusive, dynamic, and collaborative regulatory approach. It aims to foster and cultivate innovation within the structured confines of a carefully regulated environment. It encourages a delicate balance between the burgeoning creativity in decentralized insurance and the necessity to uphold established standards. These evolving trends in regulatory and legal frameworks for decentralized insurance paint a vivid and expansive picture of an industry navigating a delicate equilibrium between innovation and compliance. The global exploration of DeFi integration, coupled with the reasonable implementation of regulatory measures and international collaboration, not only sets the stage but also provides a robust foundation for a promising future where decentralized insurance can not only survive but thrive within a regulatory framework that encourages creativity while steadfastly upholding established standards.

Box 5.1: Israeli Ministry of Finance Implements Sweeping Reforms to Facilitate Insurer Licencing

The Israeli Ministry of Finance recently announced significant changes to ease the requirements for obtaining an insurer's licence in Israel. This move comes as part of a broader strategy to encourage competition within the insurance sector, which a handful of major players have historically dominated. According to a report by the Midroog Consulting Firm, the top five insurers in Israel control over 85% of total managed assets in the sector, highlighting the need for increased diversity and competition. To address this, the Ministry of Finance proposed regulations to reduce the minimum capital required for new insurance companies, thereby opening up opportunities for new players to enter the market. The proposed changes include substantial reductions in the minimum capital requirements for various insurance companies. For instance, the capital requirement for a Life Insurance Company has been lowered from NIS 52 million to NIS 15 million. In contrast, the requirement for a general insurance company has been decreased from NIS 59 million to NIS 10 million (Levitan, 2018).

These adjustments represent a significant shift and aim to lower the barriers to entry for new investors interested in establishing insurance activities in Israel. The Ministry of Finance believes these reductions will foster increased competition and pave the way for technological innovation within the insurance industry, benefiting consumers through a wider range of insurance products and potentially lowering premiums. Israeli Finance Minister Moshe Kahlon emphasized the importance of these changes, stating that they represent a broader effort to reduce regulatory hurdles and promote a new generation of technological players in the insurance market, injecting much-needed energy and dynamism into the sector (Levitan, 2018).

5.1.3 Sandbox Regulatory Frameworks: Fostering Innovation in a Controlled Environment

The exploration of sandbox regulatory frameworks emerges as a pivotal trend in the decentralized insurance sector, fostering dynamic innovation while upholding essential regulatory oversight. Countries like Canada, India, Thailand, and Singapore exemplify diverse approaches to this trend, each contributing uniquely to the global evolution of innovative insurance solutions. These frameworks serve as carefully controlled environments where cutting-edge technologies and innovative business models can undergo rigorous testing without immediate adherence to all regulatory requirements. This approach grants insurance entities the necessary flexibility to experiment with novel technologies and strategies, fostering an environment of continuous improvement and adaptation (Zhao, 2018). Simultaneously, regulatory bodies benefit from valuable insights into potential risks and benefits, ensuring that decentralized insurance development remains innovative and secure. The sandbox model, therefore, strikes a delicate balance, encouraging exploration and innovation while upholding the essential regulatory oversight needed for consumer protection and market stability.

In May 2016, FCA made a groundbreaking move by opening its regulatory sandbox to firms of varying sizes and structures, marking the world's inaugural launch of such a platform by a regulatory agency. Since its inception, the FCA has been transparent in releasing a comprehensive list of firms selected for the four cohorts that have either undergone or will undergo testing within the sandbox. Among these notable selections are several InsurTech platforms that have gained entry into the FCA's regulatory sandbox (Mueller, 2018). These InsurTech platforms include Blink, offering an insurance product with an automated claims process enabling travellers to swiftly book new tickets via their mobile devices in case of flight cancellations, and AssetVault, a platform allowing consumers to securely catalogue all their assets online, providing insights into their total value while collaborating with insurance providers to offer appropriate protection for assets. Other accepted firms encompass a diverse range of innovative solutions, such as Canlon, FloodFlash, Laka, Nimbla, YouToggle, ZipZap, Sherpa Management Services, Wrisk, Etherisc, Meet Mia, and Universal Tokens, each bringing unique offerings to the insurance landscape. Notably, of the 89 firms granted participation in the sandbox, 13 InsurTech firms have secured acceptance, representing approximately 15% of all firms admitted. Nearly one-third of the 24 firms selected for Cohort 2 were InsurTech platforms, indicating a significant presence and interest in this sector within the regulatory sandbox (Mueller, 2018).

Furthermore, as the FCA proceeds with subsequent cohorts, there has been a noticeable trend of incorporating InsurTech firms leveraging cryptocurrency or blockchain technology, reflecting the evolving dynamics and innovations within the insurance industry. The sandbox process comprises four main stages: application, selection, testing, and exit. Firms are selected based on the authenticity of the innovation they offer and its potential benefits to UK consumers (Cornelli et al., 2020). The FCA supports selected firms throughout the process, including guidance on regulatory compliance and assistance in navigating the regulatory landscape. Upon authorization, firms trial their products under regular reporting requirements, monitoring technology evolution and compliance targets. After six months, firms submit a final testing report and exit the sandbox with the option to apply for permanent authorization upon completion. The sandbox aims to attract investments towards fintech firms by reducing regulatory uncertainty and providing a platform for innovation that benefits consumers and the financial sector.

On August 7, 2018, the Financial Conduct Authority (FCA) announced the establishment of the Global Financial Innovation Network

(GFIN) in collaboration with eleven other financial regulators and associated organizations. The primary objective of GFIN is to foster communication and interaction between FinTech companies and regulators and collaboration among national regulators on innovation-related matters. The GFIN's functions were the subject of a consultation from October 14 to October 14, 2018 (Moody's Analytics, 2018). One of the primary roles being suggested is the creation of a "global sandbox," which would give FinTech companies a testing ground where they can test the products they plan to offer internationally and get the necessary input from the relevant authorities.

Thailand's Office of Insurance Commission (OIC) took decisive steps to overhaul the country's insurance regulatory sandbox. The proposed draft notification sought to streamline the project approval process by empowering the OIC with broader authority and addressing previous bottlenecks encountered under the existing framework. Notably, the draft notification included provisions prohibiting "own sandbox" testing by business operators, thereby emphasizing stringent eligibility criteria for participation. Participants were required to demonstrate robust capital, systems, personnel, and experience alongside comprehensive risk management measures. Furthermore, the draft outlined specific project requirements, mandating detailed frameworks, risk assessments, and regulation compliance. It also stipulated a capped duration of one year per project, which is extendable and subject to approval from the OIC. These regulatory efforts reflected Thailand's commitment to fostering innovation and competitiveness within its insurance sector (Tilleke & Gibbins, 2021). Establishing Thailand's insurance regulatory sandbox in June 2017 marked a significant milestone. A year later, Thailand welcomed its first InsurTech participant, Singapore-based Vouch (operating as FairDee in Thailand), highlighting its embrace of InsurTech innovation. This move aligned with global trends, as various countries championed efforts to promote InsurTech and welcomed collaboration among regulatory bodies, government agencies, and industry stakeholders to create conducive environments for insurance innovation (Asia Insurance Review, 2018).

Another example of a regulatory sandbox is Alberta, which enhances opportunities for business growth and job creation in the province. This initiative underscores Alberta's position as a growing destination for financial services and technology companies, bolstering its standing in the global economy. Approved participants may be exempt from specific requirements outlined in Acts such as the Loan and Trust Corporations Act, Credit Union Act, ATB Financial Act, Consumer Protection Act, Financial Consumers Act, and Personal Information Protection Act (Sharp, 2021). Companies must meet eligibility criteria to qualify, including maintaining a physical presence in Alberta, offering financial products or services falling under specified legislation, and demonstrating innovation. The Minister of Finance may impose terms, conditions, or restrictions on a company's acceptance certificate to ensure proper oversight and mitigate risks for consumers and the broader financial sector. Additionally, the regulatory sandbox framework mandates consumer information requirements, oversight and annual returns, and public disclosure of sandbox participant details to ensure transparency and accountability in the sandbox process. Information about each participant, including the description of products or services offered, regulatory exemptions granted, and any imposed terms or restrictions, is published online for public access and scrutiny, ensuring adherence to regulatory standards and fostering trust in the financial innovation landscape.

Hong Kong Insurance Authority In late September 2017, the Securities and Futures Commission, the Hong Kong Monetary Authority, and the Insurance Authority announced the formation of new regulatory sandboxes or enhancements to existing sandboxes (Insurance Authority, 2017). All three sandboxes were supposed to be connected at the time of the announcement, giving cross-sector FinTech product pilot trials a single entry point. To test InsurTech applications in a controlled environment and speed up the licencing process by enabling the Insurance Authority to examine suggested digital distribution channels early on, the Insurance Authority, in particular, developed two projects called InsurTech Sandbox and Fast Track. The Authority established the InsurTech Facilitation Team to assist entrepreneurs and insurers in comprehending the regulatory environment and serve as a forum for sharing InsurTech-related ideas. Beyond sandboxes, the Insurance Authority has connected with regulatory authorities worldwide. The Hong Kong Insurance Authority (IA) has started several programs that encourage innovation and integration into licenced insurers' business plans. Additionally, the IA started a fast-track process in September 2017 for applications for new insurer authorizations that use only digital distribution channels. The IA also approved basic criteria relevant to this unique permission method to protect policyholders' interests, given that insurers authorized via the Fast Track approach will not be allowed to accept business from non-digital channels. To facilitate contact with InsurTech firms actively developing and implementing InsurTech solutions, the IA has also formed an "InsurTech Facilitation Team". The Team's goals are to serve as a forum for idea sharing, offer guidance on InsurTech-related subjects, and help InsurTech providers better grasp the appropriate insurance regulatory requirements. In addition, the Insurance Industry Future Task Force was formed, and the IA collaborated with them to investigate the direction of the insurance sector in Hong Kong. The Financial Technology—FinTech group is one of its working groups; its goal is to encourage the adoption of FinTech in the insurance sector (Mueller, 2018).

The Insurance Regulatory and Development Authority of India is actively exploring the implementation of sandbox frameworks. This strategic initiative provides a controlled and monitored space for decentralized insurance platforms to test and refine their models, ensuring responsible innovation (Sinha, 2018). By carefully assessing the impact of novel approaches within a controlled environment, IRDAI contributes to developing a regulatory framework that supports innovation while safeguarding the interests of consumers (see Box 5.2 for details). The Securities and Exchange Board of India (SEBI), a stock market regulator, also initiates discussions on regulatory sandboxes that promote collaboration between decentralized insurance providers and healthcare technology companies, exploring synergies in health insurance offerings.

There are more examples of implementing regulatory sandbox initiatives globally, such as Sweden and Singapore. Sweden accounts for around one-fifth of all European FinTech investments, making it one of the leading centres for FinTech innovation. The Swedish government mandated the Swedish Financial Supervisory Authority in May 2017 to maintain these statistics. The authority then created a FinTech Regulatory Sandbox, where FinTech providers could submit their ideas, planned projects, and requests for regulatory guidance directly to the authority (Chatzara, 2020). The Financial Supervisory Authority will be in a better position to keep an eye on developments in the financial market as a result of the FinTech Regulatory Sandbox's primary assistance to FinTech companies in securing the information and guidance they need from the regulator and making sure their suggested solutions comply with all relevant regulations. The Swedish government is actively fostering innovation by establishing the Swedish National Innovation Council, led by the prime minister. Singapore is among the nations regarded as "homes" of invention. Since they actively monitor and promote technological innovation, Singapore and its capable Monetary Authority (Monetary Authority of Singapore, or MAS) are proactive regulators. To help form regulatory policies and strategies to support the use of technology and innovation to improve the financial industry, MAS formed the Financial Technology and Innovation Group (FTIG) as early as August 2015 (MAS, 2015). In May 2016, the Economic Development Board of Singapore, MAS, Infocomm Investments Pte Ltd, the National Research Foundation, the Info-communications Media Development Authority, and SPRING Singapore formed a FinTech office in response to the need for close collaboration among various competent authorities (Chatzara, 2020). The Monetary Authority of Singapore introduced its regulatory sandbox in November 2016.

Few firms have been chosen out of the over thirty submissions received since then. The first business to enter and exit the sandbox in 2017 was PolicyPal, a digital direct insurance broker that helps people purchase, manage, and maximize their insurance policies. The only InsurTech that has been approved for the sandbox is PolicyPal. Several regulatory bodies have attempted to create InsurTech-specific sandboxes in addition to the larger sandbox initiatives (Mueller, 2018). Furthermore, MAS has embraced the regulatory sandbox strategy to deter businesses from deploying cutting-edge solutions if they are unsure of their compliance with the relevant legal and regulatory framework. MAS's FinTech sandbox aims to provide a safe and regulated environment for financial institutions and FinTech startups to test new financial products and services. Regulations that normally apply are relaxed for the length of the experiment as part of the regulatory support that MAS offers innovators who enter the sandbox. MAS continues to embark on new projects and has developed into a centre for exhibiting innovation in fields like blockchain and distributed ledger technology, RegTech, InsurTech, and the future of banking, among others.

The sandbox seeks to promote fintechs' access to capital by fostering competition, innovation, and financial stability. While the long-term effects of sandboxes are still being evaluated, anecdotal evidence suggests that the sandbox has provided value to firms by offering guidance on regulatory compliance, signalling credibility to investors, and simplifying the authorization process (Rowland, 2018). By reducing regulatory uncertainty and lowering regulatory costs for firms, sandboxes facilitate innovation while ensuring adherence to regulatory standards. The sandbox's potential to reduce information problems and address regulatory restraints underscores its significance in promoting an environment conducive to fintech growth. As policies evolve and sandboxes mature, ongoing evaluation and analysis will be crucial in assessing their effectiveness in supporting fintech innovation and driving positive outcomes for consumers and the financial industry (Werbach, 2018). Collectively, these global sandbox initiatives signify a convergence towards a balanced regulatory approach, encouraging innovation while safeguarding the interests of consumers and ensuring market stability. The diverse strategies these countries adopt create a resilient and interconnected global decentralized insurance ecosystem that adapts to emerging technologies while maintaining regulatory clarity and consumer protection.

Box 5.2: IRDAI's Regulatory Sandbox Initiative

The Insurance Regulatory and Development Authority of India initiated its regulatory sandbox in May 2019, marking a pivotal moment in the evolution of the Indian insurance sector. Through this initiative, IRDAI aims to facilitate innovation and flexibility within the industry while maintaining regulatory compliance and safeguarding the interests of policyholders. Recent approvals granted to several companies for technology-driven projects in health, motor, and intermediaries insurance underscore the growing momentum of the sandbox initiative.

The regulatory sandbox is a controlled environment where insurance companies and startups can experiment with innovative products, services, and business models. By providing a safe space for testing and refinement, the sandbox enables participants to explore new avenues for growth and development while mitigating potential risks. This approach aligns with IRDAI's commitment to fostering a dynamic and competitive insurance market that meets the evolving needs of consumers.

Key objectives of IRDAI's regulatory sandbox include promoting innovation, encouraging collaboration between industry stakeholders, and facilitating the adoption of emerging technologies. By embracing advancements such as artificial intelligence, machine learning, blockchain, and IoT, insurers can enhance operational efficiency, improve customer experiences, and develop innovative solutions tailored to market demands. The sandbox initiative also reflects IRDAI's proactive approach to regulation, acknowledging the transformative potential of technology in reshaping the insurance landscape. IRDAI seeks to identify and address regulatory challenges associated with innovative products and services through structured testing and evaluation processes. By providing regulatory guidance and support, IRDAI empowers participants to navigate regulatory requirements effectively while driving innovation forward. As the regulatory sandbox continues to evolve, IRDAI remains committed to soliciting feedback, refining regulatory frameworks, and promoting best practices in innovation. By fostering a culture of experimentation and learning, IRDAI aims to position India globally as a hub for insurance innovation and technological excellence.

IRDAI Riding the Technology Wave

Since its inception, IRDAI's regulatory sandbox initiative has played a pivotal role in harnessing the transformative potential of technology within the Indian insurance sector. By accepting applications from September 15, 2019, to October 14, 2019, IRDAI signalled its commitment to promoting innovation and fostering a conducive environment for experimentation (IRDAI, 2020). The primary objective of the sandbox program is to facilitate collaboration between insurance companies, startups, and technology firms to explore emerging technologies such as artificial intelligence, machine learning, wearable technology, and blockchain. By providing participants with regulatory relaxation and guidance, the sandbox enables them to test innovative solutions, refine business models, and address regulatory challenges in a controlled environment.

Through the sandbox initiative, IRDAI aims to achieve several key outcomes, including promoting innovative startups, the development of cutting-edge insurance products and services, and enhancing customer experiences. By leveraging technology, insurers can streamline operations, improve risk assessment, and offer personalized solutions tailored to individual needs. The sandbox also serves as a platform for regulators to gain insights into emerging trends, identify regulatory gaps, and develop appropriate frameworks to support innovation while ensuring consumer protection and market stability. By engaging with stakeholders and soliciting feedback, IRDAI demonstrates its commitment to regulatory excellence and responsiveness in a rapidly evolving digital landscape.

IRDAI's regulatory sandbox initiative is poised to drive continued innovation and transformation within the Indian insurance sector. As technology continues to reshape the industry, IRDAI remains at the forefront of regulatory innovation, facilitating collaboration and fostering an environment conducive to growth and development.

Wearable Technology in the Indian Insurance Space

The integration of wearable technology marks a significant milestone in the evolution of the Indian insurance market, offering new opportunities for insurers and customers alike. With a market size projected to reach $280 billion, the Indian insurance sector is poised for rapid transformation driven by the adoption of wearable devices. Traditionally dominated by banks and government agencies, the insurance industry is paradigm shifting as wearable technology disrupts traditional models and approaches. Wearable devices enhance fitness and wellness tracking and revolutionize insurance and finance by providing real-time data insights and personalized experiences.

According to projections by the International Data Corporation (IDC), the wearable device market is expected to grow exponentially, driven by increased consumer awareness and adoption. As wearable technology becomes more prevalent, insurers can leverage data analytics, machine learning, and IoT to offer innovative insurance products and services tailored to individual lifestyles and preferences.

The entry of wearable technology into the insurance space has the potential to transform customer experiences, drive operational efficiency, and improve risk management. By incentivizing healthy behaviours, promoting preventive healthcare, and offering personalized incentives, insurers can engage customers in new and meaningful ways, fostering long-term relationships and loyalty.

5.1.4 *Supervisory Technology (SupTech)*

SupTech refers to the application of technology by supervisory authorities, such as central banks, financial regulators, and government agencies, to enhance regulatory oversight, monitoring, and enforcement functions (International Insurance Society, 2022). SupTech solutions enable regulators to collect, analyze, and interpret large volumes of data from financial institutions and markets to assess compliance with regulatory requirements, identify emerging risks, and detect potential misconduct or systemic vulnerabilities (Ocampo et al., 2022). SupTech tools encompass various technologies, including data analytics, machine learning, natural language processing, and visualization techniques, to facilitate regulatory supervision, surveillance, and enforcement activities. By leveraging SupTech solutions, regulators can improve the effectiveness and efficiency of regulatory oversight, promote financial stability, and safeguard the financial system's integrity.

As SupTech uses AI to analyze unstructured data and automate monotonous operations, augmentation should be used to prevent depending solely on model output without human judgement. Regulators must be present and positioned for the general use of blockchain and DLT. Digital and cryptocurrency assets lack a taxonomy, which makes it difficult to regulate and manage them in a global setting with several jurisdictions. Supervisory agencies may be able to gather and evaluate unstructured data—that is, data not arranged in databases—more effectively to SupTech, which may spare regulators from labour-intensive data collecting duties. Applying risk-adjusted return predictions, capital modelling, and comprehensive enterprise risk management that conforms with regulatory solvency regimes like SOLVENCY II, RBC, C-ROSS, and BASEL—as well as applying it across multiple jurisdictions to improve decision-making using a stochastic approach—are equally important applications of data analytics (OECD, 2017a, 2017b). Supervisory technology (SupTech) uses innovative technologies by financial authorities to support their work. SupTech results from digital innovation in the financial system and emerging advanced technologies, such as big data, AI/ML, and other new technologies.

The tools utilized in regulatory and supervisory functions can be categorized based on their intended uses, such as prudential supervision, conduct supervision, or both. A significant portion of these tools serves both prudential and conduct supervision purposes, with the remaining divided between those tailored for either conduct or prudential supervision. Prudential supervision tools commonly include automated dashboards showcasing key risk indicators and machine learning techniques aiding network analysis and risk scoring frameworks. These tools enable early detection of financial distress and foster preemptive engagement with supervised firms, enhancing monitoring effectiveness and promptness. For instance, the MAS is developing network analysis tools to assess interconnectedness between insurers and reinsurers, identifying concentration risks and informing stress testing exercises.

Moreover, regulatory authorities like the French Prudential Supervision and Resolution Authority are experimenting with tools to enhance the detection of fragile insurers. These tools automate the analysis of technical provisions and provide visualizations to pinpoint insurers lacking sufficient assets to meet claim obligations. Similarly, the Swiss Financial Market Supervisory Authority offers a solvency calculation tool for insurance companies, facilitating the implementation of the Swiss Solvency Test. Regulatory bodies such as the NAIC also deploy comprehensive dashboards to analyze solvency risks across various operational facets, including bond holdings, equity investments, and reinsurance.

The EIOPA is developing tools to collect and analyze data on insurance-based investment products, improving transparency and cross-border supervision efficiency. Additionally, initiatives like the Institute for Insurance Supervision are exploring tools to assess insurance contract complexity and readability, enhancing dialogue with insurers and promoting consumer-friendly policies. Regulatory authorities like the French Prudential Supervision and Resolution Authority and the Korean Financial Supervisory Service are leveraging tools to transcribe and analyze telephone conversations, identify mis-selling practices, and enforce regulatory compliance effectively.

Many of these tools serve prudential and conduct supervision functions, emphasizing data collection, validation, consolidation, and visualization processes. For instance, the Taiwan Insurance Guaranty Fund maintains a data repository system, enhancing data accuracy and enabling efficient supervisory reviews. Similarly, the Central Bank of Malaysia leverages a web portal for regulatory compliance, streamlining regulatory applications and workflow management. Initiatives like the European Insurance and Occupational Pensions Authority's Cooperation Platform aim to promote efficient information exchange between national competent authorities, addressing inconsistencies and enhancing cross-border supervision effectiveness. With advanced analytics tools, regulatory bodies can detect outliers and patterns, improving supervisory insights and fostering regulatory compliance across the insurance sector. Through continuous innovation and collaboration, these regulatory and supervisory technologies contribute to a more resilient, transparent, and consumer-focused insurance landscape.

5.1.5 *Regulatory Technology (RegTech): Revolutionizing Regulatory Compliance*

RegTech is an emerging FinTech area that uses technologies to solve regulatory and compliance requirements more effectively and efficiently. RegTech can guarantee more efficient adherence to intricate laws, especially in light of the numerous regulatory revisions implemented following the financial crisis. The technologies that are considered relevant for RegTech encompass artificial intelligence and machine learning, biometrics, application programming interfaces (APIs), and the processing of unstructured data like Facebook posts and emails. Those tools can be brought to bear on such areas as aggregating big data, modelling risk for stress testing, monitoring capital-requirement compliance, updating compliance manuals, improving anti-money laundering and KYC programs, and preventing fraud and in-house violations (Finanzmarktaufsicht., 2017). RegTech is an area where countries that have developed regulatory approaches to FinTech have benefited more from startups, with 31% of RegTech startups incorporated in the UK, as opposed to 20% in the United States. Data analytics tools, for instance, can transform financial institutions' internal data into regulatory reporting formats that the insurance industry may use. Several KYC systems may confirm a customer's identification using publicly available external data. RegTech solutions might offer an interface that makes it easier for insurers to understand their assets under management, as efforts to modernize solvency require asset managers to disclose investments on a look-through basis.

RegTech offers several insurance-related solutions, mostly focused on fraud prevention and solvency compliance. However, a new topic is how insurance firms may ensure their algorithms adhere to market behaviour laws. To ensure that financial institutions, including insurance companies, can integrate algorithms in their enterprise risk management and customer interface to align with the goal of efficiency and effective business processes while minimizing the potential risks of algorithms, some startups are addressing the unintended consequences of algorithms. A data scientist established the technology start-up ORCAA in New York for algorithm audits. The model under consideration is scrutinized from four angles: the gathering and verifying data, the algorithm's goal, the foundation upon which the algorithm has been constructed, and the tracking and modification of the algorithm (OECD, 2017a, 2017b). Algorithms are known to employ certain proxies, such as postcodes, which, depending on how the algorithm is built, may lead to specific population segments being treated unjustly. Financial regulation has been comparatively exposed to algorithms in high-frequency trading, where trading algorithms are employed to perform high-volume, high-speed automated trading in financial markets. Despite reports from financial regulators like the French Autorité des Marché Financiers (2009) and the Federal Reserve Board (2009), a mutual fund trade led to a mass withdrawal through high-frequency trading, which in turn caused the Dow Jones to crash in May 2010 (also known as the "Flash Crash").

Germany passed the High-Frequency Trading Act in 2013, requiring BaFin to monitor high-frequency trading companies that were not under its prior supervision (BaFin, 2020). Businesses must make sure that there are no disruptions or distortions to the markets. The algorithm tagging rule requires exchanges to put in place regulations requiring all exchange members to label all orders created algorithmically with a distinct key when delivered to a German exchange. As a result, the generating algorithm may assign all orders to the market surveillance system. The EU Commission has released a technical standard on implementing articles related to high-frequency trading for the Markets in Financial Instruments Directive II, which is set to go into effect in 2018 (Cave, 2016). Due to their complexity, monitoring algorithms need specialized knowledge and abilities. Supervisors and regulators frequently lack the knowledge and skills to evaluate algorithms and decide if big data is being utilized responsibly. The consumer interface is largely responsible for the recognized applications of algorithms in the insurance industry. On the other hand, insurers are probably being forced by solvency efforts to estimate solvency using algorithms. Regulators should think carefully about handling insurers' use of big data and algorithms to ensure that these tools are created responsibly and that biases and unforeseen effects are minimized. Stress testing might be done specifically to see how well robo-advice will perform under harsh market circumstances.

5.1.6 Data Privacy and Security Regulations

Big data-related technology is complicated, opaque, and sometimes difficult to understand. That's why even the people who create the technology to use big data could not completely understand the implications or proper use of data. Businesses should be able to provide evidence of their proper and bias-free use of data. Insurance companies should carefully consider privacy and data protection laws when using big data and data analytics, and they should thoroughly evaluate any use of data that raises ethical questions. Addressing this will be significantly impacted by the broader data privacy regime in this regard. Insurers also need to ensure that databases can accommodate new rules for data breach notifications when implemented.

Nevertheless, notification laws should also promote the growth of independent cyber insurance markets. For example, cross-border data transfers are prohibited under the current EU regime unless they are made to an adequate jurisdiction or the data exporter has put in place a legal mechanism for transferring data across borders (EU Data Protection Directive (95/46/EC) and EU General Data Protection Regulation (OECD, 2017a, 2017b). The GDPR will expand on the requirements from the Directive for a jurisdiction to meet to be considered an Adequate Jurisdiction. These requirements include having a fundamental rule of law, legal protection of human rights, access to transferred data by public authorities, an operational data protection agency, international commitments, and other obligations pertaining to personal data protection.

GDPR requires companies to establish legally enforceable Corporate Rules that apply to and are implemented by all members of the group of enterprises participating in joint economic activity, as well as DPA approval of the BCR, to transmit data throughout the corporate group. Distribution agreements and outsourcing arrangements must be carefully negotiated inside the EU regarding who manages and processes data. The GDPR would force insurers or data controllers to do a "data protection impact assessment" before processing personal data since the existing EU directive data protection framework prohibits processing personal data unless there are justifiable grounds to do so. Insurers are expected to establish adequate consent and efficient procedures for gathering, managing, and analyzing data. Data security and privacy regulations are becoming essential parts of legal and regulatory frameworks that support decentralized insurance and encourage innovation in the insurance industry. For insurance firms working in decentralized contexts, protecting consumer data and thwarting cybersecurity threats have become critical concerns due to the growing dependence on digital technology and data-driven procedures.

New developments in regulatory frameworks strongly emphasize adhering to data privacy laws, including the GDPR in the EU. In December 2015, the European Council and the EU Parliament reached a consensus on the GDPR (Lord, 2017). It would apply to businesses that handle personal data belonging to EU citizens, regardless of whether they offer free or paid services or if their headquarters are in the EU. It is a revision to the 1995-enacted Data Protection Directive. Under the GDPR, a company's actions that result in a data breach or loss of information might result in fines of up to €20 million, or 4% of worldwide annual sales, whichever is larger. As of May 25, 2018, it will be implemented in all member states (McCarthy, 2024). When personal data is no longer needed for the intended purpose of collection, GDPR mandates that it be deleted without delay. When a data subject challenges the accuracy of the data, the data utilized must also limit its usage. Without the data subject's consent, the company may be unable to use the data for primary or secondary purposes. Hence, the firm must keep an exact record of that consent. The introduction of new technology may be affected by the manner and location in which insurers handle their data. Furthermore, the way GDPR is implemented may impact the growth of the cyber risk insurance industry. Depending on the information gathered for various objectives, it may also affect data analytics.

The Competition and Consumer Act 2010 and the Consumer Data Rights Bill 2019 in Australia control data sharing and usage in the financial services industry, indirectly regulating AI's insurance application. The government is now developing Australia's national AI strategy. In March 2022, a government document delineated the nation's objective to emerge as one of the top 10 digital economies and societies globally by 2030 (The Geneva Association, 2023). In addition, the government is keeping a careful eye on EU developments. Through this publication, it is soliciting feedback on its regulatory strategy, which includes regulating AI choices with significant consequences. In response to these consultations, the Australian Actuaries Institute stated that current legislation already covers high-stakes choices. Current financial services legislation imposes fairness obligations on insurers that do not distinguish between choices made by computers and humans.

5.1.7 *Sustainable Integration: Carbon Credits and Climate Risk Mitigation in Decentralized Insurance Regulations*

The ongoing evolution of decentralized insurance reflects a broader shift towards sustainable practices, specifically carbon credits and climate risk mitigation. This paradigm shift is not only reshaping the operational landscape of decentralized insurance but is also being actively incorporated into regulatory frameworks. This exploration of sustainability within decentralized insurance is evident in the regulatory initiatives of Switzerland, Brazil, and Australia.

Switzerland, renowned as a pioneer in blockchain innovation, is leveraging its advanced regulatory landscape to explore avenues for integrating decentralized insurance solutions that focus on carbon credits and climate risk mitigation. This strategic move aligns with the country's commitment to fostering environmentally conscious innovations within the decentralized insurance sector. The regulatory frameworks contemplated in Switzerland seek to balance encouraging sustainable practices and ensuring compliance with established standards. The Brazilian Securities and Exchange Commission is spearheading collaborative efforts with environmental agencies to develop tailored regulations for decentralized insurance platforms in Brazil. The objective is clear: incentivising and ensuring sustainable practices, particularly in sectors related to carbon credits. Brazil's commitment to incorporating environmental considerations into decentralized insurance regulations highlights the country's dedication to fostering a more sustainable and eco-friendly insurance landscape. Australia, represented by the Australian Prudential Regulation Authority (APRA), is responding to the growing importance of sustainability in the industry. APRA is actively considering incorporating climate risk mitigation measures into its regulatory approach for decentralized insurance. This proactive stance reflects Australia's acknowledgement of the urgent need to address climate-related risks within the regulatory frameworks governing insurance practices. Germany's Federal Financial Supervisory Authority is known for its proactive approach to financial innovation. In the context of decentralized insurance, Germany is exploring ways to integrate blockchain and sustainable practices, acknowledging the potential for eco-friendly insurance solutions. The Office of the Superintendent of Financial Institutions in Canada is actively exploring ways to incorporate environmental considerations into insurance regulations. This includes discussions on integrating carbon credit-related activities and climate risk mitigation measures into the regulatory framework for decentralized insurance. As a global fintech hub, Singapore's Monetary Authority is at the forefront of integrating sustainable practices in finance. MAS actively discusses carbon credits and climate risk mitigation within decentralized insurance, contributing to the city-state's broader green finance initiatives.

The NAIC in the United States is witnessing state-level initiatives exploring integrating sustainable practices into insurance regulations. States like California are particularly active in considering measures to incentivize and ensure sustainable practices within decentralized insurance. Japan's Financial Services Agency actively promotes innovations in green finance. The FSA explores integrating carbon credits and climate risk mitigation measures within decentralized insurance regulations, contributing to the country's broader sustainability goals. De Nederlandsche Bank in the Netherlands is engaged in discussions and regulatory measures to create a harmonized approach for decentralized insurance platforms. This includes considerations for sustainability and climate-related risk mitigation as integral components of the regulatory landscape.

The Autorité de Contrôle Prudentiel et de Résolution in France actively participates in discussions to strengthen sustainability measures within the decentralized insurance sector. This involves exploring ways to incentivize eco-friendly insurance practices and integrate climate risk mitigation strategies (Banque De France, 2019). South Africa's Financial Sector Conduct Authority is extending its efforts to enhance sustainability within decentralized insurance regulations. This includes the development of regulatory measures that uphold environmental considerations and climate risk mitigation strategies. These initiatives underline the global momentum towards establishing sustainable practices within decentralized insurance regulations. The intentional integration of carbon credits and climate risk mitigation measures reflects a commitment to addressing the environmental challenges of climate change. This paradigm shift demonstrates regulatory adaptability and underscores decentralized insurance's critical role in fostering a more environmentally responsible and sustainable future.

5.2 Navigating Regulatory and Legal Challenges: Best practices and Recommendations

In today's dynamic business landscape, navigating regulatory and legal challenges has become paramount for decentralized insurance. From compliance requirements to emerging legal frameworks, decentralized insurance platforms face many complexities that demand proactive strategies and comprehensive understanding. Hence, this section explores best practices and recommendations to empower decentralized insurance organizations in their journey towards compliance and effective risk management. Embracing best practices entails collaborative engagement with regulators and industry associations to shape regulatory frameworks conducive to innovation while upholding stakeholder interests. By implementing clear and comprehensive policies, companies establish robust governance structures and internal controls, effectively mitigating legal risks while fostering transparency and accountability across their operations.

Furthermore, investments in employee training and education equip personnel with essential skills to navigate evolving legal landscapes adeptly. Engaging legal counsel proficient in blockchain technology and insurance law becomes indispensable, enabling proactive management of intricate legal matters and ensuring steadfast regulatory compliance. By leveraging external expertise and nurturing robust relationships with legal advisors, decentralized insurance entities can navigate regulatory complexities skilfully, catalyzing innovation and contributing to sustainable industry growth within evolving global regulatory landscapes (Fig. 5.1).

5.2.1 Collaborating with Regulators and Industry Associations

The journey of decentralized insurance firms towards regulatory compliance and effective risk management is a collective endeavour. It involves building bridges with regulatory bodies, cultivating collaboration within the industry, and advocating for regulatory frameworks that balance innovation and consumer protection. As decentralized insurance continues to evolve and disrupt traditional insurance models, proactive engagement

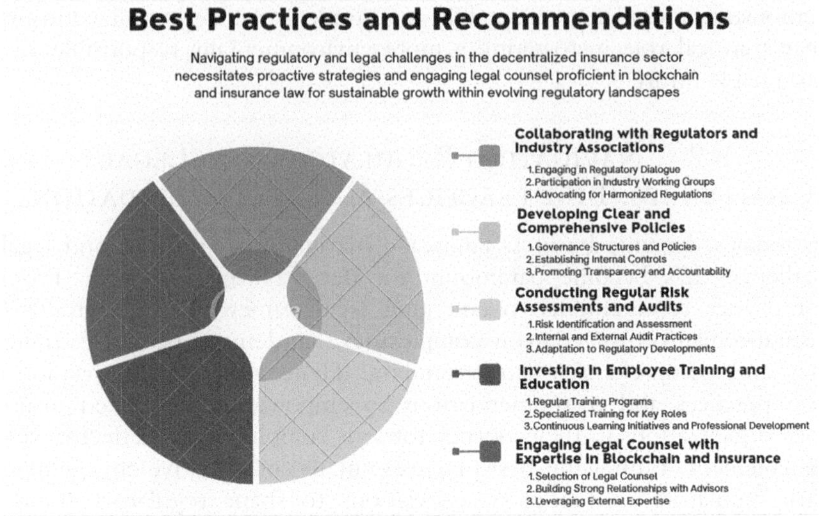

Fig. 5.1 Best practices and recommendations (*Source* Prepared by authors)

with regulators and industry associations remains essential for navigating the complexities of the regulatory landscape and unlocking the full potential of decentralized insurance solutions. Proactive engagement with these entities transcends mere compliance—it fosters an environment conducive to innovation and sustainable growth while safeguarding consumer interests and market integrity. Engaging in ongoing dialogue with regulators and industry associations is foundational for decentralized insurance firms to remain abreast of regulatory developments and to exchange insights on emerging trends and challenges within blockchain-enabled insurance. For instance, in the United States, where regulatory frameworks for emerging technologies are in constant flux, companies operating in the decentralized insurance sector have established transparent lines of communication with regulatory bodies like the Securities and Exchange Commission (SEC). Through sustained dialogue and active engagement, these entities stay apprised of regulatory updates and contribute constructively to shaping frameworks that strike a delicate balance between fostering innovation and safeguarding investor interests.

Participation in specialized industry working groups dedicated to blockchain and insurance further enriches collaboration opportunities. These serve as invaluable platforms for knowledge dissemination, fostering discussions on best practices, and forging industry standards and guidelines. For instance, regulatory bodies such as the Financial Conduct Authority (FCA) in the United Kingdom actively encourage forming industry working groups tailored to blockchain and insurance. Decentralized insurance firms engaging in these forums collaborate with regulators, industry peers, and stakeholders to collectively address legal challenges and nurture industry cohesion. By pooling expertise and insights, these working groups foster the development of standardized practices that enhance regulatory compliance and fortify industry sustainability and resilience.

Advocating harmonized regulations across jurisdictions is a strategic imperative for decentralized insurance firms operating globally. The fragmented nature of regulatory frameworks across different jurisdictions presents significant challenges for companies seeking international expansion. In jurisdictions like Singapore, which embrace fintech innovation, decentralized insurance entities collaborate closely with regulatory bodies such as the Monetary Authority of Singapore (MAS) to champion harmonized regulations. These entities aim to streamline compliance requirements across borders and facilitate cross-border operations by aligning efforts towards regulatory harmonization. Harmonized regulations alleviate compliance complexities for local industry players and catalyze the global growth of blockchain-enabled insurance by nurturing a regulatory environment conducive to international expansion and innovation.

5.2.2 *Developing Clear and Comprehensive Policies*

Effectively manoeuvring through decentralized insurance's complex regulatory and legal landscape necessitates formulating clear and comprehensive policies. Successful instances from various jurisdictions highlight the importance of implementing robust governance structures, establishing internal controls and procedures, and championing transparency and accountability as pivotal strategies to address the legal complexities inherent in decentralized insurance. At the heart of regulatory compliance lies the crafting and upkeep of clear and comprehensive policies designed to tackle key legal challenges in blockchain-enabled insurance. These policies span critical areas such as privacy safeguards, KYC/AML compliance, and intellectual property (IP) protection (Savitha et al., 2019). In Switzerland, recognized for its progressive approach towards innovation, decentralized insurance entities have adopted sturdy governance frameworks prioritizing adherence to regulatory norms. Through articulating clear policies in vital domains, companies operating within Switzerland's decentralized insurance sector manifest their unwavering dedication to regulatory adherence and risk mitigation. Beyond policy formulation, decentralized insurance firms must establish internal controls and procedures to ensure alignment with company policies and relevant laws and regulations. This involves setting up monitoring systems, automated checks, and incident response plans to detect, prevent, and address potential breaches. In Japan, where blockchain technology garners significant acceptance, companies operating in the decentralized insurance sphere have proactively instilled internal controls and procedures. Through these measures, Japanese firms fortify their capabilities to detect, prevent, and address potential legal infringements, thus contributing to developing a robust regulatory framework. Cultivating a culture of transparency and accountability stands as a cornerstone within decentralized insurance organizations. Transparent communication of policies and procedures to employees, customers, and stakeholders nurtures trust and underscores the commitment to addressing legal intricacies linked with decentralized insurance. Germany, a prominent centre for fintech innovation, serves as an exemplar where decentralized insurance entities actively advocate transparency and accountability. By transparently communicating policies and procedures, companies in Germany cultivate trust and exhibit a proactive stance in addressing legal challenges inherent in blockchain-enabled insurance. This commitment to transparency contributes to shaping a regulatory milieu valuing accountability and openness. These instances underscore the pivotal role of crafting clear and comprehensive policies as a foundation for navigating regulatory and legal hurdles within the decentralized insurance sector. Through the adoption of robust governance structures, establishment of internal controls, and promotion of transparency and accountability, companies actively contribute to constructing a regulatory framework conducive to innovation, compliance, and the enduring viability of the decentralized insurance sector.

5.2.3 Conducting Regular Risk Assessments and Audits

Effectively navigating the decentralized insurance sector's intricate regulatory and legal landscape requires a proactive stance and implementing strategic measures. Among these, conducting regular risk assessments and audits stands out as a cornerstone for decentralized insurance companies striving to ensure compliance, mitigate legal risks, and foster sustainable growth. Through ongoing vigilance and proactive engagement with regulatory bodies, decentralized insurance firms position themselves as trusted stewards of consumer protection and market integrity in the evolving landscape of blockchain-enabled insurance. Regular risk assessments and audits represent dynamic strategies decentralized insurance entities embrace worldwide. Conducting routine risk assessments is paramount for decentralized insurance entities to gain a comprehensive understanding of the legal complexities surrounding their operations. In jurisdictions like Australia, regulatory bodies such as the Australian Securities and Investments Commission (ASIC) emphasize the importance of decentralized insurance companies undertaking regular risk assessments. These assessments encompass various facets, including regulatory compliance, privacy concerns, contractual obligations, and intellectual property risks. Through proactive risk identification and assessment, companies in Australia demonstrate their commitment to understanding and managing the nuances of legal challenges inherent in decentralized insurance operations. This proactive approach enables firms to develop tailored risk mitigation strategies that effectively address specific challenges identified during the assessment process. In addition to risk assessments, decentralized insurance companies must conduct periodic internal and external audits to evaluate their compliance with applicable laws, regulations, and internal policies. In jurisdictions renowned for fintech innovation, like Germany, decentralized insurance entities have embraced robust audit practices to ensure adherence to regulatory frameworks and internal protocols. Regulatory authorities such as the Federal Financial Supervisory Authority (BaFin) stress the significance of these audits in identifying potential gaps in compliance and areas for improvement. By conducting systematic audits, companies in Germany proactively address compliance issues, thereby enhancing their resilience against legal challenges and maintaining a strong compliance posture. The regulatory landscape governing decentralized insurance is dynamic, necessitating a proactive approach to monitoring and adapting to regulatory developments. In global fintech hubs like Singapore, decentralized insurance entities exemplify the importance of actively monitoring and responding to regulatory changes. Regulatory bodies such as the Monetary Authority of Singapore (MAS) encourage companies to stay abreast of regulatory updates and assess their impact on business operations. Continuous monitoring of the regulatory landscape enables companies in Singapore to remain flexible and responsive, adapting policies, procedures, and risk management strategies in line with evolving regulations. This adaptability ensures ongoing compliance and is a proactive measure to mitigate legal risks associated with regulatory changes.

5.2.4 Investing in Employee Training and Education

Investing in employee training and education is a global proactive strategy for decentralized insurance entities. By offering specialized training programs, fostering continuous learning initiatives, integrating legal compliance modules, and collaborating with legal experts, companies equip their workforce to understand, adapt to, and navigate regulatory and legal complexities. This investment ensures regulatory compliance and cultivates a culture of legal awareness and resilience within the organization. Invest in regular training programs for employees to understand blockchain-enabled insurance's legal and regulatory requirements and your company's policies and procedures. This can help promote compliance and reduce the risk of violations. Switzerland, renowned for its blockchain innovation, has witnessed decentralized insurance entities investing in specialized training programs. These programs focus on educating employees about the legal intricacies of blockchain-enabled insurance. FINMA encourages companies to equip their workforce with a deep understanding of regulatory requirements and legal frameworks. By investing in specialized training, companies in Switzerland empower their employees to navigate legal challenges proactively. Provide specialized training for employees in key roles, such as those responsible for managing smart contracts, privacy, and KYC/AML compliance. This can help ensure that your team has the expertise to navigate the complex legal challenges of blockchain-enabled insurance. Japan, a leader in technological advancements, showcases decentralized insurance entities implementing continuous learning initiatives. The FSA encourages companies to foster a culture of continuous education, ensuring that employees stay abreast of evolving regulatory requirements. By investing in ongoing training, companies in Japan enhance their employees' capabilities to adapt to changing legal landscapes, fostering regulatory compliance and resilience. Support employees in pursuing continuous learning and professional development by providing access to resources, conferences, and industry events. This can help your team stay informed about the latest trends, best practices, and legal developments in the blockchain-enabled insurance industry. Singapore, a global fintech hub, highlights decentralized insurance entities integrating legal compliance modules into employee training. MAS emphasizes the importance of employees understanding legal obligations and compliance protocols. By incorporating legal compliance modules, companies in Singapore ensure that their workforce is well-versed in decentralized insurance regulatory frameworks. This proactive investment in education contributes to a regulatory awareness and diligence culture. In the United States, decentralized insurance entities collaborate with legal experts to enhance employee education. The SEC encourages companies to engage legal professionals in training programs, providing insights into regulatory nuances. By involving legal experts, companies in the U.S. ensure that their employees receive firsthand knowledge and practical guidance, enabling them to navigate complex legal challenges effectively. Investing in employee training and education emerges as a proactive strategy for decentralized insurance entities globally. Companies equip their workforce to understand, adapt to, and navigate the regulatory and legal complexities inherent in the decentralized insurance landscape by offering specialized training programs, fostering continuous learning initiatives, integrating legal compliance modules, and collaborating with legal experts. This investment ensures regulatory compliance and cultivates a culture of legal awareness and resilience within the organization.

5.2.5 Engaging Legal Counsel with Expertise in Blockchain and Insurance

The engagement of legal counsel proficient in blockchain technology and insurance regulations is a pivotal strategy, ensuring that decentralized insurance entities receive tailored guidance to navigate the labyrinthine legal landscape. It is imperative to engage legal advisors who are well-versed in blockchain technology and insurance to guide you through the complexities inherent in blockchain-enabled insurance ventures. Seasoned counsel brings invaluable insights into regulatory compliance, contract drafting, intellectual property protection, and dispute resolution. Germany, a vanguard of fintech innovation, accentuates the importance of securing legal professionals adept in blockchain and insurance. BaFin advocates for decentralized insurance entities to enlist seasoned legal experts capable of offering comprehensive guidance in regulatory compliance and dispute resolution, fostering a culture of legal diligence. Building enduring partnerships with legal advisors ensures a profound understanding of the business objectives and unique legal challenges. This fosters more tailored and effective advice, empowering decentralized insurance entities to address legal hurdles with efficiency and foresight. Singapore, a prominent global fintech hub, emphasizes the significance of nurturing ongoing relationships with legal advisors. MAS advocates for decentralized insurance entities to ensure that legal counsel possesses a deep understanding of their business dynamics, facilitating seamless collaboration and proactive legal strategies to navigate the dynamic decentralized insurance landscape. In addition to in-house legal counsel, tapping into external expertise, such as specialized law firms, augments organizational capabilities in addressing complex legal matters. This strategic collaboration ensures proactive readiness to tackle emerging legal challenges and access the latest legal insights. Switzerland, renowned for its innovation-friendly regulatory stance, exemplifies the strategic utilization of external expertise. FINMA advises decentralized insurance entities to engage specialized law firms proficient in blockchain and insurance, enhancing legal capabilities and enabling effective navigation of the evolving regulatory terrain. The strategic adoption of retaining experienced legal counsel, fostering enduring relationships with legal advisors, and leveraging external expertise stands as a cornerstone for decentralized insurance entities. These proactive measures, epitomized by successful practices in Germany, Singapore, and Switzerland, underscore how a collaborative legal framework contributes to blockchain-enabled insurance ventures' long-term sustainability and regulatory compliance.

5.3 Conclusion

Analytically examining regulatory and legal frameworks in decentralized insurance underscores the complex interplay between regulatory compliance, technological innovation, and consumer protection. The integration of artificial intelligence (AI) underscores the transformative potential of technology within the insurance sector. Yet, the regulatory landscape surrounding AI implementation is rife with complexities, spanning ethical considerations to consumer protection. While regulations serve as guardrails for responsible AI deployment, they also present hurdles in adapting to the rapid pace of technological innovation. As decentralized insurance entities leverage AI to enhance decision-making and streamline operations, aligning regulatory frameworks and technological advancements becomes paramount for ensuring transparency, accountability, and ethical AI governance.

Moreover, integrating DeFi Protocols within regulatory frameworks heralds a new era of decentralized finance, revolutionizing traditional insurance models and democratizing access to financial services. However, the decentralized nature of DeFi protocols poses challenges for regulatory oversight and consumer protection. As decentralized insurance entities navigate the uncharted waters of DeFi integration, striking a balance between innovation and regulatory compliance becomes imperative to foster an environment conducive to financial stability and consumer trust. Sandbox regulatory frameworks serve as incubators for innovation, providing a controlled environment for testing new products and services while mitigating regulatory risks. However, the efficacy of sandbox frameworks hinges on regulatory agility, stakeholder collaboration, and transparent governance structures. As decentralized insurance entities leverage sandbox frameworks to experiment with novel solutions, gleaning insights from these experiments and incorporating learnings into broader regulatory frameworks fosters a culture of innovation and regulatory excellence. In tandem with sandbox frameworks, the advent of Supervisory Technology (SupTech) and Regulatory Technology (RegTech) promises to revolutionize regulatory compliance and oversight. SupTech and RegTech solutions empower regulators to monitor market trends, detect regulatory violations, and enhance enforcement mechanisms by harnessing data analytics, artificial intelligence, and machine learning. As decentralized insurance entities embrace SupTech and RegTech solutions, they streamline compliance processes, mitigate regulatory risks, and enhance operational efficiency in a rapidly evolving regulatory landscape. Amidst the proliferation of digital technologies, data privacy and security regulations emerge as paramount considerations in decentralized insurance operations. With the advent of stringent data privacy laws such as the GDPR and CCPA, decentralized insurance entities face mounting pressure to safeguard consumer data and uphold privacy rights. By implementing robust data privacy and security measures, decentralized insurance entities foster consumer trust, mitigate data breaches, and uphold regulatory compliance standards in an increasingly data-driven landscape.

Furthermore, the sustainable integration of regulatory and legal frameworks is required for decentralized insurance ecosystems' long-term viability and resilience. By fostering collaboration between industry stakeholders, regulatory bodies, and technology experts, decentralized insurance entities navigate regulatory challenges, anticipate market trends, and capitalize on emerging opportunities. Incorporating insights from best practices and recommendations, such as collaborating with regulators and industry associations, developing clear and comprehensive policies, conducting regular risk assessments and audits, investing in employee training and education, and engaging legal counsel with expertise in blockchain and insurance, underscores the multifaceted approach required to navigate regulatory and legal challenges effectively. Through collaboration, transparency, proactive risk management, employee empowerment, and legal expertise, decentralized insurance entities foster a culture of compliance, innovation, and resilience, positioning themselves for sustained success and growth in the decentralized insurance landscape of tomorrow.

References

Asia Insurance Review. (2018). *Singaporean InsurTech start up first to participate in Thai regulatory sandbox*. Accessed on 19 September 2024 from https://www.asiainsurancereview.com/News/View-NewsLetter-Article/id/43442/type/AIRPlus/Singaporean-InsurTech-start-up-first-to-participate-in-Thai-regulatory-sandbox

ASIC. (2016). *ASIC releases the world's first licensing exemption for fintech businesses*. Accessed on 20 April 2024 from https://asic.gov.au/about-asic/news-centre/find-a-media-release/2016-releases/16-440mr-asic-releases-world-first-licensing-exemption-for-fintech-businesses/

BaFin. (2020). *Algorithmic trading and high-frequency trading*. Accessed on 20 October 2023 from https://www.bafin.de/EN/Aufsicht/BoersenMaerkte/Handel/Hochfrequenzhandel/high_frequency_trading_node_en.html

Bank of England. (2022). *DP5/22—Artificial Intelligence and Machine Learning*. Accessed on 20 April 2024 from https://www.bankofengland.co.uk/prudential-regulation/publication/2022/october/artificial-intelligence

Bank of England. (2023). *FS2/23 – Artificial Intelligence and Machine Learning*. Accessed on 20 April 2024 from https://www.bankofengland.co.uk/prudential-regulation/publication/2023/october/artificial-intelligence-and-machine-learning

Banque De France. 2019. *French insurers facing climate change risk*. Accessed on 20 April 2024 from https://acpr.banque-france.fr/sites/default/files/medias/documents/as_102_climate_change_insurers_en.pdf

Banque De France. (2018). *Analyses ET Syntheses*. Accessed on 20 April 2024 from https://acpr.banque-france.fr/sites/default/files/medias/documents/195ta18_as_87_etude_revolution_numerique_secteur_assurance_dw_english_so.pdf

Cave, T. (2016). *Mifid II: A cheat sheet on HFT, market data and more*. Accessed on 21 March 2024 from https://www.fnlondon.com/articles/mifid-ii-delegated-acts-2016-final-hft-algo-systematic-internaliser-20160426

Chatzara, V. (2020). FinTech, InsurTech, and the regulators. In P. Marano & K. Noussia (Eds.), *InsurTech: A Legal and Regulatory View. AIDA Europe Research Series on Insurance Law and Regulation* (Vol. 1). Springer. https://doi.org/10.1007/978-3-030-27386-6_1

Cornelli, G., Doerr, S., Gambacorta, L., & Merrouche, O. (2020). Regulatory sandboxes and fintech funding: evidence from the UK (BIS Working Papers No 901). Monetary and Economic Department. https://www.bis.org/publ/work901.pdf

Deloitte. (2024). *2024 insurance regulatory outlook*. Accessed on 20 April 2024 from https://www2.deloitte.com/us/en/pages/regulatory/articles/insurance-regulatory-outlook.html

Ferreira, A., & Sandner, P. (2021). Eu search for regulatory answers to crypto assets and their place in the financial markets' infrastructure. *Computer Law & Security Review, 43*. https://doi.org/10.1016/j.clsr.2021.105632

Finanzmarktaufsicht. (2017). *FMA focus: RegTech—using innovative technologies to optimise regulatory and supervisory processes*. Accessed on 20 April 2024 from www.fma.gv.at/download.php?d=3115

Gallo, V., & Nair, S. (2024). The EU AI Act: the finish line is in sight. *Deloitte*. https://www2.deloitte.com/uk/en/blog/emea-centre-for-regulatory-strategy/2023/the-eu-ai-act-the-finish-line-is-in-sight.html

Habuka, H. (2023). *Japan's Approach to AI Regulation and Its Impact on the 2023 G7 Presidency. Center for Strategic & International Studies*. Accessed on 20 April 2024 from https://csis-website-prod.s3.amazonaws.com/s3fs-public/2023-02/230214_Habuka_Japan_AIRegulations.pdf?VersionId=BnLSQRRqoO9jQ8u1RW3SGKOA0i8DBc4Q

IRDAI. (2020). *Regulatory Sandbox—Inviting applications for 2nd cohort*. Ref No. IRDAI/ INT/ RS/ 2nd / 08/ 2020. Accessed on 20 December

2023 from https://irdai.gov.in/documents/37343/1092396/Regulatory+Sandbox+%238211+Inviting+applications+for+2nd+cohort%2C+Aug+2020.pdf/33b1d7bd-6b29-9a57-741b-c8cf20bb3a62?version=1.1&t=1641432612961&download=true

Insurance Authority. (2017). *Insurance Authority Introduces New Initiatives to Facilitate Insurtech in Hong Kong*. Accessed on 20 April 2024 from https://www.ia.org.hk/en/infocenter/press_releases/insurance_authority_introduces_new_initiatives_to_facilitate_insurtech_in_hong_kong.html

International Insurance Society. (2022). *Regulatory Technology—The changing landscape*. Accessed on 20 April 2024 from https://www.internationalinsurance.org/sites/default/files/2022-01/Regulatory%20Techhology%201.2022.pdf

Levitan. (2018). Ministry of Finance eases requirements to obtain insurer's licence in Israel. *Lexology*. Accessed on 20 April 2024 from https://www.lexology.com/library/detail.aspx?g=7d7918a7-f835-482e-9c15-d0cae1cc67b7

Linden, T. V., & Shirazi, T. (2023). Markets in crypto-assets regulation: Does it provide legal certainty and increase adoption of crypto-assets? *Financial Innovation*. Accessed on 11 January 2024 from https://doi.org/10.1186/s40854-022-00432-8

Lord, N. (2017). *What is the Data Protection Directive? The Predecessor to the GDPR*. Accessed on 20 April 2024 from https://www.digitalguardian.com/blog/what-data-protection-directive-predecessor-gdpr

MAS. (2015). *MAS sets up new FinTech & Innovation Group*. Accessed on 20 April 2024 from https://www.mas.gov.sg/news/media-releases/2015/mas-sets-up-new-fintech-and-innovation-group

MAS. (2016). *FinTech Regulatory Sandbox Guidelines*. Accessed on 20 April 2024 from https://www.mas.gov.sg/-/media/MAS/Smart-Financial-Centre/Sandbox/FinTech-Regulatory-Sandbox-Guidelines-19Feb2018.pdf?la=en&hash=B1D36C055AA641F580058339009448CC19A014F7

McCarthy, N. (2024). *The Biggest GDPR Fines of 2023*. Accessed on 20 April 2024 from https://www.eqs.com/compliance-blog/biggest-gdpr-fines/

Moody's Analytics. (2018). *FCA Announces Creation of Global Financial Innovation Network*. Accessed on 20 September 2023 from https://www.moodysanalytics.com/regulatory-news/aug-07-18-fca-announces-creation-of-global-financial-innovation-network

Mueller, J. (2018). *InsurTech Rising: A Profile of the InsurTech Landscape*. Accessed on 20 April 2024 from https://milkeninstitute.org/sites/default/files/reports-pdf/InsurTech-Rising-12.4.18_2.pdf

NAIC. (2023). Big Data and Artificial Intelligence (H) Working Group. *MEMORANDUM*. Accessed on 20 April 2024 from https://content.naic.org/sites/default/files/national_meeting/Big-Data0813-AttB081223_0.pdf

Ocampo, D. G., Lehtmets, A., Pandey, M., & Prenio, J. (2022). Suptech in insurance supervision. *FSI Insights on policy implementation No 47*. Accessed on 20 April 2024 from https://www.bis.org/fsi/publ/insights47.pdf

OECD. (2017a). *Draft report on technology and innovation in the insurance sector*. Accessed on 20 April 2024 from https://one.oecd.org/document/DAF/AS/WD(2016)13/REV1/en/pdf

OECD. (2017b). *Technology and innovation in the insurance sector*. Accessed on 20 April 2024 from https://www.oecd.org/finance/Technology-and-innovation-in-the-insurance-sector.pdf

Rowland, D. (2018). *Innovation and technology in financial services: A regulatory perspective*. Central Bank of Ireland.

Savitha B., Banerjee S., & Shetty A. (2019). Product diversification versus technical efficiency of conglomerate life microinsurance companies: Evidence from India. *The Geneva Papers on Risk and Insurance-Issues and Practice, 44*(3), 527–547. https://doi.org/10.1057/s41288-019-00128-8

Sharp, M. (2021). *Canada's securities regulators launch fintech 'sandbox'*. Accessed on 20 April 2024 from https://www.reuters.com/article/idUSKBN1622IO/

Sinha, S. (2018). IRDAI proposes new guidelines for life insurance policies; Here's how they will benefit buyers. *The Financial Express*. Accessed on 20 April 2024 from https://www.financialexpress.com/money/insurance/irdai-proposes-new-guidelines-for-lifeinsurance-policies-heres-how-it-will-benefitbuyers/1370222/

Soliman, M. (2024). The Brussels Effect: How EU's law affects AI regulations globally. *The Indian Express*. Accessed on 20 April 2024 from https://indianexpress.com/article/opinion/columns/brussels-effect-eu-law-affects-ai-regulations-globally-9262249/

The Financial Markets Authority. (2017). *FMA allows personalised robo-advice; applications open early 2018*. Accessed on 20 April 2024 from https://www.fma.govt.nz/news/all-releases/media-releases/fma-allows-personalised-robo-advice-applications-open-early-2018/

The Geneva Association. (2023). *Regulation of Artificial Intelligence In Insurance: Balancing consumer protection and innovation*. Accessed on 20 April 2024 from https://genevaassociation.org/sites/default/files/2023-09/Regulation%20of%20AI%20in%20insurance.pdf

Tilleke & Gibbin. (2021). *Thailand's Draft Insurance Regulatory Sandbox Guidelines Open to Public Comments*. Accessed on 20 January 2024 from https://www.tilleke.com/insights/thailands-draft-insurance-regulatory-sandbox-guidelines-open-to-public-comments/

Waters, P. D., & Macro, S. O. (2023). *Locke Lord QuickStudy: Artificial Intelligence Regulation in the Insurance Industry—2023 a year in review*. Accessed on 20 April 2024 from https://www.lockelord.com/newsandevents/publications/2023/12/quickstudy-ai-2023-in-review

Werbach, K. (2018). Trust, but verify: Why the blockchain needs the law. *Berkeley Technology Law Journal, 33*(2), 487–550.

Zhao, W. (2018). *EU, US lawmakers tout 'sandbox' apprach for blockchain development*. Accessed on 20 April 2024 from www.coindesk.com/us-eu-lawmakers-tout-sandbox-approach-for-blockchaindevelopment/

CHAPTER 6

Ethical Dilemmas and Social Implications of Decentralized Insurance

6.1 Ethics Dilemmas in Decentralized Insurance

Ethics are crucial in developing, implementing, and operating decentralized insurance systems. As decentralized platforms operate on diverse principles, understanding and navigating various ethical frameworks are essential for ensuring these systems' integrity, fairness, and accountability. Furthermore, ethical considerations cannot be oversimplified, given the complexity of emerging technologies. Instead, they must be examined at multiple levels, encompassing micro, meso, and macro dimensions.

At the micro-level, ethical dilemmas primarily revolve around the technological intricacies of decentralized insurance systems. These dilemmas include designing, implementing, and operating underlying technologies such as blockchain, smart contracts, and AI. Issues related to data privacy, security, algorithmic bias, and the integrity of smart contracts are of paramount importance. For instance, in decentralized insurance systems leveraging blockchain technology, ensuring data security and user privacy while maintaining transparency becomes crucial. Additionally, addressing concerns regarding the fairness and transparency of automated processes driven by AI algorithms is essential. Ethical decisions at this level require technical expertise and a balance between competing priorities to uphold trust, transparency, and fairness within the decentralized insurance ecosystem.

N. Singhal et al., *Potential, Risks, and Ethical Implications of Decentralized Insurance*, Technology, Work and Globalization, https://doi.org/10.1007/978-981-97-5894-4_6

Moving to the meso-level, specific ethical challenges arise from applying decentralized insurance within particular contexts or industries. These challenges vary based on regulatory frameworks, market dynamics, user demographics, and the nature of insurance products and services offered. Ethical dilemmas at this level may include issues related to accessibility and affordability of insurance coverage, equitable distribution of risk, treatment of claims and disputes, and the impact of insurance products on consumer behaviour and societal norms. For example, in decentralized microinsurance for underserved populations in developing countries, ethical considerations may revolve around ensuring inclusive access to financial protection and promoting financial literacy while mitigating risks of exploitation and fraud. Addressing meso-level ethical challenges requires collaboration among stakeholders, including insurers, regulators, policymakers, consumer advocates, and community organizations, to develop policies and practices that uphold ethical standards and promote the well-being of insured individuals and communities.

At the macro level, the focus broadens to evaluate the broader societal and institutional impacts of decentralized insurance technologies. This includes examining how decentralized insurance systems interact with existing social, economic, and legal structures and their implications for systemic risks, market competition, and consumer welfare. Ethical considerations at this level encompass issues such as the redistribution of economic resources, the role of government intervention in regulating decentralized insurance markets, the promotion of social equity and justice, and the alignment of insurance practices with broader sustainability and environmental goals. It also necessitates ongoing dialogue and reflection on the ethical implications of technological innovation, with a focus on promoting ethical decision-making and accountability in developing and implementing decentralized insurance systems.

Researchers have posited that analyzing ethical challenges for emerging technologies, including decentralized insurance, must unify the three classical approaches of ethics: Teleology, Deontology, and Virtue Ethics, along with challenges peculiar to the technology (Sharif & Ghodoosi, 2022). Teleological ethics, a cornerstone of ethical philosophy, directs attention to the consequences or outcomes of actions, making it a pivotal framework for analyzing the ethical dimensions of decentralized insurance systems. At its core, teleological ethics espouses the belief that the morality of an action is contingent upon its consequences. Therefore, when applied to decentralized insurance, it is required to evaluate how deploying emerging technologies diligently may influence society, the environment, and individuals, both positively and negatively. The assessment of technological impact encompasses a broad spectrum of considerations. Hence, potential benefits, such as envisioning streamlined processes, reduced costs, and enhanced accessibility to insurance services, need to be meticulously examined. These anticipated advantages signify the potential of decentralized insurance systems to revolutionize the insurance landscape, fostering greater efficiency and inclusivity. It is also important to evaluate the potential harms of implementing decentralized insurance technologies.

Heightened attention should be paid to plausible risks, such as data security breaches, which could compromise the confidentiality and integrity of sensitive information stored within decentralized systems. There is also the possibility of job displacement within the insurance industry as automation and technological advancements reshape traditional roles and workflows. The assessment of teleological ethics in decentralized insurance underscores the importance of a comprehensive understanding of the potential consequences associated with technological innovation. It prompts stakeholders to adopt a forward-thinking approach, where the pursuit of positive outcomes is balanced against mitigating potential risks and adverse effects.

Deontological ethics, often called duty ethics, stands as a beacon of moral philosophy, emphasizing the intrinsic value of adhering to rules or duties irrespective of the outcomes they yield. In decentralized insurance, where novel technologies intersect with age-old principles, deontological ethics emerges as a guiding framework shaping the behaviour of participants and stakeholders within the system. Deontological ethics imparts a fundamental principle: certain actions are deemed morally right not because of their consequences but rather due to their adherence to ethical principles and rules. Consider, for instance, the pivotal role of transparency, fairness, and privacy within decentralized insurance platforms. These principles are not merely lofty ideals but concrete rules that govern the conduct of participants and stakeholders. Commitments to transparency ensure that processes and decisions are open to scrutiny, fostering trust and accountability within the system. Fairness is the cornerstone of interactions, ensuring equitable treatment for all parties involved. Privacy, meanwhile, safeguards sensitive information, preserving the autonomy and dignity of individuals. However, the journey towards upholding these ethical principles has its challenges. In the decentralized insurance ecosystem, where diverse stakeholders converge, conflicts may arise when different rule systems collide or when the rules are ambiguous or conflicting. Navigating these ethical complexities demands a delicate balance between adherence to established principles and adaptability to evolving contexts. Furthermore, the decentralized nature of insurance platforms introduces layers of complexity, where traditional notions of authority and governance are redefined. In such a landscape, ensuring coherence and consistency in ethical standards becomes paramount, requiring collaborative efforts among stakeholders to establish common ground and resolve conflicts in a manner that upholds the integrity and credibility of the system.

Virtue ethics, a cornerstone of moral philosophy, is concerned with the moral agent's character, emphasizing the cultivation of virtuous qualities and traits that pave the path towards a life of goodness and fulfilment. Virtue ethics transcends mere adherence to rules or consequences, focusing instead on the intrinsic qualities that define ethical behaviour. In decentralized insurance, integrity is a pillar of moral conduct, anchoring participants to principles of honesty, transparency, and trustworthiness. Upholding integrity fosters a culture of accountability and reliability, nurturing confidence and credibility within the decentralized ecosystem. Furthermore, empathy emerges as a vital virtue within decentralized insurance platforms, nurturing a sense of compassion and understanding towards stakeholders' diverse needs and perspectives. By embracing empathy, participants can forge meaningful connections, foster inclusivity, and cultivate a sense of solidarity within the decentralized community. Empathy catalyzes meaningful dialogue and collaboration, transcending barriers and fostering mutual respect and understanding. Responsibility, another cornerstone of virtue ethics, underscores the importance of accountability and stewardship in decentralized insurance. Participants are collectively responsible for upholding ethical standards, safeguarding stakeholders' interests, and contributing to the common good. By embracing responsibility, participants can navigate ethical dilemmas with diligence and integrity, ensuring that decisions and actions align with virtuous principles and contribute to the well-being of the decentralized ecosystem. However, virtue ethics may encounter criticism for assuming a universal conception of the "good life" and overlooking the diversity of values and priorities among individuals and communities. In the mosaic of human experience, diverse cultures, beliefs, and perspectives shape individuals' understanding of virtue and morality. What constitutes a virtuous life for one individual or community may differ significantly from another, reflecting the richness and complexity of human existence. In the context of decentralized insurance, acknowledging and embracing this diversity becomes essential in fostering an inclusive and equitable environment. Recognizing the plurality of values and priorities enables stakeholders to navigate ethical dilemmas with sensitivity and respect, honouring the autonomy and dignity of individuals and communities.

Applying ethical frameworks in decentralized insurance involves navigating complex interactions between technology, stakeholders, and societal values. Stakeholders must consider various ethical dilemmas such as privacy and data protection, accountability, smart contract vulnerabilities, liquidity mining and tokenomics issues, access and inclusion bias, oracle and external data sources, fraud prevention and detection, trust and reliability, and systemic risks. In decentralized insurance, privacy and data protection are paramount, necessitating robust safeguards amidst data exchange and storage. The challenge lies in harmonizing data accessibility with stringent privacy standards and navigating a delicate ethical terrain where individual rights intersect with operational imperatives. Moreover, accountability poses a formidable dilemma within decentralized governance structures. Distributed decision-making complicates the attribution of responsibility, demanding nuanced mechanisms to uphold accountability without compromising decentralization principles. Smart contract vulnerabilities further compound these ethical difficulties, highlighting the imperative for proactive measures to secure automated processes against exploitation and fraud. In tandem, tokenomics and liquidity mining introduce complexities in incentivization strategies, requiring ethical considerations to prevent market distortions and preserve integrity. Ensuring equitable access and inclusion remains a persistent ethical challenge, as platforms must mitigate biases that may inadvertently exclude marginalized demographics. Ethical concerns extend to the reliability and fairness of external data sources, underscoring the need for rigorous validation protocols to maintain trust and transparency. Fraud prevention and detection mechanisms are ethical imperatives, necessitating a delicate balance between security and user autonomy.

Trust hinges on establishing reliable frameworks that inspire confidence without compromising individual freedoms. Concurrently, addressing systemic risks demands proactive measures to safeguard against adverse repercussions on users and broader financial markets. In navigating these ethical complexities, stakeholders must engage in collaborative dialogue, drawing upon diverse perspectives to inform ethical decision-making. Transparency, accountability, and user-centricity must underpin governance frameworks, fostering an environment of trust and fairness. By prioritizing ethical considerations, decentralized insurance platforms can transcend technological innovation to become bastions of integrity, ensuring the longevity and sustainability of the ecosystem.

6.1.1 Privacy and Data Protection

The ethical dilemma surrounding privacy and data protection in a decentralized insurance model is multifaceted. This is driven by the intricate interplay between decentralized principles, digital technology, blockchain technology, smart contracts, and regulatory frameworks (Bejarano et al., 2023). For example, the immutability of blockchain, while ensuring data integrity, introduces complexities in complying with regulations such as the right to be forgotten. Blockchain is a distributed ledger technology that records data in cryptographically linked blocks. Once data is recorded on the blockchain, it becomes immutable, meaning it cannot be altered or deleted without consensus from the network participants. This immutability ensures data integrity and enhances trust in the system (Zhao, 2020), but it also poses challenges in complying with regulations like GDPR, especially concerning the right to be forgotten. Once personal data is recorded on the blockchain, it cannot be erased or removed, which contradicts the requirements of The General Data Protection Regulation. GDPR is a comprehensive data protection regulation that gives individuals control over their data. It includes provisions such as the right to access, rectify, and erase personal data. In particular, the right to be forgotten allows individuals to request the deletion or removal of their data when there is no compelling reason for its continued processing (Popovic et al., 2020). Hence, decentralized insurance platforms must balance the permanence of blockchain records and regulatory obligations. While blockchain ensures transparency and tamper resistance, it must also accommodate GDPR data privacy and protection requirements. Decentralized insurance often leverages the principles of pseudonymity and anonymity through blockchain transactions, enhancing user privacy. While blockchain transactions are pseudonymous, meaning that users are identified by cryptographic addresses rather than personal information, this does not guarantee full anonymity. It is still possible to trace transactions and infer user identities through data analysis techniques, raising concerns about privacy and confidentiality. Moreover, aligning these privacy-enhancing features with legal requirements for user identification in the insurance sector poses a significant challenge. For example, a decentralized insurance project that offers anonymous participation must navigate the legal landscape to ensure compliance with KYC and AML regulations. The absence of clear norms for data ownership in decentralized insurance prompts establishing rules and standards to delineate ownership boundaries. This addresses the privacy concerns of both insurance companies and clients. For instance, defining ownership boundaries for sensitive health or financial data stored on the blockchain ensures that data access is appropriately restricted, contributing to a more ethically sound decentralized insurance ecosystem. Smart contracts, known for their transparency, require thoughtful design to manage the exposure of sensitive data. Striking a balance between transparency and privacy involves carefully considering which information should be visible to relevant parties. Consider a smart contract within a decentralized insurance system that automates claim settlements. Ensuring that only relevant parties have access to the details of the claim while keeping sensitive information private exemplifies an ethical approach to smart contract design. Off-chain data storage solutions are often employed to address privacy concerns in decentralized insurance. Clear protocols are essential to govern how off-chain and on-chain data interact securely. For example, an insurance platform may store sensitive customer information off-chain to reduce the risk of exposing personal data on the public blockchain, thereby enhancing privacy and aligning with ethical data protection practices. User consent, encryption, and robust security measures are crucial in safeguarding sensitive data on and off the blockchain. Regular updates to security protocols demonstrate an ongoing commitment to user information protection. A decentralized insurance platform that prioritizes user consent employs strong encryption techniques and maintains up-to-date security measures, showcasing ethical responsibility in data protection. Regulatory compliance is deemed non-negotiable in the ethical considerations of data protection. Decentralized insurance platforms must design systems that adhere to global and local privacy regulations, considering jurisdictional differences. Incorporating data portability and the right to erasure aligns with regulatory standards and underscores the commitment to ethical data handling practices. The ethical dilemma in privacy and data protection within decentralized insurance emerges from the need to balance technological advantages with regulatory requirements and user privacy expectations (Deloitte, 2016). Navigating this complex landscape requires thoughtful design, clear protocols, and an unwavering commitment to ethical principles to foster trust and compliance in decentralized insurance systems.

6.1.2 Transparency and Accountability

Transparency and accountability are pivotal in establishing trust among users and stakeholders.

However, issues related to these are prevalent in decentralized insurance systems due to the distributed nature of the platform and the complexities inherent in decentralized governance structures. Decentralized insurance platforms operate on blockchain, distributing decision-making processes across nodes or participants. While decentralization offers benefits such as resilience and resistance to censorship, it can also lead to challenges in establishing clear lines of accountability and governance. The decentralized nature of the platform makes it difficult for users to understand how outcomes are determined and who is responsible for them. This opacity in decision-making undermines trust and confidence in the system, raising concerns among users about the fairness and integrity of the insurance platform. Smart contracts, which automate insurance agreements and claims processing in decentralized insurance platforms, add another layer of complexity to transparency and accountability issues. While smart contracts offer transparency by executing predetermined rules and conditions, their complexity can make it challenging for users to understand the underlying logic and mechanisms governing insurance transactions. Inadequate disclosure of information further exacerbates transparency issues, as users may struggle to access comprehensive and understandable information about insurance policies, fee structures, and risk factors. Accountability for errors, fraud, or malfunctions in smart contracts or platform functionalities may be unclear in decentralized systems. Unlike centralized institutions, where responsibility can be attributed to specific entities, decentralized platforms may lack mechanisms for holding individuals or entities accountable for mistakes or fraudulent activities. This lack of accountability undermines trust in the platform and its governance mechanisms, potentially eroding user confidence and the adoption of decentralized insurance solutions.

Moreover, disputes between users or between users and the platform may arise in decentralized insurance systems. Without a centralized authority to adjudicate disputes or enforce decisions, resolving conflicts fairly and efficiently can be challenging, potentially undermining trust in the platform and its governance mechanisms. Further, the decentralized nature of insurance platforms may create opportunities for manipulation or exploitation by malicious actors seeking to exploit vulnerabilities in smart contracts or governance processes.

Addressing transparency and accountability issues in decentralized insurance requires implementing mechanisms to enhance visibility, promote open communication, and establish clear governance structures. This may include improving user education and disclosure practices, implementing transparent decision-making processes, and exploring decentralized dispute resolution mechanisms that ensure fairness and accountability for all participants.

Nexus Mutual and Etherisc are leading examples, emphasizing transparency through smart contracts. Users can openly review and scrutinize the terms and conditions embedded in these contracts. The platform's commitment to transparency is evident, and it navigates the complexity of smart contracts by providing comprehensive documentation. This ensures that transparency exists and is complemented by user accessibility, striking a balance between visibility and user understanding. However, these platforms face challenges when dealing with errors or updates. Cover Protocol facilitates auditability by any participant to enhance transparency. However, striking a delicate balance between auditability and privacy becomes crucial. Robust mechanisms are employed by platforms, including Cover Protocol, to disclose sensitive information selectively. This approach preserves the equilibrium between transparency and data protection. The platform ensures users can access and scrutinize relevant information, contributing to transparency. These mechanisms are implemented to maintain a delicate balance, allowing for audibility while safeguarding data protection. It's worth noting that Cover Protocol experienced a notable security incident, commonly referred to as a "hack," where an attacker exploited vulnerabilities in its system. This incident underscores the ongoing challenges in maintaining security and privacy in decentralized platforms (Crawford & Piesse, 2016). Responding to such events, including transparent communication about the incident, measures taken for resolution, and subsequent security enhancements, is crucial for rebuilding trust and upholding transparency in the aftermath of security breaches.

Decentralized insurance platforms, such as Unslashed Finance, recognize the importance of governance mechanisms in ensuring accountability. Transparently outlining decision-making processes, like protocol upgrades, enhances accountability to the community. This transparency helps users comprehend how the platform evolves and ensures their interests are considered in governance decisions. The open-source codebase approach is exemplified by projects like Etherisc, which allows the community to scrutinize and identify vulnerabilities. However, maintaining transparency through open-source code requires a well-maintained repository and a clear process for code updates.

While these examples showcase effective transparency and accountability measures, new ethical dilemmas emerge. In projects like Cover Protocol, decentralized governance challenges may arise, requiring ongoing efforts to address potential power imbalances. As seen in Nexus Mutual, algorithmic decision-making introduces concerns about bias, necessitating transparent algorithms free from biases. Achieving inclusive user participation, exemplified by Opium Insurance, requires addressing barriers to entry. As observed in Unslashed Finance, balancing security and transparency becomes crucial to maintaining the system's resilience. Lastly, as practised by Insured Finance, addressing user concerns involves creating effective feedback channels and ensuring responsiveness to user feedback to maintain trust. Navigating these challenges underscores decentralized insurance platforms' ongoing commitment to ethical principles, user education, and responsive governance.

Box 6.1: The Cover Protocol Exploit: Decentralized Insurance Accountability

Background: The Cover Protocol, a DeFi project specializing in peer-to-peer coverage, faced a severe security breach in 2020 (Avan-Nomayo, 2020). The protocol, designed to mitigate smart contract failure-related risks, had recently merged with Yearn. Finance, adding to its prominence in the DeFi space. The project's security

vulnerabilities became evident when an attacker exploited the Blacksmith farming contract, leading to the infinite minting of COVER tokens.
Scenario: The attacker executed a sophisticated scheme involving depositing and withdrawing LP tokens, inflating the 'accRewardsPerToken' metric. By exploiting a bug in the Solidity smart contract, the attacker tricked the protocol into minting an astronomical 40 quintillion COVER tokens. The initial exploit liquidated over 11,700 coins on the 1inch decentralized exchange aggregator, causing a staggering loss exceeding $5 million.
Ethical Dilemma: The incident raised profound ethical concerns within the DeFi community. The unauthorized minting of tokens undermined the Cover Protocol's integrity and jeopardized its users' financial interests (Reynolds & Pan, 2020). The ethical dilemma centred on the project's responsibility to secure user funds and maintain transparency in the face of a malicious attack.
Response and Resolution: In response to the attack, Cover Protocol promptly restricted minting access to the farming contract to prevent further exploitation. The project communicated the incident to the community via its Discord group, assuring users that funds in "claim/no claim" pools remained secure. Remarkably, the attacker returned the stolen funds, albeit with a provocative note. The protocol acknowledged the return of funds and initiated an investigation into the incident.
Lesson Learned and Impact on Industry: The Cover Protocol hack is a pivotal lesson for the DeFi industry. It underscores the critical importance of robust security measures, thorough, smart contract audits, and proactive risk management. The incident prompted a broader industry reflection on the need for stronger ethical considerations in developing decentralized financial systems. Developers and stakeholders are now more cognizant of the vulnerabilities inherent in DeFi projects, emphasizing the urgency of implementing stringent security protocols to safeguard user assets.

6.1.3 Smart Contract Vulnerabilities

Decentralized insurance, enabled by smart contracts on blockchain platforms, represents a groundbreaking approach to revolutionizing traditional insurance models (Ernst & Young, 2017). However, this innovative solution is not without its vulnerabilities. Smart contracts, the backbone of decentralized insurance platforms, are written in code, and any coding errors or vulnerabilities, no matter how minor, can have significant and far-reaching consequences. The complexity of smart contract code amplifies the likelihood of bugs, logic flaws, and vulnerabilities. Unlike traditional legal agreements, smart contracts execute predefined rules and conditions automatically without human intervention. This automation is both a strength and a weakness. While it streamlines insurance processes and reduces the need for intermediaries, it also opens the door to potential vulnerabilities that malicious actors can exploit. Vulnerabilities in smart contracts can be exploited in various ways by attackers to compromise the integrity and security of decentralized insurance platforms. One common exploit is the reentrancy attack, where an attacker exploits recursive calls within the smart contract to drain funds or unexpectedly manipulate the contract's state. This attack gained notoriety following the infamous DAO hack in 2016, where attackers syphoned millions of dollars from the DAO smart contract. Another vulnerability is integer overflow/underflow, which occurs when the result of an arithmetic operation exceeds the maximum or minimum value represented by the data type used in the contract. Unauthorized access is another concern, where attackers gain unauthorized access to functions or data within the smart contract, potentially compromising sensitive information or funds. Denial-of-service (DoS) attacks, where attackers overwhelm the smart contract with a high volume of transactions or requests, can also disrupt platform operations and render the contract unusable. These attacks can lead to financial losses, reputational damage, and loss of user trust in the decentralized insurance platform. Addressing smart contract vulnerabilities requires a multifaceted approach. Developers must prioritize security throughout the development lifecycle, from design to deployment and ongoing maintenance. This includes conducting thorough code reviews, implementing best practices for secure coding, and leveraging automated testing tools to identify and mitigate potential vulnerabilities. Additionally, platforms should consider implementing bug bounty programs to incentivize ethical hackers to identify and report vulnerabilities before they can be exploited maliciously. Regular security audits by independent third-party experts can provide valuable insights into potential weaknesses and help bolster the overall security posture of the platform. Moreover, reliance on external oracles for data feeds introduces a vulnerability. False data injected through external oracles can distort the accuracy of insurance events recorded on the blockchain. For example, false information about a specific event covered by an insurance policy can lead to incorrect claim payouts or denial of legitimate claims. This undermines the reliability and trustworthiness of decentralized insurance platforms, potentially eroding user confidence and adoption. Governance risks represent another significant concern for decentralized insurance platforms. Governance mechanisms, which determine how decisions are made and executed within the platform, can be susceptible to centralization or manipulation. Suppose governance structures are centralized or controlled by a small group of individuals. In that case, it undermines the trustless nature of decentralized systems and introduces the risk of biassed decision-making or abuse of power. Front-running, where transaction order dependence is exploited, poses another challenge. Front-running occurs when malicious actors exploit the order dependence of transactions in the blockchain to gain unfair advantages in claiming or settling insurance events. By manipulating the timing of their transactions, these actors can exploit vulnerabilities in smart contract execution and gain preferential treatment over legitimate users, leading to unfair outcomes and loss of trust in the platform. The security of the underlying blockchain infrastructure is paramount for the integrity and resilience of decentralized insurance platforms. In particular, 51% of attacks represent a critical security threat. A 51% attack occurs when a single entity or group of entities controls more than 50% of the network's computing power, allowing them to manipulate transactions, double-spend coins, and potentially compromise smart contracts. A 51% attack could enable attackers to control the network and manipulate insurance contracts, resulting in fraudulent claims, incorrect payouts, and loss of user funds. Such attacks undermine the fundamental principles of decentralization, trustlessness, and immutability that underpin blockchain technology. Economic attacks represent a further concern, where manipulation of economic incentives within the decentralized insurance system may occur. Strategies such as exploiting pricing mechanisms or payout structures could undermine the fairness and viability of the platform. Regulatory compliance is another concern in decentralized insurance systems, especially regarding the security and integrity of smart contracts. Regulatory bodies may impose auditing, transparency, and disclosure requirements to protect users' interests and stabilize the financial system. Failure to adhere to legal requirements may lead to shutdowns or legal consequences. Smart contract upgradability without proper controls introduces risks of unintended changes that could compromise existing insurance contracts. Inadequate user authentication and authorization mechanisms may grant unauthorized access, posing security threats. Economic attacks represent a further concern, where manipulation of economic incentives within the decentralized insurance system may occur. Strategies such as exploiting pricing mechanisms or payout structures could undermine the fairness and viability of the platform. To address these vulnerabilities, decentralized insurance platforms must prioritize security measures. Thorough security audits, adherence to best coding practices, and engagement with the community for identifying and resolving risks are essential. Continuous monitoring and updates are critical to adapting to emerging threats and maintaining a secure and resilient insurance ecosystem.

6.1.4 Liquidity Mining and Tokenomics Issues

Liquidity mining and tokenomics issues are formidable challenges within decentralized insurance systems, profoundly affecting their sustainability, efficiency, and credibility. Liquidity mining is a foundational mechanism within decentralized insurance systems, enticing users to contribute liquidity to various protocols in exchange for token rewards. This practice, borrowed from the broader DeFi landscape, is critical in bootstrapping liquidity and fostering participation in insurance markets. At its core, liquidity mining incentivizes users to provide liquidity to liquidity pools within decentralized insurance platforms. These pools serve as the backbone for enabling insurance transactions and facilitating the smooth functioning of the platform. Users contribute pairs of tokens to these pools, allowing others to purchase insurance coverage or engage in related financial activities. In return for their participation, liquidity providers receive rewards in tokens native to the platform. However, while liquidity mining offers compelling incentives, it also presents several challenges, the most prominent of which is liquidity fragmentation. Funds become dispersed across multiple pools as users seek to capitalize on various liquidity mining opportunities across different protocols. This fragmentation can lead to shallower liquidity pools, wider bid-ask spreads, and reduced market depth within decentralized insurance platforms.

Consequently, liquidity providers face heightened risks of impermanent loss, where fluctuations in the value of assets within the liquidity pool result in financial losses for providers compared to simply holding those assets. An overreliance on liquidity mining incentives may adversely affect the ecosystem. When users are primarily motivated by short-term rewards, they may overlook the long-term fundamentals of the platform and engage in speculative behaviour. This speculative activity can artificially inflate demand for platform tokens, driving their prices to unsustainable levels. As a result, the ecosystem becomes more susceptible to market manipulation, speculative bubbles, and abrupt price corrections.

Tokenomics, the economic framework of decentralized insurance ecosystems, encompasses the principles governing token distribution, utility, and governance within these platforms. It serves as a fundamental mechanism for incentivizing user participation, fostering community governance, and ensuring the sustainability of decentralized insurance platforms.

The role of tokenomics in decentralized insurance ecosystems is multifaceted. Firstly, tokens serve as a means of value exchange, enabling users to access insurance products and services, participate in governance decisions, and receive rewards for contributing to the ecosystem's growth and stability. Tokens also play a crucial role in aligning the interests of various stakeholders, including token holders, users seeking insurance coverage, and developers responsible for platform maintenance and innovation. However, despite its potential benefits, tokenomics often faces challenges from misaligned incentives among stakeholders. Token holders, driven by profit motives, may prioritize short-term gains over the long-term sustainability and integrity of the ecosystem. This misalignment can lead to conflicts of interest and governance hurdles, where the interests of token holders may diverge from those of users or developers. Initial token distribution mechanisms, such as token sales or airdrops, may inadvertently contribute to token concentration among early adopters or large investors. This concentration of tokens in the hands of a few entities can exacerbate centralization risks within the ecosystem, as a small group of stakeholders may wield disproportionate influence over governance decisions and ecosystem dynamics. Moreover, token concentration diminishes the ecosystem's decentralization, a core tenet of decentralized finance, and may undermine the platform's resilience to external pressures and manipulations.

Ethical considerations surrounding liquidity mining and tokenomics in decentralized insurance platforms are intricate and demand meticulous attention. To navigate these challenges, platforms must employ comprehensive strategies that foster sustainable liquidity provision and mitigate the associated risks. A pivotal aspect of addressing these concerns involves designing reward structures that prioritize long-term engagement while discouraging short-term speculation. By incentivizing sustained participation, platforms can cultivate a stable liquidity environment that withstands market fluctuations and fosters ecosystem growth. This requires a delicate balance between incentivizing participation and discouraging excessive risk-taking.

Furthermore, platforms must explore mechanisms to consolidate liquidity in key markets, enhancing market depth and reducing fragmentation. Concentrating liquidity allows for more efficient price discovery and improves overall market stability. Enhanced transparency and governance around liquidity mining programs are essential to foster trust and ensure participants understand the risks and rewards. Education is crucial in empowering users to make informed liquidity mining and tokenomics decisions. Platforms should invest in educational resources to help users navigate the complexities of participation and understand the potential risks involved. By promoting financial literacy and transparency, platforms can empower users to make sound investment decisions and contribute to a healthy ecosystem. In addition to addressing liquidity concerns, decentralized insurance platforms must prioritize fair and equitable token distribution. Implementing token vesting schedules and token burns can help prevent token concentration among early adopters, reducing the risk of centralization. Decentralized governance structures ensure broader participation and representation within the ecosystem, fostering a sense of ownership and accountability among stakeholders. Transparency and accountability are foundational principles in tokenomics. Platforms must provide clear guidelines on token issuance, distribution, and governance processes, ensuring stakeholders can access relevant information and participate in decision-making processes. By fostering transparency and accountability, platforms can build trust and credibility within the community, laying the groundwork for long-term success and sustainability.

6.1.5 Access and Inclusion Bias

Access and inclusion bias can emerge as significant ethical challenges in decentralized insurance. These biases may result in unequal opportunities, discriminatory practices, or exclusionary policies that undermine the principles of fairness and equity. Decentralized insurance platforms may inadvertently create barriers that limit access for certain demographic groups, such as those with limited technological literacy, access to the internet, or understanding of blockchain technology. For instance, decentralized insurance platforms often operate on blockchain technology, requiring users to engage with digital platforms and understand blockchain principles. However, individuals with limited technological literacy, access to the internet, or understanding of blockchain technology may face significant hurdles in participating. Consider a scenario where a decentralized insurance platform heavily relies on cryptocurrency transactions for premium payments and claims processing. While cryptocurrencies offer several advantages, including transparency and efficiency, they also pose barriers to entry for individuals without access to banking services or familiarity with digital currencies. As a result, segments of the population may find themselves excluded from accessing insurance coverage based solely on their level of financial literacy or access to technology.

Moreover, these barriers can disproportionately affect marginalized communities, including those in developing regions or with limited access to resources. Vulnerable populations, such as the elderly, individuals with disabilities, or those from low-income backgrounds, may face heightened challenges in navigating decentralized insurance platforms, exacerbating existing disparities in access to essential financial services. Decentralized insurance platforms may not adequately address language and cultural diversity, creating barriers for users who do not communicate in the dominant language or adhere to the prevailing cultural norms. Imagine a decentralized insurance platform primarily operating in English, potentially excluding users more comfortable with other languages. Additionally, if the platform's user interface does not consider cultural nuances, it may be less accessible to users from diverse cultural backgrounds. A lack of educational resources and awareness campaigns about decentralized insurance can result in exclusion, as potential users may not know the opportunities or understand how to navigate these platforms. A decentralized insurance platform not investing in user education and awareness may find attracting a diverse user base challenging. Users unfamiliar with blockchain or decentralized technologies may hesitate to participate due to a lack of understanding. The algorithms used in decentralized insurance for risk assessment and underwriting may unintentionally embed biases based on historical data, leading to discriminatory outcomes. Historical data often reflects past trends, behaviours, and outcomes, which may not necessarily be representative of the diverse realities of the present or future. If the historical data used in underwriting models predominantly represents certain demographics while neglecting others, it can result in skewed risk assessments that disproportionately affect marginalized or underrepresented groups. For example, suppose past claims data is heavily skewed towards a specific demographic group due to systemic factors or historical patterns. In that case, the algorithm may inadvertently learn to associate certain characteristics with higher levels of risk. As a result, individuals from other demographics may be unfairly penalized or excluded from insurance coverage despite possessing similar risk profiles or behaviours.

Moreover, biases in historical data can also stem from broader societal inequalities and systemic injustices. For instance, if certain demographic groups have historically faced barriers to healthcare or financial services, they may be underrepresented in insurance claims data, leading to an incomplete or skewed understanding of risk. The implications of biassed algorithms in decentralized insurance are far-reaching and can perpetuate cycles of discrimination and inequality. Biassed risk assessments limit access to insurance coverage for marginalized communities and contribute to widening disparities in access to essential financial services and protection against unforeseen risks.

Addressing access and inclusion bias in decentralized insurance necessitates a multifaceted approach to ensure fairness, equity, and accessibility for all users. Firstly, platforms must prioritize enhanced accessibility initiatives, developing user-friendly interfaces, providing multilingual support, and offering educational resources tailored to diverse learning styles. Community engagement and outreach efforts are equally vital, as platforms should actively collaborate with diverse communities, including those in developing regions or with limited access to resources, to better understand and address their unique needs and challenges.

Secondly, platforms must address language and cultural diversity by ensuring their services are accessible to users from diverse linguistic and cultural backgrounds. This may involve offering interfaces and communication materials in multiple languages and considering cultural nuances in design and outreach efforts to promote inclusivity and understanding.

Investment in user education and awareness campaigns is also crucial. Platforms should provide clear and accessible information about decentralized insurance, empowering users to navigate these platforms effectively and encouraging broader adoption and participation. Moreover, platforms must prioritize algorithmic fairness and transparency. Critical evaluation of risk assessment and underwriting algorithms is essential to identify and mitigate biases. This involves implementing fairness-aware machine learning techniques, conducting regular audits and assessments of algorithms, and ensuring transparency in decision-making processes to promote accountability and trust. Lastly, promoting diversity in data collection is key to ensuring fair and equitable risk assessments. Platforms should actively seek out diverse and representative data sources, addressing gaps or biases in historical data to improve the accuracy and inclusivity of algorithmic models.

6.1.6 *Oracle and External Data Integrity*

In decentralized insurance systems, oracles and external data sources are critical components that enable smart contracts to interact with real-world events and information. These oracles act as data feeds, supplying the decentralized network with information necessary to autonomously execute predefined actions within smart contracts. The ethical considerations surrounding oracles and external data sources stem from the fundamental requirement for accuracy, security, and reliability in their data. Decentralized insurance platforms rely heavily on oracles to feed external data into smart contracts, which determine the outcomes of insurance policies, trigger payouts, or adjust premiums based on predefined conditions or events. Consider a decentralized insurance platform that offers parametric insurance for weather-related events. In this context, an oracle may be responsible for fetching real-time weather data from external sources. The accuracy of this weather data is crucial for determining whether specific insurance triggers, such as a certain level of rainfall or wind speed, have occurred. If the oracle reports inaccurate or unreliable weather conditions, it could lead to erroneous payouts, financial losses for insurers, and disputes among policyholders.

Furthermore, the integrity of oracles and external data sources is essential for maintaining the fairness and trustworthiness of the decentralized insurance ecosystem. Participants rely on the accuracy and reliability of the data provided by oracles to make informed decisions about purchasing insurance policies and managing risk. Any compromise in the accuracy or security of external data sources could undermine the entire system's integrity and erode participant trust.

External data sources can be vulnerable to manipulation or tampering if not adequately secured. Malicious actors may attempt to exploit weaknesses in oracles, introducing fraudulent information that could trigger false claims or impact the pricing of insurance products. For instance, suppose an insurance platform relies on an external data source to provide pricing information for assets, such as cryptocurrencies or stocks. In this scenario, if the oracle is compromised, malicious actors could manipulate the asset values reported by the oracle. The consequences of such manipulation can be profound. Incorrect asset values provided by the compromised oracle could lead to inaccurate premium calculations for insurance products. For example, if the asset values are inflated, policyholders may pay higher premiums based on the manipulated asset prices.

Conversely, if the asset values are deflated, insurers may underestimate the risk associated with insuring certain assets, potentially leading to inadequate coverage or financial losses for the insurer. Furthermore, the impact of compromised external data sources extends beyond premium calculations. Inaccurate asset values can also affect the pricing of insurance products and the overall financial stability of the decentralized insurance platform. Suppose the asset values provided by the compromised oracle are used to determine the pricing of insurance policies. In that case, incorrect pricing may result in financial losses for insured individuals and insurers. Overreliance on a single oracle or a limited set of data sources poses significant centralization risks for decentralized insurance platforms. Oracles act as intermediaries that fetch external data and feed it into smart contracts, enabling the execution of various functions within decentralized insurance systems. However, if a platform heavily depends on a specific oracle and that oracle encounters issues or is compromised, it can have far-reaching consequences for the entire insurance ecosystem. Consider a decentralized insurance platform that relies solely on a single oracle to determine the value of a critical asset, such as the price of a commodity or a stock. In this scenario, if the oracle encounters technical difficulties, experiences downtime, or provides inaccurate data due to manipulation or tampering, it can lead to several adverse outcomes.

Firstly, the failure of the oracle to provide accurate data can disrupt the proper functioning of insurance contracts and policies. Smart contracts rely on timely and reliable data inputs to trigger events such as premium calculations, claim settlements, and risk assessments. If the oracle fails to provide accurate data, smart contracts may execute incorrect actions, leading to financial losses, disputes, and breaches of contract terms. Secondly, widespread disruptions caused by a failing oracle can erode trust among participants in the decentralized insurance platform. Policyholders may lose confidence in the reliability and integrity of the platform if they experience delays, inaccuracies, or inconsistencies in insurance-related processes. This loss of trust can tarnish the platform's reputation and deter potential users and investors from participating in the ecosystem.

Moreover, financial losses from oracle failures can have severe implications for policyholders and insurers. Policyholders may suffer financial losses due to incorrect premium calculations, delayed claim settlements, or inadequate coverage. Insurers may face increased liabilities, reputational damage, and legal challenges arising from disputes with policyholders and regulatory scrutiny.

External data sources in decentralized insurance systems may encompass personal information, including sensitive data such as medical records, financial histories, or identity details. Improper handling of this data poses significant privacy concerns and ethical considerations for decentralized insurance platforms. Ensuring user privacy protection and compliance with data protection regulations is paramount to maintaining trust and integrity within the decentralized insurance ecosystem. Decentralized insurance platforms often rely on oracles to access and retrieve external data, including personal information, for various purposes such as risk assessment, underwriting, claims processing, and policy management. However, handling sensitive personal data by oracles introduces inherent risks concerning privacy and security. Consider a scenario where an oracle fetches medical data from external sources for health insurance contracts within a decentralized platform. Medical data is highly sensitive and subject to stringent privacy regulations, such as the HIPAA in the United States or the GDPR in the European Union. If Oracle mishandles or improperly accesses medical data, it could violate privacy laws and regulations, exposing users to risks of identity theft, fraud, or unauthorized disclosure of sensitive information. Mishandling of medical data may involve unauthorized access, data breaches, improper storage, or data transmission, violating established privacy protocols. The consequences of privacy breaches in decentralized insurance platforms can be severe and far-reaching. Violations of data protection regulations may result in legal liabilities, financial penalties, regulatory sanctions, and reputational damage for the platform and its stakeholders. Moreover, breaches of user privacy erode trust and confidence in the decentralized insurance platform, leading to diminished user adoption, increased scepticism, and potential abandonment by users concerned about the security and confidentiality of their personal information.

6.1.7 Fraudulent Activities: Prevention and Detection

Fraudulent Activities are a critical concern encompassing various deceptive practices aimed at exploiting vulnerabilities within the system. At the core of this issue lies the submission of false claims by policyholders or beneficiaries, which involves providing misleading or fabricated information regarding insured events or damages to obtain undeserved payouts or benefits from the insurance pool. Fraudulent actors exploit vulnerabilities in the claims process to obtain undeserved payouts or benefits from the insurance pool, thereby undermining the trust and financial stability of the system. This manipulation can take many forms, including exaggerating damages or losses, fabricating events, misrepresenting medical conditions, and submitting false documentation. Exaggerating damages or losses is a common tactic used by fraudsters to maximize the payout they receive from the insurance pool. By inflating the extent of damages incurred to their insured property or fabricating losses that did not occur, dishonest policyholders seek to exploit the insurance system for financial gain. Fabricating events is another method employed by fraudulent actors to file illegitimate claims. Staged accidents, fictitious burglaries, and other fabricated events are invented to deceive insurers and illicitly obtain financial compensation.

Similarly, in health insurance, individuals may falsely claim specific medical conditions or exaggerate the severity of existing ailments to receive unwarranted reimbursements for medical expenses. Furthermore, fraudulent actors may submit forged or falsified documentation to support their claims. Fake invoices, receipts, and medical records validate fraudulent claims and deceive insurers. The submission of false documentation facilitates the perpetration of fraud and complicates detecting and preventing fraudulent activities within the decentralized insurance ecosystem. The manipulation of claims data leads to several detrimental outcomes within the decentralized insurance ecosystem. It results in financial losses for the insurance pool, as fraudulent claims deplete the pool's funds intended to cover legitimate claims and ensure the system's financial health, and honest participants bear the brunt of these losses through increased premiums or reduced benefits, eroding the affordability and effectiveness of insurance coverage for all participants. Additionally, the prevalence of fraudulent claims undermines trust and confidence in decentralized insurance platforms among insurers and policyholders. It tarnishes the platform's reputation and may deter potential participants from engaging with the system, impeding its growth and viability over time.

Exploiting smart contracts represents a significant threat within decentralized insurance systems, posing challenges to the integrity and reliability of insurance processes. Fraudulent actors target smart contracts by exploiting vulnerabilities in their design or implementation. These malicious parties manipulate the underlying logic embedded within smart contracts to orchestrate fraudulent activities and illegitimately obtain insurance payouts or benefits. One method involves submitting false claims by providing misleading or fabricated information within the parameters defined by the smart contract. Furthermore, malicious actors may manipulate data inputs that interact with smart contracts to influence their outcomes. By tampering with the data provided to smart contracts, fraudulent parties can distort the information used to trigger insurance payouts or determine eligibility criteria. This manipulation of data inputs can lead to erroneous decisions and unjustified disbursements from the insurance pool. Another avenue for exploitation involves exploiting loopholes or ambiguities in the terms and conditions encoded within smart contracts. Fraudulent actors identify weaknesses in the contract logic or interpretation that allow them to circumvent intended constraints or exploit unintended functionalities. By capitalizing on these loopholes, malicious parties can extract undeserved benefits or payouts from the insurance system.

Collusion among participants introduces the risk of insider fraud, where individuals or entities within the system conspire to exploit its vulnerabilities for personal benefit. This collusion typically involves policyholders, insurers, and service providers coordinating their actions to manipulate various aspects of the insurance process. Dishonest parties engaged in collusion may employ several fraudulent tactics to exploit weaknesses in the decentralized insurance system. One common strategy involves submitting false claims, where policyholders fabricate or exaggerate information about covered events or damages to receive insurance payouts or benefits illicitly. Policyholders may bypass scrutiny and validation processes to secure unwarranted compensation by colluding with insiders, such as service providers or assessors. Collusion can manifest through providing inaccurate information during the application or claims submission process. Insiders may knowingly provide misleading data or misrepresent facts to influence eligibility criteria, premium calculations, or claim assessments in their favour. This deceptive practice undermines the accuracy and fairness of insurance transactions, potentially resulting in financial losses for the insurance pool and honest participants. Colluding parties may also manipulate the claims assessment process by exerting influence or leveraging relationships to bias outcomes in their favour. For instance, insiders involved in claims processing or adjudication may prioritize the interests of colluding parties over the principles of fairness and impartiality, leading to unjustified claim approvals or favourable treatment.

Inadequate KYC procedures and weak identity verification mechanisms can significantly contribute to fraud issues within decentralized insurance systems. KYC procedures are essential for verifying the identities of individuals and assessing their suitability and eligibility for insurance coverage. However, when these procedures are insufficient or lacking, it creates opportunities for fraudulent activities. Weak KYC procedures may allow individuals to exploit gaps or loopholes in identity verification to create fake identities or impersonate others. Fraudsters can use fabricated or stolen identity information to fraudulently access insurance coverage or benefits to which they are not entitled. By bypassing identity verification measures, these individuals undermine the integrity and credibility of the insurance platform, potentially leading to financial losses and reputational damage. Inadequate identity verification mechanisms fail to accurately authenticate the identities of individuals applying for insurance coverage. Without robust verification processes, it becomes challenging to confirm the legitimacy of applicants and assess their risk profiles accurately. This increases the likelihood of fraudulent individuals slipping through the cracks and obtaining insurance coverage under pretences. The absence of effective KYC procedures also hampers the ability of decentralized insurance platforms to comply with regulatory requirements and combat money laundering, fraud, and other illicit activities. Regulatory authorities often mandate stringent KYC standards to prevent financial crimes and protect the interests of consumers. Failure to implement adequate KYC measures may result in regulatory scrutiny, fines, or legal consequences for the insurance platform. Decentralized insurance platforms must have robust mechanisms to detect and prevent fraudulent activities. The absence of such measures can compromise the financial health of the insurance pool. A decentralized auto insurance platform without advanced fraud detection algorithms might struggle to identify patterns of collusion or false claims, leading to increased financial losses for the entire pool.

6.1.8 Potential Systemic Risks

Despite its small size, the decentralized insurance market is giving rise to risks and vulnerabilities that could, in the future, result or contribute to systemic risks, such as leverage, procyclicality, and increased interconnectedness with traditional insurance markets (OECD, 2022). Leverage poses a significant systemic risk within decentralized insurance systems, using borrowed funds or debt to amplify investment returns. In decentralized insurance, leverage can take several forms, all of which entail potential dangers if not managed effectively. One manifestation of leverage is the excessive exposure to risky assets. Decentralized insurance platforms may allocate a considerable portion of their capital to assets with high volatility or uncertain returns in pursuit of higher profits. While this strategy can enhance potential gains, it also exposes the platform to increased risk, especially during market downturns or adverse events. Another form of leverage in decentralized insurance involves an overreliance on borrowed capital to underwrite insurance contracts. Decentralized insurance platforms may leverage borrowed funds to expand their underwriting capacity and offer a broader range of insurance products. However, relying heavily on borrowed capital without sufficient reserves or risk buffers can amplify the impact of adverse events or claims, potentially leading to financial instability and insolvency. The consequences of employing leverage without proper risk management practices can be severe. Heightened financial fragility and instability within the decentralized insurance system may arise if platforms fail to assess and mitigate the risks associated with leverage adequately. For example, during periods of market stress or volatility, leveraged positions can magnify losses and trigger cascading effects throughout the system, jeopardizing the solvency of insurers and disrupting the functioning of insurance markets.

Procyclicality represents a systemic risk in decentralized insurance, characterized by the tendency of financial activities and market dynamics to intensify economic fluctuations and magnify systemic risks during periods of market stress. In decentralized insurance, procyclicality emerges due to the interconnected nature of insurance contracts, investment strategies, and risk management practices. In decentralized insurance, procyclicality can be observed in various ways. Firstly, the interconnectedness of insurance contracts implies that adverse events or market downturns can trigger a surge in insurance claims. For instance, a significant downturn in the cryptocurrency market, which often correlates with broader economic downturns, could increase insurance claims related to losses or damages suffered by policyholders holding crypto assets. Investment strategies employed by decentralized insurance platforms can contribute to procyclicality. During periods of economic expansion or market optimism, platforms may adopt more aggressive investment strategies, allocating capital to higher-risk assets in pursuit of greater returns. However, if market conditions deteriorate, these investments may experience significant losses, exacerbating financial stress and liquidity challenges within the decentralized insurance ecosystem. Risk management practices within decentralized insurance platforms may also exhibit procyclical behaviour. For example, during periods of market euphoria, platforms may relax underwriting standards or underestimate the potential for adverse events, leading to inadequate risk assessment and pricing. Conversely, platforms may become overly conservative during downturns or crises, tightening underwriting criteria and reducing exposure to riskier assets, exacerbating market downturns and liquidity constraints. The consequences of procyclicality in decentralized insurance can be profound. Market downturns or adverse events can trigger a cascade of insurance claims, depleting platform capital reserves and liquidity buffers. This, in turn, may exacerbate financial instability and undermine investor confidence, leading to further market turbulence and systemic risks.

The heightened interconnectedness between decentralized and traditional insurance markets presents significant systemic risks that merit detailed examination. As decentralized insurance platforms expand and connect with traditional financial institutions and markets, they become increasingly integrated into the broader financial system. While this integration offers numerous opportunities for innovation and diversification, it also introduces channels through which contagion and systemic spillovers can occur. The interconnection between decentralized and traditional insurance markets allows for the seamless flow of capital, information, and risk exposures between the two spheres. Decentralized insurance platforms may collaborate with traditional insurers, reinsurers, or financial intermediaries to enhance their product offerings, access broader pools of capital, or leverage underwriting and risk management expertise. Similarly, investors and participants from traditional insurance markets may seek exposure to decentralized insurance products and assets as part of their investment portfolios or risk management strategies. However, this increased interconnectedness also implies that disruptions or failures within decentralized insurance platforms can have far-reaching consequences beyond their immediate ecosystem. For example, if a decentralized insurance platform experiences technical issues, operational failures, or security breaches, it could trigger a chain reaction of adverse events propagating throughout the broader financial system. One notable concern is the potential for systemic contagion, wherein disruptions or failures in decentralized insurance platforms cascade through interconnected networks, leading to widespread disruptions and loss of confidence in financial markets. As decentralized insurance platforms become more integrated into the financial infrastructure, their failure could undermine investor confidence, trigger asset fire sales, and amplify market volatility, exacerbating systemic risks and destabilizing the financial system. Moreover, the increased interconnectedness between decentralized and traditional insurance markets heightens the risk of systemic spillovers, wherein adverse developments in one market spill over into others, amplifying market-wide vulnerabilities and challenges. For instance, if a decentralized insurance platform experiences a significant loss event or liquidity crisis, it could trigger risk aversion and contagion effects across traditional insurance markets, leading to liquidity strains, solvency concerns, and systemic instability.

Box 6.2: Decentralized Governance vs. Investor Protection

Background: In 2016, The DAO, a pioneering Decentralized Autonomous Organization, faced a substantial smart contract exploit, resulting in a large-scale fund drain. This DAO represented an experiment with a new organizational design aiming to create decentralized organizations without the need for traditional managers and hierarchies. Operating on the Ethereum blockchain, The DAO allowed investors to contribute Ether (ETH) to a smart contract, receiving tokens in return and enabling them to participate in governance and decision-making (World Economic Forum, 2022; Mehar, 2021).

Scenario: When the smart contract vulnerabilities were exploited, approximately 11.5 million ethers, equivalent to around $50 million, were drained from The DAO. The incident highlighted a critical flaw in the novel Ethereum smart contract code that managed the common pool of ETH (Mehar, 2021).

Ethical Dilemma: The Ethereum community faced an ethical dilemma regarding how to respond to the exploit. The debate centred on the principles of decentralization and immutability versus the need to protect investors and mitigate the impact of the security breach.

Response and Resolution: The Ethereum community made a controversial decision to implement a hard fork, rolling back the blockchain to a state before the exploit. This decision resulted in two blockchains: Ethereum, which followed the new rules and returned the funds, and Ethereum Classic, which continued on the original blockchain without the rollback.

Lesson Learned and Impact on Industry: The failure of The DAO highlighted the importance of rigorous security audits and the need for careful consideration of vulnerabilities in smart contract code. This incident significantly influenced the approach to smart contract development, emphasizing the implementation of secure coding practices within the blockchain industry. Additionally, the rise of numerous DAOs since The DAO incident, such as DAOstack, Democracy Earth, Decentraland, and others, showcases the evolution of decentralized organizational structures. Each DAO has unique goals and operationalizes its governance through token economies, where investors receive governance tokens based on their cryptocurrency investments. The legacy of The DAO incident echoes in the ongoing discussions about decentralization, security, and ethical considerations within the blockchain and DeFi space. The subsequent emergence of various DAOs reflects the industry's commitment to learning from past failures and advancing decentralized models with improved security measures.

6.2 Social Implications of Decentralized Insurance

6.2.1 Social Integration and Inclusion

Decentralized insurance platforms, driven by community input and leveraging blockchain technology, foster social integration and inclusion within societies (Werner et al., 2021). These platforms prioritize inclusivity by providing transparent and accessible insurance services, empowering marginalized populations to participate meaningfully in the financial ecosystem (The Geneva Association, 2023). Through initiatives like Etherisc and HurricaneGuard, blockchain-based microinsurance solutions offer tailored coverage against specific risks, catering to vulnerable communities often excluded from traditional insurance markets due to socioeconomic barriers or geographical constraints. Furthermore, decentralized insurance platforms embrace community-driven governance models, epitomized by Mutual DAOs, facilitating active participation in decision-making processes. This approach allows community members to shape insurance solutions according to their specific needs and preferences, fostering a sense of ownership and empowerment among participants (McKinsey, 2016). By involving stakeholders directly in designing and implementing insurance products, decentralized platforms strengthen social bonds and cultivate a culture of mutual support and cooperation within communities. Decentralized insurance initiatives extend beyond blockchain-based models to encompass cooperative structures that promote social and financial inclusion. These initiatives empower local groups to establish insurance collectives, enabling members to pool resources and share risks collectively. By fostering collaboration and solidarity at the grassroots level, decentralized insurance platforms contribute to developing resilient and interconnected communities where individuals can access essential financial protections regardless of socioeconomic status or geographic location. In addition to promoting community engagement, decentralized insurance platforms operate globally, transcending geographical boundaries and providing access to insurance services worldwide. Utilizing blockchain technology facilitates seamless transactions and reduces operational costs, making insurance products more affordable and accessible to diverse demographics. This global accessibility ensures that individuals from all walks of life can secure financial protection against unforeseen risks and uncertainties, thereby promoting financial inclusion and socioeconomic equity on a global scale. Decentralized insurance systems prioritize transparency, accountability, and educational initiatives to build trust and foster informed decision-making among participants. Through blockchain technology, these systems ensure the integrity and reliability of insurance processes, instilling confidence in users and promoting fairness in the distribution of risks and benefits. By promoting financial literacy and awareness, decentralized platforms empower individuals to make informed insurance coverage choices, enhancing their resilience and capacity to manage financial risks effectively.

6.2.2 *Community Engagement and Collaborative Models*

Decentralized insurance models bring about a paradigm shift not only in the way insurance operates but also in the dynamics of community engagement. Collaborative models emphasize active participation, shared decision-making, and community-driven governance. One of the key social implications of decentralized insurance is the empowerment of communities through active participation. Traditional insurance models often involve a passive relationship between policyholders and centralized entities. In contrast, decentralized insurance encourages policyholders to engage in decision-making processes actively. Users become stakeholders, voting on governance proposals, suggesting improvements, and collectively shaping the direction of the insurance platform. Platforms like Nexus Mutual, a decentralized alternative to traditional insurance, exemplify this approach. Members actively participate in governance decisions, contributing to the platform's direction and shaping the rules that govern the community.

Decentralized Autonomous Organizations exemplify collaborative models in decentralized insurance. These entities operate as community-driven protocols, allowing members to impact the platform's decisions directly. DAOs enable the creation of rules and proposals that align with the community's collective interests. Users, as part of DAOs, contribute to the platform's governance, ensuring a more inclusive and democratic approach to decision-making. Platforms like Aragon, a decentralized governance project, operate as DAOs, allowing users to impact decisions related to the platform's development directly. Members propose rules, vote on governance issues, and collectively influence the trajectory of the insurance ecosystem.

Community engagement in decentralized insurance contributes to transparent governance, a crucial factor in building trust. Transparent decision-making processes, visible to all participants through blockchain technology, create a sense of accountability. Users can scrutinize governance proposals, track fund allocations, and ensure the platform aligns with its stated principles. This transparency fosters trust within the community, a vital element for the success of decentralized insurance initiatives. Platforms like Etherisc, focusing on decentralized insurance applications, implement risk pooling where community members contribute to a shared pool. In case of a claim event, the community collaborates to provide financial support, reinforcing bonds and aligning with principles of mutual aid.

Decentralized insurance often involves collaborative risk pooling, where community members contribute to a shared pool to cover potential losses. This model fosters a sense of collective responsibility and mutual aid. In the event of a claim, the community comes together to provide financial support, reinforcing a social bond among participants. Collaborative risk pooling aligns with principles of solidarity, reducing the individual financial burden and emphasizing a communal approach to risk management. In decentralized insurance, community engagement extends to product development. Users can propose new insurance products or improvements to existing ones. This collaborative approach ensures that insurance offerings are tailored to the community's diverse needs. For example, a decentralized insurance platform focused on agriculture might allow farmers within the community to propose parametric insurance products specifically designed to address the risks associated with their crops. For instance, Unslashed Finance, a decentralized insurance platform, allows users to propose and vote on new insurance products or improvements. This collaborative approach ensures that insurance offerings align with the unique requirements of different communities, such as creating parametric insurance products for specific agricultural risks.

6.2.3 Resilience and Response to Crisis

Resilience, within the context of decentralized insurance, embodies the capacity of a society or financial ecosystem to endure and recover from various adversities, including economic downturns, natural disasters, or unexpected disruptions. Decentralized insurance platforms enhance resilience by leveraging the inherent risk distribution mechanism embedded in their operations. The risk distribution mechanism in decentralized insurance involves spreading risks across a diverse and interconnected network of participants and stakeholders. Unlike traditional insurance models that rely on centralized entities to absorb and manage risks, decentralized insurance platforms distribute risks among a broad pool of participants, including policyholders, investors, and insurers. This distributed approach prevents the concentration of risks and liabilities on specific entities, reducing the system's vulnerability to systemic shocks and crises. By diffusing risks across a wide network, decentralized insurance platforms mitigate the potential impact of adverse events on individual participants and the broader financial ecosystem. In times of crisis, the burden of losses and liabilities is shared collectively among the network participants, ensuring that no single entity bears the full brunt of the financial impact. This risk-sharing mechanism fosters greater stability and resilience within the decentralized insurance ecosystem, enabling it to withstand and recover from unforeseen challenges more effectively.

Furthermore, the innovative nature of decentralized insurance, often built upon blockchain and smart contract technologies, enhances its resilience by enabling swift adaptations to emerging risks and changing market dynamics. With its decentralized and immutable ledger system, blockchain technology enhances transparency, security, and trust within insurance transactions, reducing the likelihood of fraud and manipulation. Smart contracts, which automate the execution of insurance agreements and claims processing, facilitate faster response times and greater efficiency in managing insurance contracts and payouts. In times of crisis or rapidly evolving risk landscapes, decentralized insurance platforms can leverage smart contracts to implement dynamic risk assessment models, adjust coverage terms, and expedite claims processing, enhancing their ability to adapt to changing circumstances and mitigate potential losses.

Decentralized insurance systems offer several notable advantages in crisis response, leveraging automated processes, blockchain technology, and decentralized decision-making mechanisms to enhance efficiency, transparency, and adaptability. Firstly, automated processes driven by smart contracts enable expeditious claims processing and payouts during crises. Smart contracts execute insurance agreements and claims processing automatically, eliminating the need for manual intervention and reducing processing times significantly. This rapid response ensures that financial support reaches affected parties swiftly, helping them recover and rebuild after a crisis. Moreover, the transparency and immutability provided by blockchain technology are instrumental in crises. Blockchain's distributed ledger system records all insurance transactions transparently and tamper-proof, fostering participant trust. In times of crisis, when trust is paramount, the transparency and integrity of blockchain technology reassure participants that their claims will be processed fairly and accurately, enhancing confidence in the insurance system. Decentralized decision-making mechanisms inherent in these systems enable more effective and localized responses to crises. Decentralized governance structures empower local communities and stakeholders to participate in decision-making, allowing for tailored solutions that address each affected area's unique characteristics and needs. This localized approach fosters resilience and adaptability, as responses can be customized based on specific circumstances and challenges on the ground.

6.2.4 Environmental and Sustainable Practices

The insurance industry shoulders a critical role in addressing sustainability and climate change challenges, given its role as the provider of protection and risk management products and its management of significant premiums. Insurers have recognized the imperative to identify, manage, and monitor risks and opportunities linked to Environmental, Social, and Governance (ESG) issues (Anguiano & Parte, 2024). Various initiatives across the industry evidence this proactive stance. Munich Re stands out for its introduction of performance coverage for battery storage and the development of tailored solutions for manufacturers involved in photovoltaic projects. These solutions include compensation against guaranteed triggers, effectively mitigating risks associated with renewable energy projects. Swiss Re has boldly committed to cease providing insurance to the top 10% of the most intensive oil & gas producers by 2023, aligning its business practices with sustainability goals. Swiss Re also discontinued investing in these carbon-intensive industries, reflecting a strategic shift towards sustainability-focused underwriting practices. Generali has taken concrete steps by establishing a competence centre dedicated to underwriting risks specific to the renewable energy sector. This initiative aims to foster collaboration and share best practices, facilitating the development of tailored insurance solutions to support the global expansion of renewable energy projects. AIG has demonstrated its commitment to sustainability by creating an ESG division fund, promoting sustainable and impact investing. AIG actively promotes natural catastrophe risk modelling and climate risk anticipation/pre-emption, enhancing its ability to assess and manage climate-related risks effectively. Cigna has embraced sustainability through its strategic Sustainability Performance Plan, focusing on managing global real estate portfolios. The plan emphasizes emission reduction, energy efficiency, reusability/recycling, and waste management practices, underscoring Cigna's commitment to minimizing its environmental footprint. Liberty Mutual has shown leadership by developing a new stochastic wildfire model, adapting its existing model to align with the latest information on weather patterns and wildfire risk. This enhancement strengthens Liberty Mutual's underwriting practices and enables more accurate risk assessment in wildfire-prone regions.

These initiatives underscore the insurance industry's dedication to addressing sustainability and climate change concerns. By integrating ESG considerations into their operations, insurers contribute to a more resilient and sustainable future while fulfilling their role as financial protection and risk mitigation custodians. The insurance industry's shift towards sustainability can be amplified by adopting decentralized insurance platforms that align with environmentally sustainable practices. These platforms can incorporate eco-friendly policies directly into their insurance offerings. By providing coverage for renewable energy projects, energy-efficient technologies, and sustainable agricultural practices, decentralized insurance platforms incentivize individuals and businesses to adopt environmentally friendly initiatives. Tailored insurance products aligned with sustainability goals encourage proactive engagement in sustainable activities. Decentralized insurance platforms can incentivize sustainable behaviours among policyholders. Through rewards, discounts, or enhanced coverage for adopting environmentally friendly practices, such platforms encourage individuals and businesses to prioritize sustainability. This incentive structure fosters a culture of environmental responsibility and conservation within insurance networks.

6.2.5 Global Coverage and Niche Markets

Decentralized insurance systems are poised to revolutionize the insurance landscape by fostering global collaboration and extending coverage to emerging risks and niche markets. By transcending geographical boundaries, these systems can offer solutions that cater to the needs of a diverse, global population. Decentralized insurance platforms address emerging risks that traditional insurers often hesitate to cover, such as cybersecurity, climate change, and technological risks stemming from AI, robotics, and DeFi. These emerging risks pose unique challenges due to their limited loss history and ever-evolving nature. For instance, climate-related risks affect regions globally. Cybersecurity threats and DeFi risks are compounded by their contagious nature, potentially leading to cascading failures within ecosystems and numerous claims. Addressing such risks requires the cooperation of multiple insurers, reinsurers, and public institutions, necessitating the implementation of insurance or disaster recovery programs to manage claims and distribute risk costs. However, these programs typically incur high coordination and operational expenses due to the involvement of numerous stakeholders. Decentralized insurance models, leveraging their global reach and blockchain-based infrastructure, offer a novel solution to cover emerging risks on a global scale. Decentralized insurance platforms can serve as risk exchanges or prediction markets, channelling crypto capital to fund risks that are challenging to quantify. Blockchain technology ensures transparency and traceability, which are crucial for maintaining trust among stakeholders such as insurers, reinsurers, public institutions, and policyholders. Moreover, cryptocurrencies enable cost-efficient settlement options for premiums and claims, irrespective of geographical location. Smart contracts streamline operations and reduce the coordination required among multiple parties. Several pilot programs are underway to test the viability of decentralized insurance models in covering emerging risks. For example, Lemonade, a prominent digital insurer in the U.S., collaborates with Hannover Re, Avalanche, and Chainlink to provide parametric weather insurance for African farmers. Similarly, Deloitte has partnered with Avalanche to develop a blockchain-based disaster recovery platform, assisting state and local governments in accessing federal emergency funding more efficiently during disasters.

Additionally, decentralized insurance facilitates targeting niche markets that traditional insurers often overlook due to long product development cycles and associated costs. Examples of niche insurance products include medical insurance for individuals with severe pre-existing conditions, temporary event insurance, body-part insurance, and alien abduction insurance. Decentralized insurance platforms can theoretically pool risks globally, reducing unit costs and making coverage more affordable. Moreover, disintermediation and automation enabled by smart contracts further lower operational costs associated with individual products.

Studies and examples of blockchain-based decentralized P2P insurance models demonstrate their potential to address niche market insurance needs. For instance, a group of authors from Arizona State University showcased the deployment of a decentralized P2P insurance model to gain operational efficiencies and launch new products (Boyle et al., 2021). Teambrella, a Bitcoin-based peer-to-peer insurance marketplace, created pilot groups in various countries to cover niche categories such as pets and cycling (Shetty, 2022).

6.2.6 Consumer-centric Models and Customization

Decentralized insurance platforms are community-driven, often incorporating user input and feedback to develop consumer-centric models. Unlike traditional insurers, these platforms harness technology such as blockchain and smart contracts to enable dynamic customization of insurance policies, allowing greater flexibility in meeting individuals' or communities' specific needs and preferences. Policyholders on decentralized platforms can select coverage limits, deductibles, and other parameters tailored to their unique circumstances and risk tolerance levels. This emphasis on customization ensures that consumers receive insurance solutions that are precisely suited to their personal or business requirements, fostering a more satisfying and relevant insurance experience. By leveraging technology to enable dynamic policy adjustments, decentralized platforms empower consumers to take control of their insurance coverage, enhancing their sense of security and peace of mind. Decentralized insurance platforms also prioritize seamless communication and engagement between consumers and providers. By cutting out intermediaries and bureaucratic obstacles, these platforms enable swift resolution of inquiries, claims processing, and policy adjustments, leading to a more efficient and responsive customer experience. Direct interaction between consumers and insurance providers fosters transparency and accountability, building trust and confidence in the insurance process. Decentralized insurance platforms leverage data analytics and artificial intelligence to offer personalized risk assessment and pricing models. By analyzing consumer data and behaviour patterns, insurers develop more accurate risk profiles and offer competitive premiums tailored to individual policyholders. This data-driven approach not only enhances the affordability of insurance coverage but also promotes inclusivity and equity, making insurance accessible to consumers across diverse demographics and socioeconomic backgrounds.

6.3 Conclusion

Exploring ethics dilemmas within decentralized insurance unravels a complex tapestry woven from technological innovation, social responsibility, and ethical considerations deeply embedded in the insurance domain. Delving into multifaceted issues such as privacy and data protection, transparency and accountability, smart contract vulnerabilities, liquidity mining intricacies, access and inclusion biases, oracle and external data integrity, fraudulent activities, and systemic risks, it becomes abundantly clear that decentralized insurance systems confront a myriad of ethical challenges demanding astute attention and proactive resolutions. Privacy and data protection are paramount concerns within the decentralized insurance ecosystem, necessitating robust measures to safeguard sensitive information and uphold user privacy rights. Meanwhile, establishing transparent and accountable mechanisms becomes imperative to preserve the integrity and fairness of decentralized insurance processes, fostering trust and confidence among stakeholders. Smart contract vulnerabilities underscore the critical need for rigorous auditing and testing protocols to mitigate exploitation risks and ensure the reliability of automated contract execution.

Similarly, navigating the complexities of liquidity mining and tokenomics mandates a balanced approach to incentivize participation while averting potential market distortions and speculative behaviours. Tackling access and inclusion biases requires proactive endeavours to champion diversity and equity within decentralized insurance systems, guaranteeing marginalized communities equitable access to essential financial protections. Furthermore, maintaining the integrity of Oracle and external data sources proves indispensable to preempting manipulation or tampering risks. Efforts to combat fraudulent activities stand as linchpins in upholding the integrity and stability of decentralized insurance markets, necessitating collaborative endeavours among stakeholders and implementing robust security protocols. Additionally, identifying and mitigating potential systemic risks play pivotal roles in safeguarding the broader financial ecosystem from destabilizing influences.

Transitioning to the social implications of decentralized insurance unveils an array of considerations, including social integration, community engagement, resilience, environmental sustainability, global coverage, niche markets, and consumer-centric models. These facets underscore decentralized insurance's transformative potential in shaping inclusive, responsive, and sustainable insurance solutions. Social integration is a cornerstone of decentralized insurance, bridging societal divides and fostering inclusivity by rendering accessible and equitable insurance services. Concurrently, community engagement accentuates the participatory nature of decentralized platforms, nurturing community bonds, instilling trust, and fostering collective responsibility for risk management. Resilience emerges as a hallmark of decentralized insurance, leveraging blockchain technology and decentralized governance structures to fortify resilience and ensure uninterrupted insurance service provision.

Moreover, promoting environmental sustainability is paramount, with decentralized insurance platforms incentivizing sustainable behaviours and investments. Global coverage signifies the expansive reach of decentralized insurance platforms, bolstering financial inclusion and resilience by offering tailored insurance solutions on a global scale. Additionally, global coverage fosters cross-border collaboration and solidarity, cultivating a sense of global citizenship and shared responsibility in mitigating common risks and challenges.

References

Anguiano, D. T., & Parte, L. (2024). The state of art, opportunities and challenges of blockchain in the insurance industry: A systematic literature review. *Management Review Quarterly, 74*, 1097–1118. https://doi.org/10.1007/s11301-023-00328-6

Avan-Nomayo, O. (2020). *Cover Protocol suffers infinite minting attack, price tanks 97%.* Accessed on 6 May 2024 from https://cointelegraph.com/news/cover-protocol-suffers-infinite-minting-attack-price-tanks-97

Bejarano, F., Mazón, S., Pastoriza, A., Esteban, J., & Salgado, M. (2023). *Insurance is ready to leap forward with Blockchain and the Metaverse.* Accessed on 6 May 2024 from https://www.bcg.com/publications/2023/insurance-is-embracing-blockchain-and-metaverse

Boyle, E., Pesic, S., Jevtic, P., & Boscovic, D. (2021). *Peer-to-Peer Insurance: Blockchain Implications. Society of Actuaries.* Accessed on 6 May 2024 from https://www.soa.org/4946d6/globalassets/assets/files/resources/research-report/2021/p2p-insurance-blockchain.pdf

Crawford, S., & Piesse, D. (2016). *Blockchain technology as a platform for digitization Implications for the insurance industry*. Accessed on 6 May 2024 from https://assets.ey.com/content/dam/ey-sites/ey-com/en_gl/topics/emeia-financial-services/ey-blockchain-technology-as-a-platform-for-digitization.pdf

Deloitte. (2016). *Blockchain in insurance Turning a buzzword into a breakthrough for health and life insurers*. Accessed on 6 May 2024 from https://www2.deloitte.com/content/dam/Deloitte/us/Documents/financial-services/us-fsi-blockchain-in-insurance-ebook.pdf

Ernst & Young. (2017). *Better-working insurance: Moving blockchain from concept to reality*. Accessed on 6 May 2024 from https://assets.ey.com/content/dam/ey-sites/ey-com/en_gl/topics/insurance/insurance-pdfs/ey-marine-blockchain-pov.pdf

McKinsey. (2016). *Blockchain in insurance—Opportunity or threat?* Accessed on 6 May 2024 from https://www.mckinsey.com/~/media/mckinsey/industries/financial%20services/our%20insights/blockchain%20in%20insurance%20opportunity%20or%20threat/blockchain-in-insurance-opportunity-or-threat.ashx

Mehar, M. I., Shier, C. L., Giambattista, A., Gong, E., Fletcher, G., Sanayhie, R., Kim, H. M., & Laskowski, M. (2021). Understanding a revolutionary and flawed grand experiment in blockchain: The DAO Attack. In *Research anthology on Blockchain Technology in business, healthcare, education, and government*. IGI Global. https://doi.org/10.4018/978-1-7998-5351-0.ch069

OECD. (2022). *Why Decentralised Finance (DeFi) Matters and the policy implications*. OECD. Accessed on 6 May 2024 from https://www.oecd.org/daf/fin/financial-markets/Why-Decentralised-Finance-DeFi-Matters-and-the-Policy-Implications.pdf

Popovic, D., Avis, C., Byrne, M., Cheung, C., Donovan, M., Flynn, Y., Fothergill, C., Hosseinzadeh, Z., Lim, Z., & Shah, J. (2020). Understanding blockchain for insurance use cases. *British Actuarial Journal, 25*, e12.

Reynolds, K., & Pan, D. (2020). *Cover protocol attack perpetrated by 'White Hat,' funds returned, hacker claims*. Accessed on 6 May 2024 from https://www.coindesk.com/markets/2020/12/28/cover-protocol-attack-perpetrated-by-white-hat-funds-returned-hacker-claims/

Sharif, M. M., & Ghodoosi, F. (2022). The ethics of blockchain in organizations. *Journal of Business Ethics, 78*, 1009–1025.

Shetty, A. D. (2022). Block chain application in insurance services: A systematic review of the evidence. *SAGE Journals*. https://doi.org/10.1177/21582440221079877

The Geneva Association. (2023). *Assessing the potential of decentralised finance and blockchain technology in insurance*. Accessed on 6 April

2024 from https://www.genevaassociation.org/sites/default/files/2023-08/DeFi%20insurance_WEB.pdf

Werner, F., Basalla, M., Schneider, J., Hays, D., Brocke, V., & J. (2021). Blockchain adoption from an interorganizational systems perspective—A mixed-methods approach. *Inform Syst Manage, 38*(2), 135–150. https://doi.org/10.1080/10580530.2020.1767830

World Economic Forum. (2022). *Decentralized autonomous organizations: Beyond the hype*. Accessed on 6 May 2024 from https://www3.weforum.org/docs/WEF_Decentralized_Autonomous_Organizations_Beyond_the_Hype_2022.pdf

Zhao, L. (2020). The analysis of application, key issues and the future development trend of blockchain technology in the insurance industry. *American Journal of Industrial and Business Management, 10*(2), 305–314. https://doi.org/10.4236/ajibm.2020.102019

Index

N. Singhal et al., *Potential, Risks, and Ethical Implications of Decentralized Insurance*, Technology, Work and Globalization, https://doi.org/10.1007/978-981-97-5894-4

SPRINGER NATURE

GPSR Compliance

The European Union's (EU) General Product Safety Regulation (GPSR) is a set of rules that requires consumer products to be safe and our obligations to ensure this.

If you have any concerns about our products, you can contact us on ProductSafety@springernature.com

In case Publisher is established outside the EU, the EU authorized representative is:

Springer Nature Customer Service Center GmbH
Europaplatz 3
69115 Heidelberg, Germany